Cohen Family

D0811984

David & Beverly Cohen
1552 East 10th Street
Brooklyn, N.Y. 11230

Above
the Bottom Line

Above
the Bottom Line

Stories and Advice on Integrity

Including halachic references and commentary

by
HANOCH TELLER

New York City Publishing Company

THE RIGHTS OF THE COPYRIGHT HOLDERS WILL BE STRICTLY ENFORCED.
ISBN 0-9614772-5-3

Registered in Library of Congress

12 11 10 9 8 7 6 5 4 3 2

PUBLICATIONS
EICHLER
1429 Coney Island Avenue
Brooklyn, N.Y 11230

J. Lehmann
Hebrew Booksellers
20 Cambridge Terrace
Gateshead
Tyne & Wear

To the Memory of
Rabbi Michoel Ber Weissmandl *zt"l*
He fought for life *and* integrity.

He established a unique community in Mt. Kisco,
N.Y., rooted in *emmes*. Whoever violated this
sacrosanct precept forfeited his right to live there.
Better known for his valorous defiance of the
Nazis, Reb Michoel Ber also courageously struggled
against mankind's apathy and improbity.

One Friday, while travelling home to his yeshiva
for Shabbos, he discovered that he hadn't enough
money for his train ticket. Sensing Reb Michoel
Ber's quandary, the conductor said, "Come on,
Rabbi, I recognize you — I see you every week.
You can pay next time." But Reb Michoel Ber
feared that he might forget, or that the conductor
might not ride that line again and would always
remember that a Jew hadn't paid his fare. Thus, the
man who, under unspeakable circumstances, had
risked his life and sacrificed everything he owned
for the sake of his brethren gave up Shabbos with
his family and yeshiva that week for the sake of
ehrlichkeit.

ALSO BY HANOCH TELLER

Once Upon a Soul
Soul Survivors
'Souled'
The Steipler Gaon
Sunset
Courtrooms of the Mind
Bridges of Steel, Ladders of Gold

APPROBATION* FROM HAGAON HARAV SHIMON SCHWAB SHLITA

ב"ה

RABBI SIMON SCHWAB
736 WEST 186TH STREET
NEW YORK, N. Y. 10033

STUDY: 923-5936
RES: 927-0498

שמעון שוואב
רב דק"ק
קהל עדת ישרון
נוא־יארק, נ. י.

Tamuz 5748

Hanoch Teller has just presented us with yet another Mussar Sefer. All of his anecdotes challenge the conscience of his many avid readers. True to his name, he is not only an entertaining storyteller, but a skillful Mechanech as well. This time his topic is "Honesty". To be honest, honest בין אדם לחבירו, as simple as that. In Yiddish, a G-d-fearing individual is called "an ehrlicher Yeed" -- which means an honest Jew -- honest to G-d and man, whose yes is yes and no is no, always speaking the truth and avoiding trickery and subterfuge like the plague.

So the author portrays a gallery of "Ehrlichkeit" by גדולי תורה as well as simple folk with nobody expecting any extra credit for avoiding falsehood or betrayal.

By the way, all this used to be the accepted Jewish way of life על פי תורה but that was quite some time ago. Meanwhile, our old-fashioned honesty is fast going out of business. Even among our so called "Ehrliche Yeeden", it has often become a rare commodity. The author dishes out his menu with the silk gloves of his amusing true stories. The time is now ripe for those who are in authority of the Torah world to deliver some heavy punches of free and candid תוכחה to bring this generation back to its senses.

"כי אמת אהבתי ושקר שנאתי"

This is the message loud and clear. Thank you Hanoch Teller for your beautiful delivery, which is of great help.

Shimon Schwab

---

* Approbations are printed in the order they were received.

APPROBATION FROM HAGAON HARAV MORDECHAI GIFTER SHLITA

מרדכי גיפטער
ישיבת טלז
RABBI MORDECAI GIFTER
28570 NUTWOOD LANE
WICKLIFFE, OHIO 44092

Dear Reb Hanoch, נ״י,

I'm very happy to learn that your book "Above the Bottom Line" is about to be published, ב״ה.

I feel it will be a great contribution to Yiras Shamaim in our business dealings and many other areas of life. I sincerely hope your readers will feel and do about it.

May your latest project a "Stern Letter" achieve the desired purpose.

בברכת עליה והמשך תורה.

בהוקרה,

מרדכי ג פטר

APPROBATION FROM HAGAON HARAV
BINYOMIN ZILBER SHLITA

RABBI BINYOMIN YEHOSHUAH ZILBER

4 ABAYE VEROVOH AVE.

BNEI-BRAK   ERETZ ISROEL

Tel. 78 75 46

הרב בנימין יהושע זילבר

שדרות אביי ורבא 4

בני־ברק

טלפון 46 75 78

הרב חנוך יונתן טלר, שליט"א, זכה להוציא
לאור כמה ספרים בשפת האנגלית על נושאים מאוד
אקטואליים וביחוד על ענינים שבין אדם לחבירו
וזכה להתקרבות של גדולי דורינו כמו שראיתי את
הסכמותיהם על הספרים האלו.

וכעת רוצה להוציא לאור ספר על ענין "נשאת
ונתת באמונה" (שבת ל"א א') שזה דבר הראשון
ששואלים לאדם ביום הדין, ובעיקבתא דמשיחא זה
נחוץ מאוד שעיקר הקושי שאדם מראה בזה היתרים,
וע"ז בא מחברנו הרב טלר, שליט"א, להרחיב
הדיבור בזה. וכבר איתמחי גברא בספריו הקודמים
שנתקבלו בחיבה יתירא בחוגים רחבים וידועה הוא
השפעתם המרובה. לכן אנו מקוים שחפץ ד' בידו
יצליח גם בספר הנוכחי להגדיל תורת ההנהגה בין
אדם לחבירו להלכה ולמעשה לזכות הרבים, וזכות
הרבים יהי' תלוי בו ונזכה לביאת משיח צדקנו
בב"א.

הכו"ח לכ' התורה ולומדיה

APPROBATION FROM HAGAON HARAV
YEHUDA ZEEV SEGAL SHLITA

Rabbi J. W. SEGAL

40 BROOM LANE, SALFORD, M7 0FJ

Telephone: 061-792 2543

Principal
Manchester Talmudical College
"Saul Rosenberg House", Seymour Road
Manchester, M8 6BQ.   Telephone: 061-740 0214

ב"ה

יהודא זאב סג''ל

ראש הישיבה, מנשסתר

אי"ה תשמ"ה

שמחתי לשמוע שהאברך הי"ו הרב חנן יונתן זלה שליט"א

יואיל הואיל לאור ספר בדין ישרות הבין ממונע. בדוה"ר

היגיון ובקיאות בדין היה כמה הל"ג. מודים הי"ו לצמאם באתן

שהיו צדיקים לאחל ויונע לעבור בהסבם.

מה מאד נכאה שהגה אלקים יהויק ולא''מים המנובקרק הקלו

כהמונרה מצליים גם בדין התאור הגה שרלו כבר אחרו הל''ל

של מקסים הראו, ובדין שקרים ולאלוה וכבו' של אמר

הנפט בבין הנבון אל גל ישראל הלאו אחרת ישראל של ישיו וזלה

ולא יגברו בגב ולא ימצאו רבירה לשון ומאית.

להקפיד בדנונים את הגו בדין חזוק מאד ייר כחו ''יר חיל

של הרב המחבר ידגין מברגו שיצבה להאבק בצבורגם ההס

ונצבה לאור הקושה שלמה לגן הגאן שוחתמו ואת

יהודא זאב סג''ל

APPROBATION FROM HAGAON HARAV ELI DOV WACHTFOGEL SHLITA

בס"ד

YESHIVA GEDOLAH — ZICHRON MOSHE

- *Zichron Moshe High School*
- *College For Advanced Talmudic Research*
- *Kollel-Post Graduate School*
- *Cheder-Elementary School*

Rabbi Tzvi Abba Gorelick
Dean
Rabbi Eli Dov Wachtfogel
Rosh Yeshiva
Rabbi Yehuda Pollak
Menahel
Rabbi Elisha Dorfman
Administrator

כ"ח תשרי תשמ"ט

הריני להכיר בשער בת רבים את האברך היקר רב המעלה הר"ר חנוך יונתן
טלר שליט"א המפורסם בסיפוריו החשובים. אשר הרי הם אוצר של יר"ש
והתעוררות לתקון המדות, אהבת ישראל ולעבודת ד'.

נוכחתי לדעת שיש להמחבר כשרון מיוחד להביעה דברי מוסר והתעוררות
אמיתיים בצורה מושכת ומשפיעה. זכות גדולה נפלה לידו להיות ממזכי
הרבים בדורינו ע"י ספריו. נדיר הוא שבן תורה אמיתי מוכשר לדבר אל לב
ההמון בלי לסטות מדרך התורה כמו שעושה זאת מחברינו היקר.

עכשיו שזיכה אותנו הרב המחבר שליט"א עם ספר חדש על הנושא נשאת ונתח
באמונה אשר אי אפשר להדגיש די את גודל הנחיצות לספר על ענין הזה.
וכשם שספריו הראשונים הצליחו במשימתם כך בע"ה גם הספר הזה בענין
ישרות יחדיר נושא חשוב זה ללב קוראיו.

יהי' רצון שיזכה להמשיך בפועליו הברוכים לטובת הכלל ולהרמת קרן של
תורה; ונזכה לציון במשפט תפדה.

ישיבה דפילאדעלפיא

בס"ד

בס"ד. כ"ג מנ"א תשנ"א

לגדול ויקר הרב הגאון המופלג וכו' וכו'
הרב חנוך יונתן ראבב שליט"א

אתשל"ג דברים העומקם אל לבי וכו'
כי בקר מעני להוסיף על סגל אות אות
לבלו דינין ופלפול ולבאר... לדברי הראשונים וכו'
אף כהמזל, הבאה לאותם כי כדה הדינים אשר ישלח אל
מאות לפלפול בסוגיה ול עדקא דרא הלא ה' סמיך
דאלפא האשורית ביה.

דברינו על כמה מאלות ולהניח בו אצלינו מלא
בדקים אשר מאתר דברים עודים מילוי, ופולא כבי
הברים ולאחל אמורים, האיך ברב וא? לא' ראשי... הוא
וכן הגדול לדברים לאתקים אמורים את הקדומה עלו
לקדמות הברכ המעולה לפני. יבלא.

לאתם לזה דינין ודון ולון אל אף לא פל ע
כן הבכה הגאין להאתם לאתקת אל פניל, ומי... לצו
קלה... הגאולדקים לזרח הלא להגורו, דפוכ... המלא
המאת גדולה ותצובה... דלי... יפ 100 דק... ומלה...
להולא ואהי עדבעי הרדים ישל אל כ... שאן.
ואני הקושעה דברכת לכלאתה רבה

יד. 13. 91

Contents

Acknowledgments

I can never fully express my gratitude to the Almighty for enabling me to write this book, and to His earthbound minions, who have significantly influenced my life, outlook, and skills.

My abiding love for words — and respect for their power — derives from my parents through the osmosis of childhood. The quest to express my ideas comes from my *rebbeim* and numerous early and contemporary *gedolim* (especially those in the Mirrer Yeshiva where I learn) who have honed my thinking.

I found writing on the subject of business ethics to be a most difficult task. A colleague of mine, who, like myself, resides in Jerusalem, has written several books on ethical topics. For him, the work apparently comes naturally. And it is no wonder. Whoever has had the privilege of meeting this rabbi understands why he writes such books: he *is* what he writes.

I am the first to admit that the same does not apply to myself. But if *Above the Bottom Line* can help me, and it has, it may help others as well.

I would like to thank Rabbi Shimon Schwab for so heartily encouraging me to pursue this project; his words and example are a refreshing reminder of Rabbi Breuer zt"l's slogan, "Our products are *glatt kosher* **and** *glatt yosher*." Another *Gaon* renowned for his integrity has consented to grace this volume with his very important words. I therefore thank Rabbi Avraham Pam, and the editors of *Hamesivta*, from which the Halachic Foreword was adapted.

It is my great fortune to be acquainted with the *Roshei Yeshiva* of the Bais Binyomin Yeshiva of Stamford, Connecticut. I gain from their presence, and even more from the privilege of discussing matters with them. Rabbis Simcha Schustal and Dovid Hersh Mayer granted me an afternoon of their time to outline the principles that should be addressed in this book. I hope the result lives up to their expectations.

I draw my inspiration in an eclectic fashion, picking up a story here, witnessing an event there, hearing a *mussar* discourse elsewhere. Since joining the lecture circuit, I have been the constant beneficiary of the kind of outstanding *chessed* that would flatter and inspire the toughest of souls. Wherever I turn, I discover a thirst to hear, to read, *and* to share stories. People frequently comment, "You can write a story about this..." I often do. Their words of encouragement are most appreciated; they keep my nose to the grindstone.

I specifically would like to thank Benjie and Sussie Brecher for their ubiquitous support; Rabbi and Mrs. Dov Goldbaum for giving me a place to hang my hat; and Rabbi and Mrs. Jay Marcus for seeing to it that my plans came to fruition. I am indebted to Rabbi Yitzchak Rosenberg for his assistance and good cheer, and I am equally grateful for the help provided by Mr. and Mrs. Norman Shine and Dr. and

Mrs. Zvi White. Rabbi Paysach Krohn, Yisrael Leventhal, and Joseph Telushkin have delivered a graceful body blow to the notion that distance diminishes friendships. I am beholden to Rabbi and Mrs. Dovid Oppen for all their unstinting assistance and advice over the years. And words cannot express my appreciation to Mendy and Nechama Itzinger.

The desire to write a book is one thing, but producing a completed manuscript is another. That transition required the work and faith of my indomitable colleague, Reb Leibel Estrin. The inclusion of Daniel Taub's insights and astute suggestions also made this book far better than it would otherwise have been. As in the past, Rabbi Joseph Goldberg was kind enough to contribute his stylistic expertise, and Baruch Berniker his paste-up prowess. In addition, the book was befriended by the enormously talented Sarah Scheller, whose graphic consultation is priceless. Once again, the sharp eyes of Marsi Tabak saved me from tripping over my own words more times than I am about to admit. The other felicitous and devoted participants in this project prefer to remain anonymous, much to my chagrin. Without the Almighty's bountiful grace, the help and friendship of these people, and the determination and teamwork of New York City Publishing Company, this book would never have been. I request forgiveness from anyone whose name I have inadvertently omitted.

The debt of gratitude I owe my wife is staggering. She gives me the freedom to develop in both Torah and *derech eretz*. I pray that our children will acquire her unique attributes as well as the ideals and concepts reflected in these stories.

Finally, I offer my sincere thanks to my *rebbe*, Harav Shlomo Zalman Auerbach. For well over a decade I have had the *zechus* of learning from him and asking him my *shailos*. Permitting me to publish his *psak* on the stories in this book has elevated the contents of *Above the Bottom Line* to far more than merely entertaining Jewish literature.

I am delighted to add that the *Gaon* enjoyed the stories I related to him, and he believes they will have a positive impact on our People. I pray for the fulfillment of this vision.

"עדות ה' נאמנה" — זה סדר זרעים, שמאמין בחי עולמים וזורע (ילקוט תהילים תרע"ד). הנביטה, ההבשלה והבציר הינם תולדותם הטבעית של הזריעה. ברם המאמין יודע כי לאו בדידיה תליא אלא בידי שמים. בכך מביט הוא את פרגוד הסתר העוטה ואופף מעשי בראשית.

אמונה במשא ומתן שתולה ואמונה אף היא על פלגי מעיין קודש זה.

"קל אמונה" שהאמין בעולם ובראו (ספרי ריש האזינו). עזה תקותי שספרי זה יאמץ האימון בין הבורא לבריאה.

Hanoch Teller
Jerusalem ת"ו
20 Mar Cheshvan / October 1988

Introduction

ONE BRIGHT SUNDAY MORNING the village thief approached the house of the Rav of Shnitzelberg, his arms laden with contraband. The Rabbi, glancing out the window, was dumbstruck by this sight. Why would the village thief be bringing his stolen goods to him? he wondered. Everyone knew he would not traffic in ill-gotten items.

Without stopping to knock on the door, the thief let himself into the Rav's house. He placed everything on the table, and turned to depart.

"Wait!" cried the Rabbi. "What is all this?"

"This week's haul," replied the thief matter-of-factly.

"I gathered as much," the Rabbi conceded, "but why have you brought it to me?"

"Rabbi," the thief replied with a look of total bewilderment, "I'm surprised at you. Have you forgotten that you spoke about the mitzva of *hashavas aveida* [returning lost items] yesterday in the synagogue?

I listened to your talk with keen interest, and I hastened to comply."

The Rabbi was flabbergasted; from one sermon the village thief had repented! "D... do you really mean it?"

"Of course! And I'm all excited about it — this is the first time I've fulfilled this mitzva."

The Rabbi felt contrite that he had doubted the man even for a moment. He warmly embraced the penitent and wished him success with his new lifestyle.

A few minutes later the Rabbi frantically searched through his house for his missing watch, but it was nowhere to be found. Suddenly overcome with a sneaking suspicion, he dashed out the door to confront the village thief. "Did you just steal my watch?"

The thief sheepishly nodded his head.

The Rabbi's anger knew no bounds and he demanded an explanation. "Here you purport to be a *baal teshuva* eager to perform the mitzva of returning stolen items, and a second later, you're back to your old ways?!"

The village thief rolled his eyes at the Rabbi's naiveté. "What does one thing have to do with the other?" he asked innocently. "*Hashavas aveida* is a mitzva but stealing — that's my *parnassah*!"

This unregenerate robber eloquently articulated the problem that, as Rabbi Shimon Schwab describes it, "plagues" our generation. *Above the Bottom Line* attempts to eradicate this plague, the primary symptom of which is religious schizophrenia. Time and again, we see *parnassah* invoked to justify actions that are undeniably antithetical to the Torah precepts we hold dear.

Theologically, religious schizophrenia is untenable;

morally it is repugnant. The prophet Eliyahu cried out to his contemporaries to adopt a single stance. "How long will you go limping between two opinions?" (*Melachim* I 18:21) he asked. Over one hundred years ago, Rabbi Samson Raphael Hirsch wrote to a friend, "One could write a whole treatise on the damage that has been done and is still being done by the fact that the *Shulchan Arukh* did not appear from the very beginning in one volume. That is how it came about that many a person has thought and still thinks he is a perfect Jew if he merely observes the laws of *Orach Chaim* [daily rituals]... A good deal of *Yoreh Deah* and *even more* [emphasis mine] of *Choshen Mishpat* [money matters]... is neglected."

More recently Rav Hutner wrote to a student who was leaving yeshiva to embark on a career, "I can never agree to the concept of a 'double life,'... all aspects of your life must revolve around a oneness that does not permit a double standard."*

As a young teen, I was once a guest in the home of Rabbi Shmuel Blech of Lakewood, New Jersey. My host, who was perusing his mail when I entered, pointed to an uncancelled stamp and related a story about the Chafetz Chaim. Whenever that saintly scholar received a letter by courier, the tale went, he would immediately tear up a postage stamp lest the government suffer a loss of revenue as a result of the circumvention of its postal service.

---

*A free translation.

Since then I have heard Rabbi Blech's story retold numerous times, with numerous variations. But it wasn't until much later that Rabbi Dovid Hersh Mayer placed the incident in the proper perspective by relating, "People are very cautious now about the stamps they use, but often forget to contemplate the legality or propriety of the contents of the envelope to which the kosher stamp is affixed."

On occasion, stolen money finds its way not only into envelopes, but into newspaper headlines. Thus certain financially unscrupulous people have not only shamed their brethren but desecrated the Holy Name as well. There is a general assumption that a religious individual will not place himself above the law but, rather, will assiduously obey it; when he fails to do so, his crime appears all the more execrable.

The recklessness of such a person and the extensive damage he causes is reminiscent of Leon Trotsky and the effect of his draconian decrees on the Jews of Russia. A Moscow rabbi appealed to the revolutionary leader, whom he remembered from earlier days when the apostate was known to his co-religionists as Leibel Bronstein. Past association, however, was of no help to the rabbi; Trotsky remained intractable. His parting words to the architect of the Russian Revolution were, "The problem is that the Trotskys make the revolutions and the Bronsteins have to pay the price." And the price is heavy indeed.

Years ago, driving on the Merrit Parkway, it occurred to me that I might have inadvertently handed a twenty-dollar bill to the toll collector instead of a single dollar. On my way back to the city I pulled over to the toll station in Greenwich, Connecticut, and explained my suspicion to the manager. The man took my name and address and told me, "No problem. At the end of every day we make a tally, and we can account for every penny. If an error was made you'll receive your money back in the mail."

That episode happened a decade ago, but I still remember the manager's words, "we can account for every penny." If only I could make the same statement! (Four days later I received notification that I had *not* overpaid.)

A more moving incident occurred during a recent visit to the Mirrer Yeshiva in Brooklyn. Located in the heart of the Syrian Jewish community of New York, the yeshiva draws students and passersthrough from all across the globe. Sitting directly behind me on that Tuesday afternoon, in the last row of the *beis midrash*, were three Sephardic businessmen engaged in a heated discussion.

"What position," one entrepreneur asked his colleagues, "do you want to be in when you die?"

I was shocked. Of all places to discuss such a frivolous matter, and in a clearly audible tone, no less!

"I want to be sleeping," came the response. "They say that's the best way to go."

His partner suggested a different pose. The inquirer then stated his preference: "I want to be seated at my desk in my office."

By this time I could no longer feign being absorbed in the *sefer* open before me, and my temper rose. "They had to abandon their fancy offices to conduct this absurd discussion here?" I fumed. "Speaking nonsense in a yeshiva — disturbing everyone within earshot — is bad enough. But *chutzpah* of *chutzpahs*, to declare that one wishes to spend his final moments in his office negotiating one last deal! A lot of good it will do him then."

"I want to be at my desk," the businessman continued, "so it can testify that I never took a dollar that did not belong to me. Let the walls serve as witnesses that whenever I was in doubt, I passed the money on to the customer and never kept it for myself..."

I was ashamed of myself not only for violating the tenets promulgated in *Courtrooms of the Mind*, but for being incapable of the same declaration as this Sephardic merchant.

I regret that a number of no less compelling stories about integrity could not be included in this volume. Bowing to deadline pressures, brief mention is made below of some extraordinarily inspiring episodes in the lives of Torah luminaries.

Reb Aharon Kotler was known for his meticulous observance of *mitzvos*, including those relating to money matters. When his son was wed at Beth Medrash Govoha, the *Rosh Yeshiva* kept a careful account of every cup or plate broken and any other minor expense incurred during the *simcha* so he could later reimburse the yeshiva.

Because he often stretched out to rest during his commutations from Lakewood to New York, occupying more than one seat on the bus, Reb Aharon would insist on paying double fares.

His wife was no less concerned about finances. Since food was supplied to her by the yeshiva, she assumed that it was meant to be consumed only within Lakewood city limits. Therefore, whenever Rebbetzin Kotler travelled to New York, she would calculate exactly how much food to bring along for the journey.

As a matter of course, she purchased only inferior fruit and vegetables for her own family so as not to overtax the yeshiva budget. Stale bread from the yeshiva's dining room reappeared in her own to complement the yeshiva's leftovers, which the Kotlers ate six days a week.

The same woman who would never throw out food provided by charity funds would also never accept a check from the yeshiva until she had depleted all her cash resources. (Rabbi Simcha Schustal)

❀

Reb Aharon's son, Reb Shneur, carried on the family tradition. Once a California millionaire with no relatives made out a check to the Lakewood Yeshiva after Reb Shneur had visited him and encouraged him to increase his yearly donation of one hundred dollars. The very same day, the *Rosh Yeshiva* received a call from the tycoon's aide informing him that the benefactor had passed away before he could fill in the amount on the check. "Rabbi," the aide asked, "tell me how large a check you'd like. There are millions of dollars sitting in the bank and no heirs to collect them. It's either Sacramento or Lakewood."

Reluctant to take more money than the donor might have intended to give, Reb Shneur promptly responded, "One hundred dollars, like every year." (Rabbi Dovid Hersh Mayer)

❀

The Vishka Illui lived in a low-income project on New York's Lower East Side. As soon as any money came his way, the Illui would inform his housing office, lest the new revenue disqualify him from living there. The great scholar would also never ride the elevator down from the *shiur* he delivered in the Anshei Maamad building so as not to incur an additional, "unnecessary" expense to the shul. (Rabbi Simcha Schustal)

⚶

Rebbetzin Kaplan, who devoted her entire life to Bais Yaakov, felt duty-bound to respond to every student who called or wrote her. She kept a copious account of all the telephone calls she made, since she didn't consider it a direct school expense, and deducted their cost from her salary.* (Rabbi Dovid Hersh Mayer)

⚶

Rabbi Yosef Eliyahu Henkin would not allow his Ezras Torah organization to raise his salary. Although he was hardly well-paid, Rav Henkin was loathe to take a single superfluous penny of public funds.

Ezras Torah's board of directors, however, urged the *Gaon* so incessantly that he finally relented. But when they went over their books at the end of the fiscal year, they discovered that somehow the salary increase had been

---

*When Mr. Yitzchak Nebenzahl, a devoutly observant and conscientious Jew, became comptroller of the State of Israel, he had a second telephone line installed in his government office — at his own expense — from which to make private phone calls (Rabbi Aharon Lopian).

refunnelled back into the organization. (Rabbi Simcha Schustal)

⚘

Heading home from his yeshiva on Shabbos, Reb Leib Mallin was frequently delayed by inquisitive students. On these occasions he would be compelled to eat *seudah shlishis* in the yeshiva, but he would later reimburse the administration for the meal. Likewise, Reb Moshe Feinstein would "settle" with his yeshiva for every unscheduled meal he ate there. (Rabbi Dovid Hersh Mayer)

Stories such as these, as well as those involving more intricate plots and lesser-known individuals, inclined me toward giving this volume a different title: Although *Above the Bottom Line* very much reflects the contents (Rav Gifter, commenting about the sad state of people's integrity today, quipped that a more accurate description might be "*Below* the Bottom Line"), an equally appropriate title would be *Profiles in Courage*. Unfortunately, that particular title was taken — by the thirty-fifth president of the United States. The sheer fortitude required to resist monetary temptations is an aspect of courage all too often overlooked.

John F. Kennedy writes in his book: "Courage is a diamond with many facets, and it owes much to its setting.... Sporadic instances of courage on isolated and unimportant issues have no great significance. To be important, courage must be exhibited on behalf of some large cause or rule." I can think of no larger cause than Torah and no greater rule than *Halacha*.

Public opinion need never be a criterion for the Jewish conception of courage. The men and women portrayed in this volume demonstrate farsightedness, intelligence and, most of all, profound faith, the compass that steers their conscience clear of compromise.' They are all blessed with the courage to do what's right despite financial consequences or personal loss.

The student of history will see in these stories a refreshing departure from the conventional understanding of courage and valor. Generally human heroics is a blinding, all-consuming drive, often a screaming for glory as reflexive as the howling of a dog. The protagonists of this book all responded to a higher, far more subtle calling.

Reb Yaakov Wiesenfeld related an incident involving a needy couple from the Stamford Hill section of London and the board of governors of their son's school. Noting the family's dire financial straits, the governors excused them from paying tuition — but both parents objected.

"I could take on another job [in addition to the three she already held down]," the mother insisted.

"Why should the other parents have to subsidize our child's education?" the father protested. "It may take ten to twenty years until I can get the money together, but *please* don't absolve us."

This is the Jewish conception of courage: "clean hands and a pure heart." (*Tehillim* 24:4)

Israel's first president, Chaim Weizmann, sought to have the management of the country's Orthodox community under the aegis of the Chief Rabbinate. To this end he even launched a personal appeal to this plan's most vehement opponent: Rabbi Yosef Chaim Zonnenfeld.

Reb Yosef Chaim, the undisputed leader of the Yishuv,

lived alone in a hovel in Jerusalem's Old City. The president knocked on his door just as Reb Yosef Chaim was futilely attempting to ignite his kerosene stove.

When Weizmann entered the Rabbi's house, he gasped at the appalling conditions and winced at the pitiful activity to which Reb Yosef Chaim had been reduced. "What do you need all this for?" he asked. "Look at yourself and your surroundings. If you accept the position I am offering you in the Chief Rabbinate, you will never again have to debase yourself with such menial labor... your attendants will see to everything."

Reb Yosef Chaim rose from the stove and held his hands up to the president. "You are a renowned man of science," he said. "Can you tell me why hair grows all over the body but not on the palms?"

Puzzled by this apparent non sequitur, Chaim Weizmann could only shrug.

"The reason," the venerable rabbi explained, "is that there should be nothing on the palm at all: no dirt, no grease. I will not allow my hands to be sullied by your offer."

Not long afterward, Rabbi Moshe Klierst, a brilliant scholar in Tiberias, was presented with the same offer. "Accept the position in the Rabbinate," he was assured, "and we will never interfere with your job or decisions."

Rabbi Klierst had no delusions about either his integrity or the corrupting influence of money and security. He responded, "If you pay me, you will not have to interfere — I will *seek* your intervention!" (Rabbi Yosef Zeinwert)

Selecting a subtitle for this book was no simple matter. *Above the Bottom Line* is not intended as a definitive treatise on business ethics; topics such as monopoly and restraint of trade, rivalry in the marketplace, resource mobility, business pricing, etc., are notably absent. It is rather a volume about a word that defies translation: *ehrlichkeit*. "Integrity" is only a close approximation.

Free enterprise places a premium on the values of competition, economic freedom and personal gain. *Ehrlichkeit* places a premium on concern for the needs and possessions of others.

As in the past, all the stories herein are true but character names and story locales have generally been changed to insure the privacy of those concerned, and the sensibilities of community members. Since numerous stories in this book involve instances of impropriety, it was especially important to disguise identities. I trust that all the appropriate precautions have been taken. All stylistic liberties were taken either to address this concern, or to enhance the impact of the lesson. Elements of certain stories are works of the imagination, yet they are woven of fact.

The "bottom line" is universally understood to connote money. "What's the bottom line?" means "What is the true cost?" or "Where is the profit in this endeavor?" My wise and talented literary mentor, Marsi Tabak, remarked that for people of conscience, certainly for Jews, there is a different "bottom line": life itself. There are times, and we should only be spared such trials, when rising above the bottom line entails a willingness to endanger our very existence.

This cogent comment resulted in the inclusion of the last chapter of this book, which celebrates the highest form of integrity.

Halachic Foreword
by Rabbi Avraham Pam

The Chafetz Chaim writes that whoever wishes to engage in business must learn the second section of *Shulchan Arukh Choshen Mishpat*, especially the laws germane to fraud.

Just as a slaughterer must study the laws relevant to slaughtering, and a scribe must learn those pertaining to a *sefer Torah*, a businessman must be well-versed in the laws governing business. Furthermore, just as a slaughterer must be ordained before he can practice, it would be advisable to test a businessman in all the relevant *halachos* before permitting him to engage in business.

❀ Defective Goods

If a person sells a defective item, he must point out the defect to the purchaser if it is normally considered a drawback. Failure to do so invalidates the sale and entitles the buyer to a refund (he must be certain, however, that the damage did not occur after his purchase). And it makes no difference if the purchaser is a Jew or a gentile, for defrauding a non-Jew in weights, measures or numbers is forbidden by the Torah (*Vayikra* 19:38).

✦ Customer Responsibility

If currency values have changed and the seller is unaware that his merchandise has increased in value, the purchaser must inform him.

One who accidentally damages an item in a store may not replace it on the shelf and walk away. Rather, he must pay for the damage. (This is especially relevant for men who inspect *lulavim* and inadvertently split the leaves at the tip.)

✦ Truth in Advertising

A merchant who recommends inferior merchandise to an unsuspecting customer violates the Torah prohibition against placing a stumbling block before the blind.

If a customer requests a particular item or a specific color that isn't in stock, a merchant may not say, "They have stopped making that, but I can show you something even better..."

೫ Naming a Price

When contractors and employers are reluctant to discuss prices during their initial meeting, they often end up in disputes, with each person feeling cheated. If they don't forgive each other (even if they do not outwardly argue) the result is stealing. If they do not determine rates beforehand, the contractor must pay the worker however much is locally customary for such labor. Since such customs are difficult to ascertain and a miscalculation results in stealing, all terms and payments should be arranged in advance.

As indicated in the Introduction, all the stories and events depicted herein are true, in part or in whole; locations and characters' names have been changed in most cases.

Balance Sheet

Months	Chessed	Teshuvah	Torah	Tefillah	Tzeddakah	Aveiros
Tishrei						
Cheshvan						
Kislev						
Teves						
Shevat						
Adar						
Nissan						
Iyyar						
Sivan						
Tammuz						
Av						
Ellul						

Profitable Losses

Prepared by

Date

Index No.

המצוה הזאת של השמירה מגזל היא מן המצוות המושכלות שאילו לא נתנה התורה ימצאנה האדם בשכלו והנה זה מז׳ המצוות שנצטוה אה״ר וצריך שאדם שישא ויתן באמונה ויהיה נקי כפיים מן הגזל כדי שיהיה זוכה לעלות בהר הקודש אלקים...

שפת תמים פרק ג׳

Refraining from stealing is a mitzva that appeals to reason; even if the Torah hadn't commanded it, man's reason would have dictated its observance. It is one of the seven mitzvos *that Adam was commanded, and man must be very careful to deal in good faith and bar his hands from thievery. Thus he will be able to ascend the holy mountain of the Lord.*

Sfas Tamim: 3

Robbed Blind

AVENUE U, Brooklyn. This was little Little Italy. By seven-thirty in the morning the neighborhood was already redolent of the distinctive aromas of fried sausage, Di Noble cigars, meat sauces, steamed clams, olive oil, and red wine.

Still decades before the advent of the supermarket, and a lifetime before the shopping mall, most of the business in the area was conducted on the street. Fruits and vegetables — the neighborhood staples — were hawked from Dom's ancient, creaking truck. Other foodstuffs were purveyed by pushcart peddlers who trekked up and down the avenue.

Crammed into these mobile emporia was every edible an Italian could want: exotic vegetables, baked goods, butter and eggs, mussels (the vendor proclaiming that his mollusks were fresher than the ones at Coney Island), and Italian olive oil. Naturally the biggest trader was the wine merchant who sold his wares in five gallon jugs. (All Italians drink wine — red wine, a beverage rumored to have restorative and medicinal powers. Even the children indulge, although they usually mix it with cream soda.) If you sat at the curb of Avenue U long enough, and were Italian, an entire meal — course after lavish course — could be placed at your feet.

For added ambience, delicacies indigenous to the populace were prepared outdoors, generating a spontaneous culinary symposium on cooking methodology, gastronomic lore, and traditional recipes. By ancient rite and sacrosanct custom, food preparation was the exclusive domain of women, particularly grandmothers. Unless the dish in question was *cabutzel*.

Innate feminine squeamishness precluded their involvement in the preparation of this favorite, made from half a lamb's head. But while the distaff side found *cabutzel* rather offensive, the menfolk had no qualms about gazing at the steaming remains of a still-recognizable lamb's head, while one roasted, unseeing eye gazed back; in fact, they considered it a rare treat. The Arabs have nothing on the Italians when it comes to arcane cuisine.

I N THE MIDST of this homogeneous hodgepodge of little Little Italy was a merchant as unfamiliar with the local delicacies as he was with the nuances of dialectical Italian. For that matter, he wasn't particularly well-versed in English expressions or American fare either. An emigrant from the Ukraine, Reb Hirsh Moshe Cohen was a simple, God-fearing Jewish peddler who plied his dry goods in this Italian neighborhood.

Reb Hirsh Moshe was something of a curiosity in the area. He looked different, dressed differently, talked differently, and acted differently from all the natives. Avenue U, like smaller Italian enclaves, was closed to outsiders, and his presence was tolerated only by virtue of his virtue: his honesty and forthrightness had earned him the grace of the upper stratum of society: the bookies.

These businessmen, who ran the biggest operations in the area, were highly respected entrepreneurs. As such, they were frequently called upon to render binding arbitration or settle jurisdictional and other disputes. In their service to the community, they were recognized by all as no less vital than the sanitation department, Con Ed, and Ma Bell. Since they were local talent, they knew everyone, but they were slightly sharper than the populace at large. Like E.F. Hutton, when they spoke, their minions listened. They determined who were the VIPs and who the *personae non gratae*.

While Hirsh Moshe Cohen's favorable status did not protect him from robberies or competition, it did place him in a much better position than the undesirables on the local chieftains' list. To say that his business was flourishing, however, would be a gross overstatement.

Reb Hirsh Moshe's success was hampered by what he considered merely a minor handicap: in fact he was legally blind. Aided by neither a cane nor a guide dog, he could just barely see. His children were constantly apologizing for their father and explaining away his foibles as the result of his poor eyesight.

BUT FOIBLES were one thing, and hazardous vision was quite another. On two occasions, Reb Hirsh Moshe was struck down by a speeding car whose approach took him by utter surprise. Neither of these encounters were mere brushes or sideswipes; they were major collisions, and only boundless Providential blessings and an equal amount of public and private prayers were responsible for his survival.

After one of these accidents, the patrolman who picked up the pieces of Reb Hirsh Moshe didn't even see the need to rush to the emergency room. The poor man was a goner, he figured, another appalling statistic in the toll of pedestrian recklessness. Given the empirical evidence, the officer's assessment was not far off. But Hirsh Moshe Cohen, as his family can readily verify, was practically impervious to the norms of nature.

Apparently the man's impeccable integrity and meticulous performance of *mitzvos* had found favor with his Maker. It is written that the Almighty despises the haughty; from this we infer that He treasures the humble. Few men were as humble as Hirsh Moshe Cohen, and the light of the Lord shined through his dim eyes.

ON ONE FATEFUL DAY an Italian woman and her daughter purchased several yards of bedding fabric from Reb Hirsh Moshe's pushcart. As was his custom, he rounded down the price to an even $2, which the customers gladly proffered.

Reb Hirsh Moshe placed the cloth on a sheet of newspaper, carefully wrapped it, and handed the package to the woman. After they departed, he felt the money they had given him, using his hands as his eyes. His careful rubbing of the crisp new bills revealed that two of them had been stuck together and there were actually three dollars in his possession instead of two.

Accepting money that was not rightfully his was anathema to the honest peddler, and he quickly darted after his customer. The woman and her daughter had already ascended the steps to the el (elevated subway platform) and Reb Hirsh Moshe followed.

Returning the extra dollar was a noble act to be sure, but it was equally foolish and negligent. He had left his pushcart unattended in an area where trafficking in "hot" items was a way of life. Of course stolen goods were never identified as such; but enormous quantities of merchandise merely and inexplicably shared the same fate of having "fallen off a truck."

N O ONE in the vicinity of Avenue U needed Newton to teach him the law of gravity; once an item hit the ground it was fair game. Anything from plumbing supplies to ritzy raincoats could take a tumble from a truck and within hours, if not minutes, the inventory would be liquidated.

Reb Hirsh Moshe understood this, but he understood the immorality of taking that which was not his even better. In his talmudically unhoned mind, the evils were not equal, nor did they cancel each other out. Better he be robbed clean, he reasoned, than retain another's money.

Indeed, by the time he finally scaled the el platform and located the woman who had overpaid him, the assault had commenced on his solitary earthly possession. Miraculously, two gun-toting cops happened to be strolling up the block just as Hirsh Moshe abandoned his cart, but everyone, except one kid (a novice), had enough sense to wait until the cops had passed before they set the forces of gravity into action on the dry goods.

The kid didn't get very far before the police nailed and cuffed him. In that era justice was swift, and the very next day Vinnie Carboni was arraigned before a judge in the presence of Hirsh Moshe Cohen. The attorney hired by the Carbonis filibustered for an hour before the court and the victim describing the embarrassment this affair would cause the boy's family were it to become publicized. Furthermore, he added — straining pathos to its emotional limits — the Carboni's impoverished state was embarrassment enough.

Although the hardened judge was not moved, Reb Hirsh Moshe obviously was, and he waived all the charges so as not to force the family further into debt. He even appealed to the defense attorney to forgo his fee, lest he overburden the unfortunate.

T HE NAME OF GOD was mightily sanctified that day in Brooklyn Juvenile Court. Hirsh Moshe Cohen's humble demurral elicited a lengthy sermon from the judge on the morals and enviable example set by the poor-sighted merchant. The judge dropped the charges as requested and, in an extraordinary gesture, asked an officer to drive the plaintiff home.

Reb Hirsh Moshe's chauffeur turned out to be none other than the very patrolman who had driven him to the hospital after one of his near-fatal accidents. The officer was visibly moved by the proceedings in the courtroom, especially since the protagonist looked so distinctly familiar. He asked his passenger if they'd met before. Mr. Cohen apologetically responded that with his feeble eyesight he could not possibly distinguish one policeman from another.

That's all the driver had to hear.

"You de blind Jew peddler got hit offa Coney?"

Reb Hirsh Moshe nodded.

"No kiddin'!" the cop said in thorough amazement. "I'm de cop brought youse to de hospital! Between you, me and de Commish, I never t'ought you'd make it, ya ole sonova gun.

"But I got it now. Ya got Someone Up Dere watchin' out for ya." He hooked a thumb skyward. "Must be de way you act, iz why youse still here. You somethin' else, man."

Reb Hirsh Moshe was touched by the officer's compliment, even though between the Carbonis, the judge, the attorney, the lady customer, and her daughter, he had already received a total of thirteen "bless you Mr. Cohen"s in the space of twenty-four hours.

T HE FOLLOWING WEEK, as if nothing had happened, Reb Hirsh Moshe Cohen resumed his beat, peddling dry goods on Avenue U. Hirsh Moshe had stocked his cart to capacity that day, hoping that this day he might merit the blessing so many others had wished him.

Hirsh Moshe Cohen knew that his success in business, like everything else, was dependent exclusively on the will of God. Nonetheless, he felt that an element of confidence and preparation for the "big sale" was necessary on his own behalf.

Only an optimist could have looked at things this way, but that was one advantage of Reb Hirsh Moshe's optic disability. His blindness often enabled him to see more clearly than others, unencumbered as he was by the practicalities and considerations that normally obstruct man's vision. He could focus, as one should, only on the good in others, and remained blissfully blind to their deficiencies.

And even if his neighbor happened to be a punk thief, Reb Hirsh Moshe could see the good in him, too. Certain people are imbued with such lofty vision, but very few — perhaps no more than thirty-six in a generation — can maintain this farsightedness when they themselves are the victims. This is the true eye test, and apparently the Lord was pleased with the results.

FROM UP AVENUE U a mob of Italian women and their retinues began to descend upon Hirsh Moshe's pushcart. They were talking a mile a minute at the top of their robust lungs and his four little cubits on the street took on the flavor of a Neapolitan market. Dozens of women began removing roll after roll of material from the bowels of his cart. At first, Reb Hirsh Moshe feared they were going to clean him out, gravity-style. But he then noticed, to his great relief, that some congenial Sicilian chaperones were overseeing the proceedings and nodding their approval.

As long as the Sicilians were on your side, Reb Hirsh Moshe had learned over the years, there was nothing to worry about. Their approach was fairly simple: whatever worked in Italy worked over in Brooklyn, especially in terms of their conception of justice.

While the more industrious women were fighting over fabric, the more sentimental began kissing Hirsh Moshe

Cohen's hands and drooling all over his sleeves. It was quite a sight, but with the stocky Sicilians — their slicked-back hair gleaming and their chunky pinky rings glittering on their chunky pinkies — guarding the premises, Hirsh Moshe, as nauseated as he was, was in no hurry to close up his cart for the day.

Before the vendor fully grasped what was happening, tens of dollars had been pressed into his hands, punctuated by garlic-doused busses. His pushcart was sold out and the women, from what he could decode of their "English", wanted more. Reb Hirsh Moshe promised to be restocked early the next morning and they vowed to return with their fellow parishioners. And then, as abruptly as they had materialized, the entire lot noisily retreated up Avenue U.

What had happened, Reb Hirsh Moshe learned from the subsequent days of booming business, was that the woman whose dollar bill he had returned was the mother of the priest of the largest church in the area. Italians from all over Brooklyn — and, it seemed, from all over Italy — attended his church, and the previous Sunday his sermon had been devoted to the poor peddler who had risked everything he owned in order to return money to his mama. "This man is a living saint," the priest declared, "and we must pay homage to him." And pay they did.

Heard from: Rabbi Dovid Cohen

"You Are My Witness"

WITH OBVIOUS DISTASTE, Janousz rammed the leg brace of the workbench between the big vise and the dog blocks. The claw of his hammer gripping a bent sliver of steel and his shoulder inclined for better leverage, he wrenched a rusted nail from the crumbling wood.

"This is a job for a master carpenter?" he challenged, holding the remains of the nail up to the light and twisting it this way and that to see if it could catch a glint. He extended the hammer to his addlebrained apprentice, who was busy sanding cabinet handles. "What do you say, Igor?" he shouted over the rasping noise. "Can you believe this idiotic assignment?"

Igor's reply was a stertorous grunt — about the most eloquent response Janousz could hope to elicit. Apparently it satisfied his need for dialogue, for he continued his tirade.

"I got the finest hardwoods money can buy. I got hickory that will last a century. I got birch and fir without a single flaw, and oak like iron! But do they want any of those? No-o-o. They want I should use this antique. Whatever happened to plain old pine boxes? Answer me that!"

Igor grunted again and Janousz disgustedly hurled the nail through the open door of his carpentry shop and out onto the sidewalk where a pile of its brothers was mounting in a makeshift monument to his exasperation.

Normally the veteran cabinetmaker would have dropped salvaged nails into one of the large pockets of his dull gray apron, but these he discarded as though they were contaminated. "This is no work for an artisan," Janousz declared. "It's a job for a junkman! Am I right, or am I right?"

The apprentice's misaligned eyes lit up with a semblance of glee at the mention of the word "junkman," for this had been his father's profession. His grunt was significantly more enthusiastic this time. But his master paid him no heed.

"I MUST MAKE FIFTY, maybe sixty, coffins a year," the carpenter raged on, "and never was anyone so persistent over something so absurd. Sure, you always get people who want a casket made out of mahogany or walnut. But out of this garbage?" Janousz yanked a small plank out of the bench and thrust the decayed wood in front of Igor's face. "This stuff wouldn't even be good for kindling! Am I right, or am I right?"

Igor snorted in agreement as Janousz smashed his hammer down again, leaving the workbench without a leg to stand on. "I just don't understand," the carpenter ranted, punctuating his every thought with a resounding *wham!* "My father was buried in a plain pine box. *His* father was buried in a plain pine box. And for all I know, *his* father was buried in a plain pine box. It was good enough for them. Yet here am I, the greatest carpenter in all the Oberland, known near and far as a coffin specialist, submitting to this nonsense! Did my own father make any special requests of me? No-o-o, sir, he did not. *He* trusted me. That's right. Trusted an expert to do the job right." *Wham!*

"Igor, think of all those tall, beautiful pine trees chopped down for nothing. Clear pine I would have given him, with no knotholes, and he wants this... this... firewood! It's an embarrassment to the forests, I tell you. Am I right, or am I right?"

The apprentice grunted emphatically and smacked the sawhorse with his meaty paw as if to emphasize the foolhardiness of the undertaking.

"**I** COULD UNDERSTAND," Janousz continued, "if this workbench were something special, if it were finely finished or well-built. Maybe then they could justify saving on materials. But look at this! Igor, *you* could have done a better job. I really mean it! See? It's never even been sanded. Not one nail was driven in straight." To illustrate his point, he tore off another plank, which came away with a *screech!* "The stretcher is crooked and the tool well is practically upside-down. A bench couldn't be so rickety unless it started off wrong.

"This must be at least fifty years old; it's crumbling in my hands! Look here — dry rot and woodworm. Eech! It's teeming with termites and carpenter ants. Igor, this isn't normal. Am I right, or am..."

Before he could complete his rhetorical interrogative, Igor supplied the desired gutteral response and knocked over the heavy sawhorse with his elbow.

"You know what the explanation is?" Janousz concluded with fatherly certitude. "The poor guy thought he could take it with him. I once heard about a rich landowner who had his gold melted down to line his coffin. And that old dame — the one who wanted all her jewelry packed in with her body. She said she was afraid no one would take care of her precious gems after she was gone. Stupid woman — the graverobbers took care of them, all right. But this Jew, Abish — his workbench was all he had. What do you say, Igor, am I right or..."

֍

"**I**'M RIGHT, husband," the tailor's wife was saying.

"Shha, Mama," Abish replied, cradling a garment between his bowed head and crossed knees, "I'm counting."

"I know you are counting, husband. Counting stitches. You'll ruin your eyesight for sure. Can the counting not wait until daylight?"

The tailor carefully folded the coat, smoothing the wide lapels and straightening the pocket flaps. He then went on to appraise each dexterous stitch of his *piéce de résistance*, the shoulder, from which more than twenty individualized parts of the coat must hang in harmony and allow for fluidity. "The Baron is sending for his overcoat tonight," he explained, "and I must calculate the price to charge him for my work."

Avraham Eichler, better known as "Abish the Tailor," was a meticulous man, meticulous about his workmanship and meticulous in his accounting.

S INCE THE DAY he opened his business, he had allowed for only two factors in his prices: labor and material. The "going rate" was irrelevant to this pious man. Indeed, even the fee for his labor was based not on how much work had actually gone into the alteration, but on how much *should have*. If after mending an article Abish discovered that his patch was imperfect, or that he'd misaligned the pattern at the seam, he would redo it properly at no extra charge.

Abish recognized that the nature of his profession entailed an inherent trial of faith — in one sense, for his patrons, and in an altogether different sense, for himself. While commercial establishments such as groceries and bookstores would have set prices for stock items, a handicraftsman could not. Standard items of merchandise had standard prices, but there was no such thing as a standard rip, a conventional waistband, or two identical hemlines. No two inseams were the exact same length, and no hand-tailored suit ever had a twin. Minor alterations, button sewing, and cuff pressing varied from one garment to the next. Only the tailor himself was aware of every factor involved, and a patron could either have faith in the man's integrity or take his business elsewhere.

"You see, Mama," Abish explained patiently, "every bill I submit is a test of my customers' faith in me. If I make an error, they lose that faith." He shrugged his heavy, sloping shoulders in a familiar gesture, a small smile quirking at his lips. "Makes sense, no?"

BUT ON ANOTHER LEVEL entirely, being a tailor was a test of faith for Abish himself, as he was acutely aware. Most people go through their entire lives without ever touching someone else's money, and are spared this test of their integrity. Abish, however, was tested every day. While others draw a salary or stipend from some anonymous entity like a company, school, or government, their probity is never probed. But Abish was intimately acquainted with each and every person who contributed to his livelihood.

They were the men with whom he *davened* in shul, and the citizens he met on the streets and in the shops. He knew when they overindulged on *Yom Tov*, for they'd bring in their trousers to be let out. He knew their vanities and foibles — those who clung to styles too youthful for their years, and those who sought to create a high-fashion wardrobe with low-priced fabrics. He could follow the rise and fall of their fortunes by the orders they placed.

Although assessing their means was child's play for Abish, calculating his customers' bills was a less exact science. A patron's ability to overpay could never justify an overcharge. Despite the *Gemara*'s generalization, "*Rubam b'gezel*" — most people have some contact with theft — Abish was determined never to succumb to this temptation. His responsibility to man and God was woven into every fiber of his consciousness.

The material which his customers submitted to be fashioned, how they wished it pleated or tapered, and how they wanted the fabric's seams to be sewn were all clues to their financial standing. And their fur collars and high-crowned hats were not lost on his wife. "What difference would it make," she nudged, "if you charged a little extra to a man whose raiments are always made of the finest silk?"

Abish smiled, for they both knew the answer: all the difference in the world. To steal a single, solitary *groosh* was as sinful as embezzling a thousand crowns.

I T WAS STANDARD PROCEDURE for Abish to inspect every article of clothing he tailored for *shatnes*. If he ever discovered the forbidden combination of wool and linen, he would summarily remove it and insert permissible fabric in its place. He would then carefully restitch the area, but he never billed customers for this invaluable service. Hundreds of coats, jackets, suits, dresses and trousers were rendered free of *shatnes*, free of charge.

A mountain of apparel in need of mending routinely formed before every holiday. Abish would not commit himself to scaling this precipice before *Yom Tov*, but since he knew his customers very much wanted their garments back in time for the festival, he would do so anyway.

Yes, Abish's propriety was legendary. In his book, a shoddy alteration was also a form of stealing, as was the use of an inferior fabric to mend a tear. No job was ever refused for being too difficult or time-consuming. Scores of Jews and gentiles throughout the Oberland patronized this virtuous tailor without ever requesting a receipt for the items they deposited with him. So honest was Abish that no customer even dreamed of haggling over the price he quoted. If Abish charged it, it had to be fair.

A BISH'S MENTOR must have been the primordial Chanoch, a cobbler who the Midrash attests was *"miyached yichudim"* with his every stitch, accomplishing sublime spiritual feats beyond the ken of mortal man.

Chanoch bore the customer's comfort in mind with every seam he sewed and every nail he hammered. He worried how the shoes would feel and if they would stand up to wear and tear. Would they fit properly? Would they be ready on time? And would his price accurately reflect the labor invested?

Reb Yisrael Salanter explained Chanoch's spirituality as a function of his work ethic. His professional pride, concern for others, and pathological aversion to stealing elevated him to the angelic state of *"miyached yichudim."*

Like Chanoch the Cobbler, Abish the Tailor's integrity transcended the four walls of his shop. Once, when Abish was travelling on a train with the renowned and revered Nitra Rav, the conductor inexplicably failed to sell tickets in their car. When Rav and disciple reached their destination, the two of them — without prior discussion or pangs of conscience — headed straight for the ticket counter to make amends by purchasing tickets which they ripped and discarded.

ABISH AND HIS KIND, for whom honesty and good citizenship went hand-in-hand, were not destined to merit the grace of their countrymen when they needed it most. After the Austrian revolution Jews escaped to Hungary, hoping to settle where they wished, build homes and be permitted to wed. Little did they know that virulent vestiges of anti-Semitism would sail across the bloody Danube and dock at Budapest, reviving the cycle of Jewish history with vicious fury.

The year was 1919. Hungary was bleeding from a war into which the nationalists claimed they had been drawn by Germany, Austria and the Jewish-inspired left. In response, King Charles seceded from Austria, a popular but unwise move that left the country defenseless. Serb, Czech, and Rumanian troops installed themselves and began to devour their hosts. The Hungarian government moved radically to the left, and Bela Kun, a Jew, seized power and guaranteed his compatriots Russian protection against the Rumanians. That succor never arrived, however, and Kun's doctrinaire Bolshevism, enforced by a "red terror," antagonized the entire population.

Like so many of his People, Abish was accused of being a Bolshevist and was warned of the consequences. Tempers soared and matters came to a head with the Treaty of Trianon, which ceded economically and militarily strategic territories and non-Magyar populations. With one stroke of the pen, Hungarian plenipotentiaries were forced to relinquish two-thirds of that which had belonged to the Crown of Saint Stephen for more than a thousand years. The very populations and lands that had been inextricably intermingled in the Marches of Hungary were no more.

The populace was incensed and the rancor simmering for years exploded. Jews were murdered and their properties looted. With anti-Semitism its declared policy, the new regime promptly unleashed the "White Terror."

From one end of the country to the other, people fell upon the Jews with untamed cruelty. Mass hangings and assassinations, brutal lynchings and torturous dismemberments were executed with a ferocity determined to purge Hungary of the Bolshevist Israelites forever. Thousands of Jews rushed to the churches of Budapest to be baptized while others fled into hiding. The victims of the riots and atrocities have been estimated at three thousand, although there is no way of gauging those plundered in the countryside.

As soon as the violence subsided the Numerus Clausus Bill was passed, restricting Jewish activity in virtually every area. This was followed by the "Jewish Laws," which terminated the livelihood of 250,000 Hungarian Jews.

ABISH WAS FORTUNATE to retain his tiny shop but his destitute customers — now only fellow Jews — could no longer pay for his work. But the absence of remuneration did not dissuade him from carrying on. Hungry and impoverished, he was grateful to serve God and his brethren however he could, especially when he painfully recalled the thousands of martyrs robbed of this privilege.

But what the self-proclaimed "awakened Hungarians" could not do, nature itself was accomplishing. At his advanced age, Abish found his everyday tasks more and more taxing. Simply hauling an overcoat onto his workbench became a tedious chore which left him exhausted, and threading a needle strained his senescent eyes.

Abish the Tailor looked around his modest shop and realized that his long career was coming to an end. Suit orders were as scarce as supplies, and the heaps of clothing waiting to be mended had dwindled to a shadow of their once-Carpathian proportions. Worse yet, he sensed that his few remaining customers felt they were doing him a favor by reluctantly entrusting their finest garments to his shaky, enfeebled hands.

"Maybe," he thought to himself, "I should close the shop for good and spare them their twinges of guilt that make them patronize me."

It was an agonizing decision to make. He knew that he was dying and that his days left on this earth were preciously numbered. The war and its subsequent pogroms had ravaged practically everything material he owned; but he knew that would not be his legacy.

ABISH'S RHEUMY EYES began to swim and a lump lodged itself firmly in his throat. He saw his years as a trusty tailor pass before him, and he recalled each incident where his integrity had prevailed. He'd calculated every stitch, and withheld nary a shred of fabric that did not belong to him. Not once was a customer ever overcharged or misinformed.

Abish looked lovingly at his workbench, and traced his tremorous fingers along its rough edges. He had built it himself more than half a century earlier. Although it had always rocked a bit and had never even been properly sanded, it had served him well. Decades of inadvertent buffing with lengths of serge and gabardine had endowed it with a slight sheen and the tailor could almost discern his image reflected in the surface.

Tears rolled down Abish's wrinkled cheeks and splashed onto the wood. "You are my witness," he whispered to his silent companion. Feeling faint, he gripped the workbench with both hands and repeated, "You are my witness."

Heard from: Rabbi Dovid Hersh Mayer

Home, Sweet Home

ACCORDING TO THE LADIES in the neighborhood, Sam Levine wasn't much of a landlord. It was common knowledge that he could get four or five times the rent he charged old Mrs. Kaplan. Why, according to their calculations (which were extremely precise, since it was someone else's money rather than their own), he was actually losing money.

That's right. Losing money, when you figured in depreciation, wear and tear, lost income, found income, the effect of the elderly on the ozone layer, and a myriad or so of other details too petty to mention.

"Mr. Levine," accused Mrs. Nudnik, "I'm surprised at you. My friend has an apartment just like yours and she's asking $150 a week. If I'm not mistaken, you're only charging Mrs. Kaplan $150 a *month*. Don't you know she can afford much more than that? She's loaded!"

"That's right," Mrs. Mandelbaum chimed in. "I know it for a fact. I heard it from Sylvia Fine. And she heard it from Gloria Buchsbaum, who heard it from Mrs. Kaplan's sister-in-law's cleaning lady! According to Mrs. Kaplan's sister-in-law, she earned thousands and millions of dollars on the stock market!"

"And cash!" cried Mrs. Zalmanowitz. "I bet she's got more money lying around her apartment than we've ever seen! Yet she never spends a cent — never! She even used to ask for my boy's outgrown clothes for her children!"

"*GENUG!* Enough!" Sam protested. "In *Pirke Avos*, we find that Envy, Desire and the need for Honor drive a person from this world. It sounds as if you ladies want to travel first class!"

"Mark our words, Mr. Levine. She's using you. She could afford to live in a mansion, with servants waiting on her hand-and-foot. But you're just as good. You don't charge her much. You buy her things. Sometimes you even cook for her!"

"I don't want to hear any more, Mrs. Mandelbaum. Or I won't save you any chicken feet for your Shabbos soup!" Instantly, she was quiet.

S AM LEVINE was the neighborhood butcher. Every day, he sawed, sliced, cubed, and ground meat for friends, family, and the few strangers who wandered into his tiny shop off Grove Street.

"Who cares if Mrs. Kaplan has put away a little money?" Sam told the crowd of women. "It's probably not as much as you think. And even if it is, that's nobody's business but hers."

"Well, don't say we didn't have your best interests at

heart," Mrs. Zalmanowitz piped up.

"Thank you very much, Mrs. Zalmanowitz. And the next time I need advice, I'll know exactly whom to call."

As the flock of ladies trooped out of the store, chattering away about this and that, Sam sighed with relief. "I don't know where they get their ideas or why they carry on like that, but I sure wish they would stop!"

EVERY NIGHT when Sam returned home, he would knock on old Mrs. Kaplan's door to make sure she was all right. After a couple of minutes, he could hear the sound of tiny footsteps slowly making their way to the door, followed by a squeaky "Who is it?"

"It's Sam, Mrs. Kaplan. Can I do anything for you today?"

"Why, yes, as a matter of fact. Please come in."

Sam would gently open the door to find a small wisp of a woman in her late eighties. "How can I help you?" he would ask.

This evening's request was a familiar one. "Mr. Levine, I want to move my furniture around. Could you help me?"

"*Oy vey*, not again!" he thought to himself. Every *Montag und Donnershtik*, she was rearranging her apartment. The first few times Sam did the mitzva because he felt sorry for her. But now it was becoming a habit; and a bad one at that. Still, if it made her happy...

"All right, where do you want the piano to go this time?" he inquired.

"Over there, next to the end table. And move the

potted rubber tree to the other side of the living room... That's better. Now if we can just manage to slide the sofa between the wall and the wing chair."

"Mrs. Kaplan, it won't fit. That's a five-foot space. You've got a six-foot sofa."

"Can't you just try?"

"I tried the last time, and the time before that."

"Please?"

"Okay, okay... But it's not going to work."

It didn't.

"Oh my, you're right. Could I trouble you to put everything back where it was?"

If Heaven gave an Academy Award for acting, Sam Levine would have walked away with it.

After it was all over, the ever-grateful Mrs. Kaplan said sublimely, "Thank you, Mr. Levine. You're such a sweet dear!"

Mrs. Kaplan had her own children: two boys and a girl. They were all grown up but neither they nor their children ever visited. On rare occasions, they would call or write. But that was the extent of the communication. Mrs. Buchsbaum claimed it was because she didn't spend money on them when they were children. But Sam didn't pay any attention to her. "It's not my business!" he would exclaim. "And contrary to popular belief, it's not even yours!"

Sam's patience with his tenant was legendary. When Mrs. Kaplan turned 75, she naively asked if he wouldn't mind switching apartments, as she was too old to climb the stairs to the second floor. Any other landlord would have given her the name and phone number of a senior citizens' home. But not Sam. He said he would think about it. And sure enough, a week later, he helped her move all her things downstairs.

"I've always wanted to move up in the world," he told his gawking neighbors. "And now the Almighty has enabled me to do it."

F OR CLOSE TO TWO DECADES Sam Levine and Mrs. Kaplan lived in the same two-family home. Then one day, it all came to an end.

As usual, Sam knocked on Mrs. Kaplan's door when he got home from work. When she failed to respond, he knocked again, shouting "Mrs. Kaplan! Mrs. Kaplan!" But there was no answer.

Concerned, and more than a little scared, he hurried upstairs to find his key to her apartment. He searched his broom closet where the extra key usually hung, rummaged through his junk drawer, and finally found it in his old jewelry box, alongside six pairs of late-fifties-style cuff links.

Sam darted back down the steps. The old key fit neatly into the lock and with a twist and a click, the door was open. Sam rushed into the kitchen, calling Mrs. Kaplan's name.

"Here. Over here." Her voice sounded weak and hollow.

Sam sped into the dining room, but she wasn't there. She wasn't in the living room, either. He peeked into the bedroom. No luck.

"Mrs. Kaplan, where are you?"

"Here..." Her voice sounded weaker still.

Sam pushed open the bathroom door and found Mrs. Kaplan lying on the floor. He dropped to his knees. "What happened? Are you all right?"

"I fell... hit my head..." she responded.

"Don't move. I'm calling an ambulance!"

Sam raced to the phone and dialed 911, the code for Emergency Medical Technicians. Every second seemed like a minute, and every minute like an hour. Eventually the operator answered.

Sam tried explaining what had happened, but the words wouldn't come out coherently. He was forced to repeat everything slowly, including his name. "Sam Levine... Not Ravine. L-E-V-I-N-E!"

After an interminable delay, the operator told him an EMT ambulance would be there in five or ten minutes.

Sam hung up the phone and ran back to the bathroom, only to find Mrs. Kaplan unconscious.

F INALLY, Sam heard the sirens. He bolted out of the house to make sure the ambulance wouldn't pass him by. It screeched to a halt in the middle of the road, lights flashing, and a man and a woman jumped out. "She's in here," Sam said, flailing his arms and leading them to the bathroom.

The two technicians leaned over Mrs. Kaplan. They checked her weak pulse and ran for the stretcher. In seconds, they were back, gingerly securing the frail octogenarian in the portable bed. Then they inserted an intravenous needle and some sort of solution began dripping into her veins. As they hoisted the stretcher up into the ambulance, Sam climbed aboard.

"Are you a relative?"

"Well, yes and no. I mean, I'm not related. But I take care of her."

"If you're not a relation, I'm afraid you'll have to follow us in your car."

Sam reluctantly agreed, the door closed, the lights immediately turned on, the engine turned over, the siren whooped, and the ambulance charged off.

Sam tried to stay behind the ambulance but it was hopeless. It was a long, traffic-infested drive to the hospital and after just two short blocks he got caught at a red light. By the time he reached the Emergency Room, Mrs. Kaplan had already been transferred...

Sam rushed to the front desk. "Mrs. Kaplan... what's her condition?"

The attending physician looked up at the trembling butcher. "Are you her next of kin?" he asked.

"Next of..." Sam's voice trailed off.

"I'm sorry to say..." the doctor hesitated, employing the stock medical phrase that physicians resort to when they don't know what else to say. His words felt like a knife plunging into Sam's heart. He closed his eyes.

"I'm sorry to say she's gone..."

SAM TOOK HIS TIME going home. "I suppose I've got to make all the arrangements," he muttered to himself, trying to keep a clear head. "First thing I should do is notify her kids. But how? I don't even know where they live."

Pulling into his driveway, he noticed that in his haste he had left the front door to Mrs. Kaplan's apartment wide open. He went inside. "I'd better look for some letters or a phone bill or something. Maybe that will tell me how to get in touch with her children."

Sam began his search in the living room and worked his way into the kitchen. Mrs. Kaplan was always a very tidy woman, yet he couldn't even find the electric bill, much less a letter from loved ones.

He entered the bedroom and felt extraordinarily uncomfortable, as if Mrs. Kaplan would suddenly appear and ask what he was doing. With a twinge of trepidation, Sam opened her dresser drawer. Hidden among an array of head scarves, he discovered a small shoe box. "This must be it," he thought.

Sam lifted the surprisingly heavy box, removed the lid, and stared at the contents in disbelief. It was crammed with dollar bills: tens, twenties, fifties — hundreds of them!

Sam could see the money was old because the bills were not "Federal Reserve Notes" but "Silver Certificates." They were not only old, they were rare, and their worth far exceeded their face value. Sam's heart began pounding loud and fast. He pulled out another drawer and came upon a second box. This, too, was filled with money. Sam's eyes opened as wide as silver dollars, appropriately enough, since that was precisely what he saw: close to a thousand of them!

Quickly yet methodically, Sam Levine searched Mrs. Kaplan's bedroom. From her six dresser drawers, he recovered twelve boxes stuffed with cash and coins. In her closet, he found another five and under her bed ten more.

Her room also contained an old steamer trunk that was locked, and inordinately heavy. Sam was still looking for a way to contact her kids, he reminded himself, and a second later the trunk lock was broken open. Inside there were yellowed stock certificates, containers of coins, cash and more cash.

Sam was stunned. He had broken into a treasure trove worth hundreds of thousands of dollars.

The landlord walked out of the bedroom in a state of shock. All these years, he had pitied her. All these years, he'd never raised her rent. All these years, he'd fetched her groceries, moved her couches, run her errands.

Sam Levine felt like a fool.

HE RETURNED TO THE KITCHEN to resume his search for a name, address, phone number — any clue of Mrs. Kaplan's children. As his hands emptied out drawers, his mind sorted out thoughts: "By rights, some of that money belongs to me. After all, I took care of her. Her children never did that. If I wanted to, I could hide it all. Her kids would never know. I suppose that would be stealing. But taking a couple thousand wouldn't. It would make up for all the shlepping I did."

Finally, sandwiched between plastic-coated recipes for "Sweet and Sour Stuffed Derma" and "Diet-Delight Kugel," he found what he was looking for: a small, battered address book. Sam flipped to the Ks, and there were the phone numbers and addresses of her two sons.

He picked up the phone and then replaced it, consumed by curiosity. "Maybe I should count the money," he rationalized. "I'm sure her sons will want to know how much there is."

For the next three hours, the same fingers deft in cleaving feet and hacking away gristle riffled through piles of bank notes. Sam patiently counted and stacked hundreds of bills, tallying the results on a large sheet of paper. The total came to $72,589 in cash, and Mrs. Kaplan's bank books listed $843,755 in assets (plus interest). There were also untold numbers of stocks and bonds of indeterminate value.

"Just ten thousand dollars," urged a persistent little voice inside him. "That's all. You don't have to be greedy."

Sam shook his head to get rid of the thoughts, but they came roaring back. "C'mon, ten thousand isn't even five percent... Think of the tzeddakah you could give... I'll bet her children won't say Kaddish. With a couple thousand, you could pay a kollel Rabbi to say Kaddish for a year. Mrs. Kaplan would want that! She would probably be willing to pay you for it. After all, she relied on you for everything else."

Mustering all his strength of character, Sam marched back into the kitchen, determined to make the phone call. "Don't tell them," the inner voice bargained. "See how they act first. Maybe they couldn't care less about their mother's passing. Maybe they'll leave you with the funeral expenses."

Sam looked at the phone and then at the stacks of bills. He scratched his head and cogitated, and then he stared again.

"**H**ELLO, this is Sam Levine," he said to the man who answered the phone. "Are you Carl Kaplan?"

"Yes I am."

"I was your mother's landlord. I'm sorry to tell you this... but your mother passed away this morning."

"Oh, my gosh..."

"She left you and your brother and sister some $72,000 in cash along with several bank books and stock certificates."

❦

Mrs. Mandelbaum and the other ladies in the neighborhood will be happy to tell you the rest of the story. How the children came and ransacked the apartment looking for more cash. How they carted away all the money and didn't give Sam Levine a dime. How they didn't even thank him for all he had done over the years.

Yes, according to the ladies in the neighborhood Sam Levine wasn't much of a landlord. But the true landLord must have considered him a special man indeed.

Heard from: Ruthie Buckler

Balance Sheet

Months	Chesed	Teshuvah	Torah	Terillah	Tzeddakah	Aveiros
Tishrei						
Cheshvan						
Kislev						
Teves						
Shevat						
Adar						
Nissan						
Iyyar						
Sivan						
Tammuz						
Av						
Ellul						

Operating in the Black

Prepared by

Date

Index No.

※

מרמה נקרא... אפילו אם אין בעצם השקר
נזק והפסד לחבירו אך יתכן בו לעשותו סיבה
אל הנזק ואל הרע...

שפת תמים פרק א'

Even if a lie does not result in damage
or a loss, it is still considered fraud if
the intention was destructive or evil.

Sfas Tamim: 1

Special Delivery

THE EL AL jingle resounded through the jumbo as it commenced its taxi down the runway. Most eyes were focused on the screen at the head of the cabin, where a stewardess on film delineated the designated smoking areas and emergency exits and explained where to stow baggage, and how to lock one's tray table, adjust one's seat position, and fasten one's seat belt.

But two passengers sitting directly in front of the screen were oblivious to the video. Young American women in their twenties, and sisters-in-law for four years, they were thoroughly engrossed in their discussion. Since Devorah Katz's two young daughters were already sound asleep, and Chani Rosenfeld's son was being lulled into dreamland in his mother's lap, there was nothing to distract them.

"How do you feel?" Devorah asked for the fourth time.

"Like I said, I'm fine, really. The doctor said I'm not due for another six weeks."

"I sure hope so," Devorah said with a grin.

"You sound like Eli Meir. You know what his last words were to me after check-in? 'Don't do something silly like give birth in the air.' Some sense of humor he has. Anyway, you both have nothing to worry about — Shragi here was two weeks overdue. He takes after his father — always late."

Devorah laughed.

"You know, if this baby is as late as Shragi was, I'll be spending Pesach in the hospital."

"I wouldn't worry about it."

"I'm not worried: whatever happens, happens — here, there, or anywhere. I just wish Eli Meir could have come back with us. He won't be returning for another three weeks."

"You'll manage," Devorah said confidently.

"I know that," Chani responded with maternal assurance. "I just wonder if *he* will."

"I was wondering the same thing about Yehoshua," Devorah added.

"I wasn't referring to the daily chores of cleaning up, making meals, and doing laundry," Chani explained. "I mean Eli Meir's condition. He is simply beat.

"On Tuesday Shragi developed a high fever and, amid all the preparations for the trip, Eli Meir had to shlep him to the doctor, get the medicine, have a test taken; he's been running around for three days straight. The house looks like a tornado hit it and decided to stay."

"You know," Devorah added, thinking in turn of her other half, "Yehoshua said he has been looking forward to our leaving so he can have a little quiet for a few weeks."

"That's my brother for you," Chani quipped. "He knows how to make everyone feel needed."

"What do you think Eli Meir is going to do in a big apartment all by himself?" Devorah pressed.

"Well, there's no question about tonight. If I know him, the second Yehoshua drops him off he is going to close all the shutters, unplug the phone, write 'DO NOT DISTURB' on the door, and go to sleep until Shabbos."

"Chani," Devorah yawned, fluffing up her skimpy airplane pillow, "I think Eli Meir is on to something."

"DEVORAH, wake up. Wake UP!"

"Wh... Whaddya want?" Devorah mumbled without opening her eyes.

"I'm having a baby," Chani whimpered.

"I know you're having a baby," Devorah responded, pulling the cover back over her head.

"I mean now!"

"Now? NOW?!"

"Now."

"Now!!!"

Devorah jumped out of her seat as if scorched by a live wire, discharging a sleeping infant on the way. "Oh no," she began to scream hysterically. In seconds Devorah was running back and forth in the aisle, screeching that her sister-in-law was having a baby. This did nothing to help the situation, but it did alert the entire plane to the development.

IT WAS FOUR O'CLOCK in the morning Israel time, but everyone roused himself out of his seat to discuss the news and contribute to total pandemonium.

"Who's having a baby?" "She is." "Who?" "The one up front." "Where?" "Here." "No, where's she sitting?" "In front of the screen." "Oh, I thought that was part of the movie."

Firmly yet politely, the stewardesses took charge. First, they got most of the passengers out of the aisles and into their seats, by no means a simple enterprise. Then they devoted themselves to Chani, clearing a few seats to enable her to stretch out and shielding her from the rush of onlookers converging from all directions.

A flight attendant asked over the P.A. if there was a doctor on board. A few minutes later, Melvin Frentic, M.D., reluctantly reported to the stewardess stationed at row nineteen.

She escorted the visibly nervous physician over to the expectant mother's chairside. Distressed by the doctor's decidedly unprofessional air, a crew member asked what his specialty was. "P... po... po... podiatr... ist," came the reply.

The stewardess gravely explained that his prognosis would determine whether they would continue on schedule or make an emergency landing.

"Oh my," Melvin Frentic cried, bracing himself for the momentous task assigned to him. Spluttering in a half-whisper, he asked Chani to remove her shoe for an examination.

"She's giving birth!" the stewardess exclaimed. "Her foot is irrelevant!"

"R... right you are," Melvin conceded. "I better take her pulse." Frentic placed his sweaty fingers on Chani's ankle and felt for a beat. But even after an alert steward guided him to her wrist, he was hopeless. Every few seconds he started making a calculation by counting his fingers, presumably in an attempt to calculate an average from the few times he stumbled across the pulsation.

B Y THE TIME the good doctor had demonstrated his inability to diagnose anything more complex than a bunion, a flight attendant had announced that although they were directly over Amsterdam, the Dutch authorities had refused them landing rights. They would soon commence their initial descent on Heathrow Airport in England, however, where they had been cleared for an emergency landing.

Minutes later, the captain announced that he was turning on the "fasten seat belt" sign in preparation for an unscheduled landing in London. A raucous buzz swept through the plane.

"Unscheduled landing? What does that mean?" "It means an 'emergency landing!'" one armchair pilot with an especially loud voice broadcast. Total panic erupted and once again everyone stood up as the stewardesses raced through the aircraft, calming and sitting people down.

Devorah informed Chani that she was coming with her.

"But what will we do with the children?" Chani protested between contractions.

"I've already taken care of that," Devorah reported. "All the kids are sleeping and this couple across the aisle has offered to deliver them to my parents in New York." Chani grunted what Devorah assumed was agreement.

AS SOON AS the jet taxied to a halt, the door closest to row nineteen burst open and two British policewomen appeared at the gangway. Behind them were two men, who carried Chani down the steps in a wheelchair.

"Since you have not cleared passport control," one officer of the law informed the two startled Americans, "you are to remain in our custody." With no further ado, the police accompanied the foreigners to the Middlesex Maternity Hospital, where to Devorah's apoplectic consternation, their officious escorts attached themselves to their ersatz suspects and monitored their every move.

With her sister-in-law in good hands, Devorah ran to a pay phone to tell Eli Meir about the funny thing that had happened to them on their way to America. But the international operator would not honor her credit card for a call to Israel. She did manage to get through to her mother-in-law in America, however. It was early Friday morning.

❀

E LI MEIR FUMBLED for the keys to his apartment, rummaging through the used tissues, medicine bottles, and cookie crumbs nestled in his pocket. Three days of attending to Shragi and packing for his wife had taken its toll. He tried to recall his last decent night's sleep, but his memory failed to reach back that far.

The bachelor of one hour turned on the light in the entryway and desperately maneuvered his way through the junk to his bedroom. He had never navigated such a mess, but for the time being he couldn't have cared less. He had only one thing on his mind.

He flung his jacket onto a chair in the living room, and his vest was discarded a few feet later. His tie must somehow have joined its companions on the floor because by the time he made it to the bedroom it was no longer around his neck. Zombie-like, Eli Meir hermetically sealed every window and drew every shade. Then, with the help of gravity, he did a free fall into his bed.

Ten seconds later he leaped out of bed, unplugged the telephone from the wall socket and resumed his earlier pose.

A FEW MINUTES LATER, or so it seemed to the extraordinarily fatigued man, a nuclear attack was launched on his front door. It started with incessant knocking punctuated by ringing doorbells and followed by kicks and knee slams, which rapidly built up into a crescendo of battering-ram thuds and hoarse shouts.

Squinting one eye open at a time, Eli Meir struggled

over to what remained of his front door and looked through the peep hole to discover his brother-in-law busily engaged in house wrecking. A stinging fear of tragedy gripped Eli Meir's soul. As premonitions of a hijacking or engine trouble, God forbid, swiftly wreaked havoc upon his conscience, he flung open the door.

"Get dressed!" Yehoshua Katz panted, rubbing his bruised palms and massaging his wounded shoulders. "You're having a limey baby!"

"What?!" cried Eli Meir, both eyes suddenly wide open.

"You heard it. At this very hour Chani may be giving birth in London. My mother called twenty minutes ago with the news. She couldn't get through to you. Lemme tell you, I feared that I wouldn't be able to, either."

"What... what do I do now?"

"The custom is for the husband to be present when his wife gives birth. I've already done it twice — it's S.O.P. Barring geographical problems, the father usually attempts to arrive at the scene of the *simcha* as expeditiously as possible."

Eli Meir didn't find his brother-in-law's sarcasm especially amusing at the time.

"Do you have any money for a ticket?" Yehoshua asked.

"Not a penny."

"That makes two of us. You get hold of a travel agent who can get you on any flight to England and I'll try and scrounge some money. We'll meet back here in an hour. Until then, pack a suitcase or clean up this mess, for Heaven's sake!"

SLEEPY BUT SYMPATHETIC, Eli Meir's travel agent informed him that there was only one flight that day to England, which was leaving at 10:30. And at such late notice, El Al would only accept reservations at the airport. She reckoned that getting on the flight was a long shot, but considering what had happened since Chani boarded, anything was possible.

Eli Meir had barely put down the receiver when Yehoshua returned, out of both breath and time.

"I thought you said you would be back here in an hour," Eli Meir said.

"That was before I found out that there is only one flight to England today. We better hustle if we want to make it."

"I don't think I have a chance," Eli Meir shrugged.

"Don't worry," Yehoshua asserted with the confidence of an intrepid diamond merchant who was once marooned in Detroit, "I'll get you on that flight, please God."

ELI MEIR hastily shlepped his suitcase downstairs as Yehoshua gunned the motor of his car. He had barely closed the door behind him when his brother-in-law floored the gas pedal, hurling him straight into the dashboard. Stock-car racers had nothing on Yehoshua Katz.

"I heard there is a new route to the airport through Givon," Yehoshua hollered over the protests of the engine. "We can save four minutes."

"Please! Don't try anything new," Eli Meir begged. "We're in a big enough rush as is; now isn't the time to start experimenting!"

"It's not really so new," Yehoshua retorted. "It's supposed to be right off the Ramot Road, and I certainly know where *that* is."

ELI MEIR would have voiced further objection to a driver who was obviously under the assumption that the way to an airport must be a runway, but decided to devote his energies to holding onto his seat. Besides, he knew better than to argue with a driven man.

Gritting his teeth and bearing down on the steering wheel, Yehoshua forced his little car up the incline to Ramot as fast as it would go. The scenery became a kaleidoscope of fleeting images and Eli Meir had to ask Yehoshua once again if he was sure he knew where he was going.

"Just look for a sign to Givon," Yehoshua instructed.

"All I can see is a distinct blur," Eli Meir cried.

"There it is!" Yehoshua suddenly announced triumphantly, but by the time he hit the brakes, the sign was easily 150 meters behind them. Yehoshua deftly spun the car around on two wheels, which screeched in pain. So did the oncoming traffic.

In no time Katz completed his U-ee and let instinct navigate him past the sign and onto a narrow, unpaved road lined with olive trees. Even on this rocky surface, he managed to maintain his breakneck pace until a huge truck loaded with chickens appeared on a direct collision course.

Eli Meir yelped in a desperate attempt to articulate his fear, but the speed demon was busy plotting how to proceed uninhibited by the most obstructive presence imaginable on such a tiny road. Yehoshua shot through the first hiatus in the olive trees and continued across what appeared to be a wheat field.

"Do you realize what you are doing?" Eli Meir demanded, aghast at the mowing being perpetrated by his brother-in-law.

"Of course," Yehoshua reacted nonchalantly, "I'm making shredded wheat."

A T HIS FIRST OPPORTUNITY, Katz jerked the car back onto the unpaved road, swerving to miss a sign. "TO GIVON," the billboard beckoned innocuously, but it was flanked by six of the largest German shepherds ever to roam the Middle East.

Each one displayed a frightening set of teeth dripping with a Pavlovian reaction of unusual intensity. Devouring a half a ton of steel and its contents would clearly pose no difficulties to those ravenous-looking creatures.

Barking at the top of their robust lungs, the canines chased the car in between chickens, over cow paths, around piles of hay, through a row of tractors and away from occasional cyclists. Miracle of miracles, even on their own turf the beasts were no match for man's second-best friend: four-wheel drive. Their prey managed to escape intact, which was more than anyone could say for the moshav. "I wouldn't have minded stopping to pick up some eggs," Yehoshua quipped, "...but I suppose we're in a rush.

"Speaking of which, we should be there by now," the automotive aficionado shouted as they burned rubber back to civilization. "Keep your eye out for the tarmac."

Craning his neck as many degrees as humanly possible, Eli Meir shrieked with delight as the highway came into view. "There's the airport!" Eli Meir exclaimed.

"Not so fast," Yehoshua commented sourly at the surrealistic sight arrayed before him: troops, battalions, platoons, and regiments of the Israel Defense Forces were double-timing across the road. Even fearless Yehoshua Katz was not prepared to take on the entire Israeli Army to get his brother-in-law on a plane. "Now what?" Eli Meir asked.

"Don't worry."

"Do I have a choice?"

"I'm thinking, I'm thinking."

OBVIOUSLY without investing too much thought, Yehoshua proceeded to commit the biggest driving error in the book. He drove onto the highway from the only point of entry available: the exit ramp. The last things Eli Meir saw before covering his eyes with his clenched fists were the WRONG WAY signs positioned strategically on both sides of the ramp.

Driving faster than an exiting car ever would, Yehoshua darted out onto the highway heading away from the airport. "Don't worry," he said with the same confidence that marked the journey from the outset, "all we need is one little, or make that big, U-ee to get us back on the right track." And with that, Yehoshua pulled the car around as four lanes of traffic screamed, honked, brayed, and escaped from the motorized menace up ahead.

"It really paid to take the short cut," Yehoshua proclaimed with total ebullience as he pulled his vertiginous vehicle up in front of the departure terminal of the airport. "Just like I said, we saved four minutes."

"What a bargain," Eli Meir muttered.

THE TWO ROAD WARRIORS dashed into the airport and went straight to the El Al counter. "I must get on the 10:30 flight to England," Eli Meir blurted out.

"Let me see your ticket," the hostess responded.

"Well, I... er, don't have one."

The hostess punched a few keys. There was room on the plane, she explained, but he'd have to purchase a ticket at the cashier. Relieved that their efforts had not been in vain, Eli Meir pushed his way over to the cashier and asked for a ticket: Tel Aviv, London, New York, Tel Aviv.

"Will that be cash or charge?" the clerk asked.

"Charge, please."

"That will be $1,314."

"What?" Eli Meir gasped.

The cashier repeated the astronomical figure. It dwarfed his meager budget.

"Are you sure?"

"Yes, but if you pay in cash it's only $997." Eli Meir thought quickly. He had exactly one thousand dollars. If he paid for the ticket in cash, that would leave him with precisely three dollars to get to the hospital, not to mention his other expenses. He hesitantly removed the money from his wallet and handed it to the clerk but didn't offer, "Keep the change."

CONSUMED BY his financial constraints and unable to find anyone in possession of *Europe on $3 a Day*, Eli Meir spent the entire trip dreaming up imaginative, inexpensive modes of transportation. Fortunately, all his far-fetched calculations and scenarios proved superfluous, for he was met at the gate by an El Al agent.

"Mr. Rosenfeld?"

"Ye... Yes?"

"Mazel Tov! One hour ago your wife gave birth to a girl. Mother and baby are just fine. We have a car outside waiting to take you to the hospital."

ELI MEIR was escorted directly to Chani's room, which had been brightened with a generous bouquet of flowers. They had seen each other just a half a day before, but so much had transpired during the last twelve hours.

"Mazel Tov!" Eli Meir greeted his jubilant wife. "How are you?"

"*Baruch Hashem*, just wonderful. And so is the baby. She's small as Shragi was. How did you manage to get here so fast? How was your trip, the drive to the airport?"

"Uneventful," he replied, struggling to keep a straight face. "Where are all these flowers from?"

"El Al. I don't know where I'd be without them. Their people even visited me an hour ago."

"I don't know how they found this place. Where are we?" Eli Meir inquired.

"You should know better than I do," Chani responded. "I came here in the middle of the night, and I wasn't exactly sightseeing at the time. I know we're not in Picadilly Circus or Trafalgar Square, or London for that matter, and from what I've noticed of the people here, they're not exactly cosmopolitan."

"I'm going to go take a look at the baby, and then I better get into town to buy some food for Shabbos and find a place to stay."

"That's all taken care of."

"What?"

"The airline sent over sixteen kosher meals and they also made reservations for you and Devorah at the only hotel within walking distance, the Victorian Palace."

WITH SUCH AN AUGUST NAME, Eli Meir feared that the Victorian Palace must be the local equivalent of the Ritz. He had already spent enough on this *simcha* and could do without any more unnecessary expenses. Looking around the cavernous ward, Eli Meir wondered, "It's almost Shabbos — why can't I sleep here?"

"I don't think they'll go for that," Chani said. "Don't forget, you're in England... but you can try."

Eli Meir approached the head nurse, explained his situation, and asked if he could spend the night in his wife's enormous room.

The woman's eyes dilated to their fullest. She seemed so extraordinarily shocked that Eli Meir was sure she hadn't understood him, so he repeated his request.

The nurse straightened her carriage and answered curtly, "It wouldn't be 'propaw.'"

C HANI had been right. They were a long way from Israel, and he wasn't about to alter Her Majesty's subjects regarding their conception of propriety. He would have to make do with what was provided.

Back at his wife's side, he asked what had happened to Devorah.

"She went out shopping. She was all excited about going to Harrods. You know Devorah... She asked, 'how could I come to England without shopping?' and off she went."

News of Devorah's escapades put a damper on Eli Meir's happiness and his anger began to rage. "I thought she came to be of help, and off she goes galavanting *erev Shabbos* on a shopping spree!"

"No, no, she went for nappies."

"Nappies?! There are beds here!"

"Nap P I E S."

"Linen she wants?"

"No, that's what they call diapers. Over here, you must supply your own diapers for your baby. And if you don't bring nappies, well then..."

"I got the picture. I also got no time. It's almost Shabbos. Where can I call a cab?"

"Try the front desk... and make sure your request is 'propaw.'"

ONE OF THE NURSES informed Eli Meir that it would take at least forty minutes for a taxi to arrive, and there was no public transportation to the inn. Panic-stricken, he set out on foot, huffing and puffing his two suitcases along the road. Every minute he glanced at his watch, willing it to slow down, but it refused to cooperate.

Shabbos was minutes away and he still had a long way to the hotel. In desperation, he mustered nerve he didn't know he had and begged a man watering his garden to drive him over to the Victorian Palace. He realized how foolish it must have appeared to be staying at a lavish resort and be shlepping luggage by hand. "You'll be handsomely rewarded," Eli Meir promised, alluding to more esoteric recompense rather than his remaining three dollars. "I can always throw in a kosher airline meal or two to sweeten the pot," he thought to himself.

But the Cockney gardener gawked at Eli Meir. He understood that he was being spoken to, but in what language? "Whatcha talkin 'bout, mate?"

"I need a ride to the Victorian Palace. If I don't make it before the Sabbath, I'll be stuck here with all my bags!"

THOROUGHLY BEWILDERED, the man turned to his wife as she was coming out of the house. "What yer reckon this geezer's on about, luv?"

Eli Meir gesticulated madly as if grasping a steering wheel.

"Like a cuppa?" the wife offered.

"What?"

"Cuppa tea?"

"No, no, I don't want any tea, I just came from the maternity hospital and..."

"'Trouble and strife' is thataway, mate."

"What?"

"'Trouble and strife' is a wife."

"...And I have to get to the hotel up the road real fast."

"Oh, you wanna thumb a lift in my mo'er, mate." The man's eyes lit up in sudden comprehension. "Why didn't you say so?"

TWO MINUTES before sundown, Eli Meir Rosenfeld checked in to the Ritz of Middlesex, England. Had he had even one more minute to spare, he would have checked out and sought less "propaw" accommodations.

Clearly, El Al's sole criterion in arranging this lodging had been propinquity. Spending Shabbos in rural England on a few hours' notice was disorienting enough for this *yungermann*; being thrust into a decadent British subculture was downright harrowing. The lobby was crowded with a sight Eli Meir had never seen or imagined in his wildest nightmares: rockers wearing heavy metal, rivet-studded leather vests, graphic Kodachrome tattoos, earrings that made their lobes look like they were under acupuncture, and hair streaked in a rainbow of colors, apparently the latest thing in teen attire in that locale. The odor of fulsome incense mingled with other burning weeds contributed to an unusually revolting aroma.

"Culture shock" would be a woefully inadequate description of Eli Meir's reaction. "Culture upheaval" would be more accurate.

"HELLO, is this the Katz family?"

"... Yes."

"This is Gideon Ben Dror, captain of El Al Flight 001. We are vectoring in on New York and I would like to ask you some questions before we land."

Had Mrs. Katz not already been woken up that night with the news that her daughter had given birth in England, she would have dismissed the call as a prank. But under the circumstances, she was ready for anything.

"As I'm sure you know, several hours ago we made an unscheduled landing in Heathrow. Now that that crisis is over, a new one has arisen and we cannot resolve it. Your daughter was escorted off the plane by her alleged sister-in-law, leaving three children sleeping on board. We're not sure whom they belong to."

Mrs. Katz gasped.

"We have been led to understand that Shraga Rosenfeld is the son of the woman whose passport reads, 'Chana Katz.' Penina and Bina Zippora Katz are supposedly the daughters of Devorah Shwartz. Do you follow our identity crises? The children don't match their mothers. Wouldn't it make more sense for the two girls whose last name is Katz to be your daughter's daughters?"

AT FIRST Mrs. Katz was stymied. All three kids were her grandchildren and she knew very well who their mothers were. But how could their passports be mistaken?

Then it came to her: "Of course! My daughter Chana Rosenfeld's passport is still in her maiden name, 'Katz.' But, naturally, the kids have the same last name as their father, Rosenfeld. My son's wife, Devorah Katz, also never bothered to have her name changed on her passport so it reads 'Shwartz', even though her children bear her married name, 'Katz.'"

"Thank you, Mrs. Katz," the pilot said with audible relief. "We should be landing in about two hours. I hope you will be at the airport to collect your grandchildren, and Mazel Tov on the latest addition."

SUFFERING from a minor case of bedbugs and a major case of punk rockers, Eli Meir counted the minutes until Shabbos would be over and he could abandon the Palace. Over Shabbos he kept his wife abreast of his sociological discoveries and informed her in no uncertain terms that *motzei Shabbos* would augur a new venue for the three of them.

It also presented a new challenge for the Middlesex Maternity Hospital. The facility had never served a foreigner before and didn't know how to bill someone not covered by Britain's national health insurance. "If we ever figure it out, we'll make sure to let you know," was the hospital administrator's parting blessing.

The Rosenfelds saw Devorah off to the airport, rented a conventional hotel room near the Golders Green section of London, and busily proceeded to arrange their own departure from Britain. Sunday morning, *Rosh Chodesh*, Eli Meir took a taxi to a synagogue. He would be able to name his daughter that morning, entitling her to a birth certificate and a passport.

The worshippers at shul were quick to extend not only their Mazel Tovs but their assistance as well. They explained that a birth certificate is only issued in the county where the baby is born. Thus, Eli Meir would have to return to Middlesex to acquire the document. The congregants thoughtfully arranged a driver and other conveniences for the rest of the Rosenfelds' stay.

Needless to say, the Middlesex Registration Bureau was closed on Sundays, so Eli Meir used the spare time to arrange their flight to New York Monday evening. He dialed the El Al office and asked for Reservations.

El Al's next connecting flight to the States, however, was not until Wednesday. Furthermore, it would not fly with any infant younger than eight days old. The next option was British Airways, which had seats open on its 6 P.M. flight on Monday.

TO AN AMERICAN, everything in England seems to be done slowly. To an American in a rush, nothing seems to be done at all. First thing Monday morning, Eli Meir stood outside the Registration Bureau clasping the hospital record of his daughter's birth. His driver was parked on the street, ready to leave immediately for the American consulate to secure a United States passport for the baby.

When the door finally opened, and when the clerks finally assumed their positions behind their desks, and when everything was finally set to serve the public, Eli Meir noticed to his horror that no one was manning the desk marked, "Births."

"Surely the clerk is just taking her time about showing up," he hoped, but after a significant wait there still was no sign of life at "Births." Eli Meir went to one of the other desks to inquire and was informed that on Mondays they only deal with "Deaths."

Eli Meir was stunned. He couldn't think of anything un'propaw' about births, or any reason why they should be penalized on Mondays. He tried his hardest to explain his predicament, lingering over every tearjerking detail, but the apathetic officials remained unsympathetic. Monday was deaths, and they wouldn't think of tampering with such a time-honored tradition.

A desperate man, Eli Meir drew on his untapped wellsprings of dramatic flair. He begged, he got down on his knees, he cried, and when even that failed, he threatened to do something so drastic that it could be registered on a Monday.

Even though he provided an offer that "could not be refused" in the end, an appeal to the steely British sense of logic proved more persuasive than any amount of Yankee histrionics. Once a quick-witted clerk ingeniously grasped the connection between births and marriages, which were registered on Mondays, the Rosenfeld baby became a legitimate statistic.

ELI MEIR grasped the document that was his ticket to a passport for his daughter and raced outside to his waiting driver. The chase to the American consulate was on.

Unlike Yehoshua Katz, the driver Eli Meir got this time was a native of England and a scrupulous student of road-safety rules and courtesies. Ironically, his lackadaisical pace made Eli Meir as nervous as Yehoshua's record-breaking run of a few days earlier.

They arrived at the American consulate at 1:01 in the afternoon, but the door was already locked. Eli Meir tried to force it open, or at least attract the attention of those inside. After several loud bangs, he was awarded a response by G.I. Joe: a towering black marine charged exclusively with keeping people from assaulting the door. The snarling sentinel pointed his weapon toward a sign that read: "CLOSED FROM 1:00 P.M. TO 4:00 P.M."

Eli Meir reverted to his beg-and-plead routine, but the marine maintained his military posture. So Eli Meir stayed put until four o'clock, unceremoniously collected his daughter's passport, fetched his family and headed for the airport, incredulous that this odyssey was finally coming to an end.

"**Q**UITE AN ADVENTURE," their trusty chauffeur chuckled from the front seat. "Tell me, how are you going to pay for all this fuss?"

"Pay for it?" Eli Meir said slowly.

"That's right, mate," the driver remarked.

The proud father explained that the people he had met in shul in Golders Green were kind enough to lend him money to cover his local expenses. "No, no, not this pittance," the driver emphasized.

All at once realization dawned on Eli Meir.

Like jarring background Muzak the driver started listing debits and what he estimated their cost to be... "You got yer unscheduled landing — that's thousands of quid right there. They also had to drop fuel, which costs tens of thousands more. I s'pose there's those baggage handlers, taking on more food — and those Kedassia meals cost a fortune; refueling for takeoff — an easy ten G's; overtime for all the staff..."

The driver went on and on in a monotonous dirge, spelling out a bill so colossal that it would place the Rosenfelds in debt for the rest of their lives, no matter how long they lived. Eli Meir and Chani looked at each other and realized that their bundle of joy was probably the most expensive baby ever born.

Trying to take charge, Eli Meir suggested that first they had to get on their America-bound flight, and then they could start worrying about less immediate problems.

"Maybe she can be a stewardess for life," Chani suggested. Eli Meir reminded her that there were child-labor laws against that kind of thing. Besides, El Al certainly wouldn't be interested in her until she was at least eight days old.

The family arrived at the BA check-in counter at 5:41 and a sweaty Eli Meir nervously surrendered his family's tickets, hoping that the ground hostess hadn't interned at the Registration Bureau. His fears were quickly dispelled as she deftly punched in the information and handed out boarding passes. "You better hurry," she advised, and the Rosenfelds hoofed over to the departure gate.

&

ADJOINING OFFICES on the third floor of El Al's headquarters in Ben-Gurion Airport could hear the grunts and shouts emanating from the head of Ground Operations. The man was obviously furious and was having great difficulty keeping it to himself.

"How am I supposed to balance my budget at the end of the month?" he bellowed to his secretary. "It's just one bill after another. This flight cost us more than our entire operating expenses for a week! And this isn't even all of it! Get me Flight Operations on the line."

Dani Ettinger's secretary dutifully obeyed. "Ami," the Ground Operations chief roared to a department head one building away, "wait till you see the paperwork on Flight 001 this week."

"I know," the head of Flight Operations responded, checking if he was hearing Ettinger through the phone or through the window, "I've got it right in front of me."

"So why are you so calm? Practically every item is five digits: dropping fuel; an unscheduled landing; ground facilities; landing fees; handling; overtime for getting our staff out there in the middle of the night; catering; maintenance; fuel for takeoff..."

"Dani, I know, I know — it's all here..."

"A six-minute phone call made in mid-flight, sixteen kosher meals, a bouquet of flowers, taxi fares..."

"I know, I know, not to mention the inestimable damage..."

"That's right, a delayed takeoff from New York, disgruntled passengers, relatives who drove for hours and had to wait around for the flight to come in."

"You forgot about the people who missed their connecting flights. They'll be trying to bill us for the loss."

"And the bad press! Here we go again with the jokes that El Al stands for Every Landing Always Late. We're going to stick this Rosenfeld for every penny, that's for sure."

"Dani... I don't know about that."

"What?"

"Look at it from their perspective: True, she shouldn't have boarded so late in her pregnancy, but she certainly had no intention of costing us so much or causing others harm. If you bill this family, I don't care how rich they are, they will resent their child for the rest of their lives."

"Spare me the psychology. That's not my problem, and it's not yours, either. We're responsible for this company's profits, which are going to be non-existent unless we slap them with every last expenditure right down to the flowers!"

"Dani, it's simply not fair. What is the point of charging someone more than he can pay? You're asking for too much."

"But why should we lose out?"

"Because we are in the business of helping people, not just making a profit, and sometimes this entails more than just transporting people, luggage, and cargo."

"Ami, you've got to stop hanging around our P.R. people! We are a poor country and El Al is the national carrier. Why should the people of Israel bear Mr. and Mrs.

Rosenfeld's expense?"

"My father used to say that if you do the right thing, like not billing someone who cannot pay, then you really don't lose. You may have less money, but you haven't lost."

"Don't be ridiculous. Now is no time for sentimental nostalgia and your father never saw a bill like this! But if you wish, you can take the matter up with the president."

L ATER THAT AFTERNOON Ettinger informed the president and general manager of El Al of the expenses of the unscheduled landing in Heathrow. He went on to explain to a most sympathetic audience why he intended to bill the Rosenfelds for the entire cost.

The head of Flight Operations tried to voice his opposition but the president cut him off. "We are not a private company," he chastised. "We cannot act in accord with our whims or emotions. We have a government to answer to, plus a Knesset committee, the Minister of Transportation, and the Minister of Finance, who go crazy every time we run a promotional campaign, print calendars, or even order mugs with our names on them. We cease to be a business the moment we decide to forgive every person who owes us money!"

"Compassion," Ami insisted dramatically, "is the hallmark of our People and our State. I hope you would weigh this decision carefully."

"I shall," the president responded, sounding very reassuring. But when Ami left the presidential suite, the boss instructed Ettinger in a conspiratorial tone, "Send me the details. I want that bill to go out directly from my office!"

EL AL אל על

Rosenberg, Eliyahu Meir and Chana

משרד	אסמכתא	תאריך
office	reference	date

re: expenses for unscheduled landing on flt 001 TLV-NY

Landing Rights
Notification
Special Privileges $4,200

Dropping fuel
Refueling for takeoff $19,680

Ground crew
Handlers
Maintenance
Catering $3,470

Mid-air phone calls
Other air arrangements $71

El Al staff
Overtime
Security Arrangements $910

Ground courtesies, London $128

Total expenses incurred: **$28,459**

Please remit payment to our New York office within the next 15 days.

GRATIS

EL AL ISRAEL AIRLINES LTD. בעמ אל על נתיבי אויר לישראל בעמ

Head office: P.O.B. 41, Ben-Gurion Airport, Tel: (03) 9716111, טלפון: 41, ת.ד, המשרד הראשי: נמל תעופה בן-גוריון,
Israel 70100, Cables: Israelal, Tel-Aviv, Telex: 371107 טלקס: ישראלאל תל-אביב, מברקים: 70100, מיקוד

Heard from: Nachman Klieman

The Best Policy

CHESTER DAVIS let his eyes flicker over the letter he had just written. Heaving a sigh, he crumpled it and sent it to join its companions in the waste basket next to his desk.

He looked out the window of his fifth-floor office for inspiration. The reversed letters of the name "Interstate Rock Insurance Inc." emblazoned across the glass obscured his vision. Had his seven months of working for the company similarly clouded his view of the outside world? Another sigh escaped him as he went back to his troublesome letter for the fourth time. He read the finished product with ambivalence.

```
Mrs. Sylvia Carpenter
7751 N. Fernwell Drive
Wichita, Kansas  67202
                    June 6, 1988
Dear Mrs. Carpenter,
    We are sorry to inform you that
the loss of your necklace was not
```

reported to us within the required
six week period. Accordingly, we
cannot process your claim for $400.
    We understand that you were
visiting your grandchildren in Kansas
at the time, and were unaware of the
lapse of the notification period.
Nonetheless, our regulations do not
give us discretion to waive the
reporting requirements.
    We regret this unfortunate
occurrence, but we trust you will
continue to place your confidence in
us in the future.

                    Yours faithfully,

                    Chester Davis
Interstate Rock Insurance Inc.

cc: Todd Nichols, Collections V.P.

Poor woman, Chester mused, but rules were rules. Maybe they could've made an exception just this once for this elderly woman with — judging by her policy — so few worldly goods. But his supervisor wouldn't hear of it, and nearly went through the roof when he had suggested it.

THAT'LL HAVE TO DO, thought Chester, reaching for the next letter in his in-tray. As he read it, disbelief widened his eyes and furrowed his brow. He scratched his head and began to read it through again, trying to ignore the banter coming from the other side of the office.

"Would you mind removing that ruler from your head?" Mike requested.

"Leave me alone, Mike, I'm trying to make an important calculation."

"Don't tell me, you've decided once and for all to calculate the diameter of your cerebrum."

"Na, I was just thinking that about a pint and a half of applesauce could fit into my skull if it wouldn't be so crowded with vital fluids and gray coils of wit and memory."

"Oh no, Charlie, don't tell me you're measuring the symphonic fidelity of your Walkman again."

"Pardon me, but this is no *Walkman*! This is my WM-D6C with quartz lock and disc drive! With this portable deck the Monteverdi Choir no longer sounds like the Sax Kittens, a guitar reclaims its missing midsection, and the bass builds a floor you can walk on. Here Mike, listen to Siouxsie and the Banshees — the sound is breathtaking. Hills and mesas and Andes arising from an ocean of silence..."

"Gentlemen, I hate to interrupt what sounds like a discussion of earth-shattering importance," cried Chester, looking up from his letter, "but wait till you hear this. A client in Denver has refunded us, I repeat, refunded *us* $1,000!"

"Give me a break, Chet," Charlie muttered, "I'm trying to teach Mike the finer elements of scientific development and you have to butt in with science fiction?"

"Listen, I ain't making it up:

ב״ה

June 2, 1988

Interstate Rock Insurance Inc.
422 Bloomfield Dr.
Hartford, Conn. 06002

Dear Sirs:

On February 12, 1988, I filed a claim for the loss of my silver Chanukah candelabra, valued at one thousand dollars. As I am sure you recall, I enclosed its evaluation by a local jeweller and a xerox of its detailed inclusion in my coverage.

Now, three and a half months later, I have discovered that the candelabra was not stolen after all, but has been sitting at my silversmith all this time. I had taken it in for repair, and, I'm afraid, completely forgotten about it.

I feel terrible for having caused you the trouble of issuing my coverage and embarrassed that I made such an outrageous error.

I enclose a cheque for one thousand dollars, please accept my most sincere apologies.

Yours, Truly
Chaim Stern

"**T**HIS IS A FIRST: there's no doubt about that,**"** Mike said in a mixture of amazement and relief — amazement over the content of the letter, and relief over the termination of Charlie's litany regarding the finer points of high fidelity.

"Now what am I supposed to do?" Chet continued. "In the seven months I've been working for the Rock, we've never received a refund."

"You got a point," Charlie added. "This company is designed to receive money for policies and send out money for claims — but that's it."

"This is a real doozy," Mike contemplated, rubbing his troubled temples. "You know, before I made it up here to Hartford, I was all over. I even sold policies door-to-door, and nothing like this ever happened. This is not only a *first*, it's history in the making!"

"Why don't you take the letter to the Marketing Department," Charlie suggested, "and find out where this account came from?"

"I've been there already," Chet said with a note of desperation. "They didn't know what to do with it so they passed it on to the Underwriters Department. Underwriters kicked it over to the Accounting Department, and Accounting brought it back to the Claims Department, and Claims — you guessed it — dropped it on the desk of Chet Davis, with an inter-office memo that looks like a scorecard from a Ping-Pong match.

"So fellas, what do I do with this weirdo and his thousand bucks?"

"Hey, c'mon," Mike said defensively, "how're we supposed to know? We ain't executives. We ain't even 'suits,' we're just a bunch of yuppies."

"Pardon me!" Charlie interrupted, "but the latest poll has indicated that a 'yuppie' is anyone and everyone who eats out more than once a week, carries a MasterCard, knows that wine comes from California, and owns, or has owned, a yellow necktie. Therefore I do not qualify."

"Charlie, will you cut it out already?" Mike interjected as his colleague started measuring his cranium once again. He shrugged and turned back to Chet. "This one's over our heads; even Mr. Stereophonic Sound doesn't have the technology to deal with it. You better take this to the top, to the 'Boss' himself, and you're in luck because the board is in session."

"Are you serious?" Chet wheezed in exasperation. "You expect me to go to the board with this? They're probably deciding what premiums the President should pay on the White House. They're probably deciding what..."

Before he could finish his sentence, Chet was escorted, or more accurately *lifted*, by two human hydraulics named Charlie and Mike and deposited in the boardroom right in the middle of a heated argument:

"I say we travel to the Hillcrest Course — it's just 25 miles out of Phoenix and has hosted the Ladies' PGA Tour for the last four years."

"Month after month we pass up going to Ojai Valley. Where else can you find a 6,100-yard course surrounded by mountains?"

"We are not going to Ojai! Just last week all the regional CEOs went to Maui and that's enough exotic courses for this season. As president of this company I am entitled to make some decisions!"

"Sorry, Boss."

"**H**EY, what are those guys doing in here?" Around the room a dozen fleshy faces looked up from their leather-bound desk pads to stare at the intruders. "Don't they know we're busy deciding important company matters and cannot be disturbed? What's the matter with you, can't you read English? There's a big sign outside the door that reads, 'Board in Session.'"

Mike ribbed Chet to speak, but he was intimidated into nervous silence. Charlie took up the initiative:

"Excuse him, Boss, he's got this problem, but it's better if he explains it."

"O.K., let's hear," the Boss said, his curiosity piqued. "What in the world could be so important that you decided to interrupt the board?"

"Well, eh... you see we got this letter here," Chet fumbled, holding up the document to provide an air of authenticity, "and it has baffled the entire staff of the company. We just don't know what to do, and in desperation I was advised, er, to come to you, sir."

"What is it? A government decision to downgrade all policies?"

"No."

"Aetna went ahead with its plan to undercut SBLI?"

"No, it's... kind of different."

"Oh, I know: no one is issuing life insurance without compulsory blood tests. And we better adopt the same policy before we're stuck with all the goners. No, no, you don't have to make any more gesticulations. We were just about to tackle that problem after we finished attending to the other pressing matters at hand."

"But..."

"But what? I told you we're in the middle of important business."

"I'm trying to explain that the letter is about an entirely different matter."

"It is?"

"Yes, Boss, it's from a client who returned money."

"Who what?!" the entire board chimed in in unison.

"He filed a claim for something he thought was stolen, but a few months later he found it and immediately returned what we paid him."

A palpable silence wedged itself between the panelled walls of the boardroom.

"I understand," the Boss finally pronounced, as his deputies chorused murmurs of assent. "Just leave it with us, and we'll put it on our agenda."

Chet hurriedly placed the letter and the enclosed check on the enormous mahogany table and darted out of the room with an audible sigh of relief.

THE HEAD OF THE ACCOUNTING DEPARTMENT picked up the letter and his eyes began to dilate. "Hey, Boss," he gasped in shock, "we really have a problem here. This guy is right out of them fairy tales. If we don't cash his check immediately he'll probably call us, or launch a letter campaign to find out why."

"Don't worry," the Boss replied with a wave of his

hand, "there has got to be some easy way to bury the money. How much is it?"

"A thousand dollars."

"A thousand bucks?! Is this guy normal? It doesn't pay to be moral for that kind of money."

"The way he writes, I bet he would have returned a larger sum, too."

"Tell Pat to have the check endorsed," the Boss ordered. "Then hand it over to our dealer in exchange for $1,000 worth of office supplies."

The head of Purchasing removed his glasses and shook his head. "Sorry, Boss, we just completed our order for this year and our storerooms are full."

"O.K.," the Boss responded, "take the money and have all the reception rooms painted."

Now, the Services manager started shaking his head. "They've been wallpapered for the last eight months, sir."

"Why can't we just enter the money," the head of the Underwriters Department put forward, "as coverage returned due to improper filing?"

"What?" several CEOs demanded. "We can do no such thing! The paperwork alone would run us over a thousand bucks!" The stuffed shirts were stumped but not for long.

"I know how to bury the money," the Boss said with a gleam in his enterprising eye. "Where's this client from?"

"Denver."

"Great," the Boss beamed with total ebullience. "Let's get that junior fellow, you know, the one who burst in here, to go investigate the case. We'll tell him he's going to adjust a claim. There aren't any direct flights out of Hartford so it will be an expensive ticket, and he'll have to kill a night or two there before he can catch a flight back. Best of all, the time he'll waste on this ridiculous mission talking to this 'straight nut' will teach him that next time he gets a letter like this, he should accidentally-on-purpose lose it instead of wasting valuable executive time."

T HE ENTIRE BOARD sat in awe of their boss' brilliant idea. At times like these, they realized it was more than being the son of the founder that made him the "Boss."

"As a matter of fact," the object of their admiration added, settling back into his chair, "get that kid back in here. I'll assign him the mission myself. That'll really make him feel like hot stuff."

The boss' secretary punched out a number on the intercom and issued a directive for Chet Davis to report immediately to the executive conference room. In a matter of minutes a trembling, quivering, speechless young recruit from the Claims Department was brought back before his officer-in-chief.

"Junior, er... I mean, young man," the Boss began, "I really liked your detective work. You really know how to sense a problem and bring it to the attention of the appropriate authorities right away."

Chet managed a half-smile.

"Therefore, I think you are just the man to investigate

this matter. After all, it is rather out of the ordinary for a client to return coverage, so maybe there are some details here that require some checking. Who knows? Maybe this client is hiding something; perhaps it's all a smokescreen to conceal coverage he has collected illegally."

All the exec veeps present nodded gravely in agreement and muttered similar suspicions. The Boss eyed his board and then fixed his company's greenhorn with a solemn stare. "Junior," he declared, "the Rock is entrusting a major mission to you." He then began to pour forth a dizzying array of insurancese:

"Keep your eye out for individual variable annuity contracts, fiduciary capacity, antedating, indemnities relating to flexible premium payments, and most particularly, master contracts with a noncontributory group."

Chet's hand raced across his pad, struggling to catch each vital phrase.

"Don't forget disclosure to MIB and riders relating to the beneficiary," cut in the high-pitched voice of the Services manager, getting caught up in the torrent of jargon.

"Guaranteed insurability options are often problematic," added the head of Marketing, "not to mention disability premium waivers."

"Double indemnities," cried Sales.

"Deferment clauses," shouted Underwriters.

Chet's face turned chalky and he began hyperventilating. He gave up on note-taking and resorted to nodding wildly in all directions as the board members all competed simultaneously in offering increasingly obscure proofs of their expertise.

"Fifth-dividend options..."

"...current conversion..."

"...automatic premium loans..."

"...multiple-line coverage..."

As the crescendo peaked, Chet's jaw dropped low in gaping incredulity. Meanwhile, the bigwigs clutched their stomachs and tried their hardest to refrain from laughing.

"Now listen here, Junior," the Boss continued, struggling to regain his composure. "I have selected you for this mission because I know that you are a shrewd, keenly observant, perspicacious, judicious young man. Don't be taken in by any of this guy's honest, goody-goody talk. You better examine everything very well before you return with your report."

Still in shock, Chet barely noticed the compliment, but he tried to feign a Sherlock Holmes expression.

"**I** EXPECT you back next week," the Boss concluded. "We will anxiously await your findings. So godspeed, and don't be concerned about the expenses. Money's no object when a company man is on an important mission."

The smirk-ridden executives all affirmed the claim and rose to pat the tyro on the back and shake his hand.

The Boss slung a solicitous arm around Davis and escorted him to the door. "Go down the corridor to the end," he instructed, "take a left and ask for Chris, the company's in-house travel agent. Just tell her you need an immediate itinerary and I have approved it."

C HET FIDDLED NERVOUSLY with the handle of his attaché case as he stood outside the Stern residence. In view of the board's warnings he had decided not to call in advance. If this Stern character was really a sly snake, he wanted to take him by surprise. Chet was determined to do Hartford proud.

The fellow who answered the door was not exactly Davis' stereotypical conception of a Midwesterner. Or a snake. He wore a large skullcap and sported a long, brown beard and spaghetti-like fringes drooping down from his shirt.

"Eh... Hello," the Hartford emissary fumbled, extending his sweaty hand. "My name is Chester Davis and I represent Interstate Rock Insurance and, well, that sure was a mighty nice gesture of yours to return your coverage, and we just wanted to show you how much we appreciated it. I hope you don't mind if I ask you a few questions."

"Why, of course not," Rabbi Stern answered, motioning the insurance man into his house.

"Yeah, like I was saying, it was so unusual of you to return the money — you see, that doesn't happen too much in our company. I was wondering if you wouldn't mind repeating exactly what happened."

Rabbi Stern sat his guest down, brought him a cold drink, and began to recollect:

" A BOUT FOUR MONTHS AGO, I noticed that our silver candelabra was missing. This was no ordinary candelabra, or *menorah* as it is called in Hebrew. I purchased it years ago in Israel and our festival of Chanukah wouldn't be the same without it.

"Naturally, this isn't the sort of item we would misplace. So we informed the police, but they failed to come up with any leads.

"Much as we hated to do it, we began to suspect our maid, Juanita. We wanted to give her a fair hearing, but since she barely speaks English and we don't know Spanish, it was an exercise in bilingual futility:

Juanita, did you clean the breakfront? *Si, Señor.*

Did you dust the *menorah*? *No se, Señor.*

Didn't you clean everything inside? *Si, Señor.*

So why is one of the items missing? *No se, Señor.*

Maybe you took it out and forgot to put it back? *Nunca, Señor.*

Maybe you wanted to show it to someone and now you want to return it? *Nunca, Señor.*

Are you sure? *Si, Señor.*

Who else do you think might have removed it? *No se, Señor.*

Do you want to think about it? *Si, no se, Señor.*

Do you want to forget about it? *Si, Señor.*

What should we do? *No se, Señor.*"

Chet found himself smiling at the Rabbi's unexpected gift for dramatization. "Go on," he said.

RABBI STERN continued his tale: "Although we couldn't be sure Juanita was responsible, we reluctantly let her go. This didn't help us find our *menorah* of course, but at least we hoped we wouldn't have to worry that more things would disappear. In the meantime we filed a claim with your company, and eventually your payment came through.

"Four months later, however — that is, two weeks ago — I noticed that my wife's candlesticks were cracked. I immediately brought them to the silversmith, who promptly asked me where I'd been all this time. Before I could figure out what he meant, he went to the back of his shop and brought out our *menorah*. 'Do you know how long this has been sitting here?' he inquired.

"Suddenly I knew very well. In my terrible absentmindedness, I had totally forgotten that I had brought the *menorah* in for repair right after Chanukah. And the silversmith couldn't even get in touch with me since he didn't have my phone number and wasn't sure of my name. I can assure you that he was careful to take down all my particulars when he took the candlesticks.

"As happy as I was to have our *menorah* back, I felt terrible at having dismissed Juanita and very much wished to apologize to her. Both my wife and I made numerous attempts to locate her, but she had apparently moved out of state.

"In any event, since we had our *menorah* back, I had to return the coverage."

CHET WAS TAKEN ABACK by the story. He had little reason to doubt Stern's sincerity, aside from the Boss' warnings. The last thing he wanted, however, was to return to Hartford a laughingstock and stand accused of being gullible and naive. He would have to find some kind of guarantee that Stern was legit.

"Rabbi Stern," Chet began, "I'm not sure I fully understand why you felt that you had to return the money."

"Because it wasn't mine."

"Of course it's yours. The check was made out to you."

"But you only issued the coverage on the assumption that my *menorah* was missing."

"All right, but no one is asking you to give it back now."

"I repeat, the money isn't mine. If I don't pay it back now, I will have to pay it back later."

Chet nodded wisely and whispered, "You were afraid that we would launch a criminal investigation and accuse you of fraud?"

"No, nothing like that. It's just that everyone is accountable for his actions."

"Accountable?"

"To Heaven, to God."

Chet shifted awkwardly in his seat. "Oh, oh, I'm sorry."

"You don't have to be sorry, but you should be aware. Let me explain: according to Judaism, stealing involves far more than just putting your hand into someone else's purse. Shortchanging, making a call from the office without permission, pocketing paperclips, and even misleading someone or disturbing a person's sleep all fall under the biblical interdiction of 'Thou shalt not steal.'"

"Yeah,... well, I mean, I knew that," Chet stammered,

his mind racing to find a more comfortable topic of conversation. "By the way, while I'm here, maybe I could interest you in one of our other policies?"

"Look around you," Rabbi Stern said. "Does it look like we need insurance on anything other than our few pieces of silver?" Scanning his surroundings Chet realized he had a point.

"You see, the silver has religious value for us; otherwise why should we squander our money on such luxuries?"

"Lots of people do... er, I mean lots of people buy valuables."

"True, but we believe that the more you have, the more you worry, and once you have this you'll always want that. I think it's more important that we look after what we already have."

"I don't follow."

"You know, our children, our health, our virtues. For example, since your company is probably paying for your trip here, I assume you are being very careful to watch your expenses. You wouldn't want to bill them for money you didn't spend, would you?"

"Huh?... I mean of course, I guess... As a matter of fact, I agree with you that — how'd you put it? — 'If you don't pay it back now, you'll have to pay it back later.'"

Rabbi Stern pumped Chet's hand and led him to the door. "I hope I've been of some help."

"Oh yes, you most certainly have. You really straightened me, I mean, this matter out. Goodbye now."

THE NEXT DAY Chet was back at the Rock and eager to file his report. He made it just in time, for the board was reportedly just about to depart for an important conference somewhere outside of Phoenix.

Chet was ushered into the Boss' office and planted his feet in the shag with newfound confidence.

"O.K., Junior, what's the scoop?" the Boss asked, looking forward to hearing about his flunky's fiasco.

"Well," Chet said breathlessly, "the bottom line is that the guy, I mean the Rabbi, honestly thought his candelabra was stolen, so he filed for theft. But by the time he'd discovered it at the silversmith's, Juanita had left town."

"Juanita?"

"Yeah. So he had to send us back the check. You see?"

"I think you'd better back up."

Chet dutifully shifted into reverse and explained the whole story, but afterward his boss still didn't seem very enlightened.

"What is this guy, some kind of lunatic or something?"

"I'll tell you the truth," Chet conceded, "at first I thought he was really off the wall, like the kind of guy who takes nursery rhymes seriously. But after meeting him and being in his home a couple of minutes, I realized that he and his folk actually live it. Truth and honesty and ethics and all those kinds of things really mean something to them. No wonder you never see any rabbis running for office."

"All right, all right, I guess this case is finally closed. Just report your expenses to Accounting."

"No problem, I got it all written down here." Chet rifled through his datebook until he found the appropriate page, which he ripped out and proudly presented to the Boss.

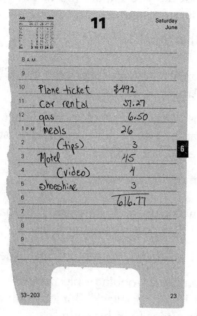

July 1988			**11**			Saturday June
8 AM						
9						
10	Plane ticket			$492		
11	car rental			37.27		
12	gas			6.50		
1 PM	meals			26		
2	(tips)			3		
3	Motel			45		
4	(video)			4		
5	shoeshine			3		
6				616.77		
7						
8						
9						

53-203   23

A LOOK OF INCIPIENT NAUSEA gripped the president. "Junior, did you fall on a rock while you were out in the Rockies? Your assignment was to lose that thousand bucks."

"Huh?" Chet gulped, all astonishment and stupefaction.

"How in the world could you come back with such a bill, for heaven's sake! I never heard of anything so preposterous!"

"But Boss, these were my expenses, every one of them."

"Nobody with an ounce of sense, or a milligram for that matter, would turn in an expense record like this. This bill should have totalled $999.98 at least!"

"But what did you expect me to do?" Chet implored, still not understanding.

"Lose the grand."

All at once Chet grasped what his CEO, and all of corporate America, was promoting.

"But Boss, that's the whole point. That's what I learned from the Rabbi. You're not supposed to swindle, even a penny, certainly not $383.23."

"Ah, c'mon! Wake up to reality!"

"I did wake up — to integrity. We have no right to take money that doesn't belong to us."

"I'm not telling you to rob anyone," the boss insisted.

"Do you think robbing only means holding a victim at gunpoint in a dark alley?" Junior countered, suddenly aware of the audacity in his tone.

The Boss flailed his arms to put an immediate end to the discussion. "O.K., Davis," he said, his patience depleted, "if that's the way you want to play it, then you find a way to work it into the Rock's ledger."

With a note of finality, he turned his back on his young employee and gripped an imaginary golf club, and, arching his back, teed off towards his vast picture window.

"Our customers out there trust us," Chet muttered. "I think we should be deserving of that trust." But his words fell on deaf ears.

BACK AT HIS DESK, Chet took out his wallet, counted out $16.77, and added it to a check he had drawn from the Claims Department for $383.23. This time he had no need to look out his office window before writing his next letter.

Dear Mrs. Carpenter,

In view of the unusual circumstances of your case...

Heard from: Rabbi Meyer Yerucham Schwab

The Great Estate

BOSTON has always been known as one of the most fashionable cities in the world. Ralph Waldo Emerson called it "the hub of the universe." And with good reason: Boston was, and still is, the cradle of American civilization. As you walk the streets, you can almost feel the spirit of Paul Revere, Sam Adams and all the other radical revolutionaries who presumed to replace the king's rule with their own. The Boston Tea Party, the North Burial Ground, and the U.S. Constitution all make the Boston area one of historical renown.

Boston is equally famous as the home of Boston University, Harvard, M.I.T., Tufts University, and numerous other institutions of higher learning. A center of academe, Boston boasts over one hundred thousand full-time students.

But lately, Boston has acquired another reputation... as one of the hottest real-estate markets in the country. This metamorphosis has a lot to do with the high-tech industry and the giant defense contractors that can be found along Route 128.

Yet perhaps the greatest reason for the rise in real estate values has been the rise of real-estate developers, who knew when something was almost too good to be true and who took advantage of it. These men and women turned Boston's turn-of-the-century row houses into some of the most fashionable condominiums on the East Coast. In fact, the cost of property in the Boston area has swelled above and beyond what any affluent individual, even a millionaire, would expect. Like mushroom clouds over the Nevada Nuclear Test Site, the prices of homes have reached astronomical proportions: $300,000 for a two-bedroom condo; $500,000 for a luxury apartment; $750,000 for a detached house; and more. In the rush to develop, the poor, the elderly, and the ill have been displaced, along with all their worldly possessions. There was money to be made, and the smart people were determined to make it.

And they did. By the millions. Real-estate speculators, development companies, and even bored housewives-turned-brokers have all gotten in on the "gold rush" of the 1980s.

There were a lot of exceptions, of course — men and women who didn't have the cash, the courage, or the charisma to wheel and deal. For them, the boom was more of a bust.

NATHAN SHAPIRO was one of those. A lifelong resident of Massachusetts, Nate knew the area from the Back Bay to Brookline block by golden block. He was a real-estate agent who made most of his money renting apartments to college kids. On occasion, he also sold houses, land, and even businesses. Yet it was always someone else who ended up rich.

It's not that Nate was unaggressive or a bad businessman. On the contrary, he was very "buttoned up." Whenever he had a house or two for sale, he listed them in the right papers, showed them to the right people, and made sure his clients knew all the right tricks: "Put out flowers. People love flowers. Have some bread or cake baking in the oven. People want a home that smells and feels like a home. And get rid of any extra furniture. You want the rooms to look as large as they can."

No, it's not that Nate was unsophisticated or a *nebbach* case. It's just that for him, money wasn't the name of the game. People were. Although he represented the seller, he would often end up working just as hard for the buyer. Invariably, he would end up trying to convince people to virtually give their property away, along with his commission: "C'mon, they're newlyweds. If you ask for so much, they won't go for it," he would cajole his clients. Or "Look, I'm telling you the house isn't worth it. Even the mice have left!" he would sometimes say.

HIS POOR WIFE, Goldie, was happy to be married to such a *gutte yid*. It was Nate's creditors who were upset. It got so bad, Goldie was afraid to answer the phone.

RRRRRing. "Mr. Shapiro, this is Brookline Office Supply. You placed an order seven weeks ago but still haven't even made the downpayment. We're cancelling your order."

RRRRRRRRRing. "Hello? Mrs. Shapiro, I'm calling from Boston Gas. I'm afraid you haven't paid your bills for three months and as of tomorrow we will terminate your service."

RRRRRRRRRRRRRRRRing. "Shapiro? This is Shusterman, the butcher. *Nu?* You know I won't make up your *Yom Tov* order unless you pay in advance."

When confronted with all of the above, Nathan Shapiro would merely shrug his shoulders and say, "It's a *lebidike velt* when you've got the *gelt*."

EVERY DAY, Nate *davened* at the New England Chassidic Center on Beacon Street. After fifty years of *davening* three times a day, you might think he would be one of those who seemed to finish before the rest of the *minyan* even got started.

You'd be wrong.

While the *minyan* ran at a fast clip, Nate *davened* at a slow trot. Word for word, he went through the *siddur*, patiently praying to his Maker. As a result, he was usually the last man out of the shul. ("Even God leaves before Nathan Shapiro!" the guys in shul would joke.)

Even ever-patient Goldie encouraged him to speed it up just a little. "Listen, the whole world starts work at 8:30. Why do you have to start two hours later? Maybe you could ask a Rabbi for permission to say less. After all, *parnassah* is as big a mitzva as prayer."

"*Davening* less and working more doesn't guarantee a better *parnassah*," he replied. "Reb Levi Yitzchak of Berditchev once said that a person who runs to earn a *parnassah* may actually be running away from it."

"That was easy for Reb Levi Yitzchak to say," she retorted. "His court probably paid all his bills..."

"Don't worry," Nate would say, "*Hashem* will provide..."

And while that's exactly what happened, it didn't come easy.

One day, Sol Shaffer, a lawyer and non-paid *gabbai* of the daily *minyan*, came to Nathan with an offer. "Listen, Nate. A colleague of mine is presenting the court with the deposition of the old O'Hara estate and he owes me a favor. Let me talk to him and see if he'll let you handle it."

"Sure," Nate said to Sol. "Why not?" But to himself, Nate said, "Fat chance I'm going to get it. Every real-estate agent and development company around is going to go after Sol's lawyer friend."

NATE WAS RIGHT. The O'Hara estate was one of the last pieces of prime property left in the area. It was originally owned by one Seamus O'Hara. At one time, he had been the driving force around Boston. Literally. Around the turn of the century, he had the largest fleet of handsome cabs in town, those light, elegant two-wheeled carriages designed by Joseph Hansom in 1882. That fleet, along with O'Hara's own ability to make friends in high places, gave him a real edge over the so-called "independents," the few individuals recklessly brave enough or foolish enough to try to compete with him.

In any event, Seamus O'Hara bought a vast piece

of land as a tribute to his own success. The mansion he built thereon, all forty rooms of it, was a symphony of brick and oak and walnut. Colorful in-lays of stained glass glimmered throughout. Smaller cottages, which housed his myriad drivers, dotted the property, and there were several stables for his horses and cabs, a harness shop and tack room, and even a garage for the horseless carriages that later proved to be his company's demise.

For over sixty years, O'Hara lived like a feudal lord on his estate. After he went to the great cab company in the sky, his daughter Kate took it over. She lived until the ripe old age of eighty-six, then left the land to the living. And to the Commonwealth of Massachusetts.

With its massive mansion, numerous cottages, and exquisitely landscaped grounds, the O'Hara property was a developer's dream. It could be used for anything from a college campus to a condominium complex. The price was bound to be in the millions. And some lucky real-estate agent was going to get a nice chunk of that pie, along with the battery of take-charge lawyers representing various could-be, would-be, and should-be relatives; the City of Boston; the Commonwealth of Massachusetts; and the Internal Revenue Service, as well as dozens of other interested parties.

E VEN THOUGH Nate believed in miracles, he knew the odds of his getting the business could be conservatively estimated at ten thousand to one. So it's no surprise that he promptly forgot the entire pipe dream, until the next morning, when, at precisely 8:30, the phone rang.

"Hello, this is Raymond Kearns of Kearns, Adler, and

Tewksberry, Attorneys at Law. Is Mr. Shapiro available?"

"This is his wife. I take care of all the bills. So if you're trying to collect money, you're better off talking to me."

There was a slight pause, almost a hesitation. "Excuse me?"

"I said, I'll get to you as soon as we can. Just tell me whom you're collecting for and..."

"Pardon me, but I'm not from a collection agency. I would like to speak with Mr. Shapiro regarding an important business matter. Is he available?"

"Not until 10:30," she replied.

"Could you please have him get back to me, as soon as possible? It's rather urgent."

As soon as he hung up, Goldie said to herself, "I wonder what's happened now. Maybe one of the students Nate rented an apartment to shot the landlord. Or maybe we're being investigated for under-reporting our income. No, that's impossible. We have no income! I better go to the shul and hurry him up."

IN MINUTES, Golda was standing inside the Chassidic Center. She spotted her husband, a lone figure sitting in the middle of a long, wooden bench, quietly *davening* to himself and his Creator.

What followed was one of those conversations that only husbands and wives who have been married for many long years can have, conversations that take place after *Baruch She'amar* and before *Tachanun*. (To make things easier on the reader, a free translation of their dialogue appears in parentheses.)

"Nate, Nate."

"Huh? Uhaahhaa." (What's wrong? What are you doing here?)

"Listen, a lawyer just called. His name is Kearns. He wants you to call him right away."

"Uh uh. Aahhh uhhh." (Not now. After *davening*.)

"What does he want?"

"Uhaahua uh." (I don't know.)

"Well, can you hurry up? He says it's urgent."

"Uh uh!" (No!)

"Come on. It won't hurt. He sounded very serious!"

"*Nuuuu!*" (*Nuuuu!* Don't bother me! I'm *davening!*)

"All right. All right. I'll see you when you get home."

A T EXACTLY 10:30, Nathan Shapiro trudged up the thirty-nine steps to his third-floor apartment, put away his *tallis* bag and proceeded to make what might have been the most important phone call of his life.

The line was busy.

"I'll call back later," he told his wife. Unfortunately, Nate had an unusually busy day. What with two or three rentals and a closing, he never got around to making this all-important call.

The next day at 8:30, the phone rang again. It was Mr. Kearns. His message was short and sweet. "Please tell your husband I must speak with him. It's about the O'Hara estate."

When Nate got home, Goldie was ready. She took his coat, hat, and *tallis* bag, dialed the number, and gave him the phone.

"Kearns, Adler and Tewksberry," a female voice sang, "good morning."

"Hello? Is Mr. Kearns in? This is Nathan Shapiro." In spite of his outward calm, inwardly Nate's heart was beating like mad.

A few seconds later, Goldie could hear the garbled whisper of a voice on the other end of the line. From her position on the edge of her seat, the one-sided conversation sounded like a man arguing to himself. And losing.

"Mr. Kearns? Sorry I was unable to reach you yesterday. You see, I was in the synagogue till late. Then I had a closing... You want me to meet you tonight at seven? I'm sorry, I have to be at the synagogue for the evening services... Tomorrow morning at 8:30? No, I'm afraid that's not open, either. Listen, could I suggest the mid-morning?... I see, you're in court. How would I like to meet you for lunch? Uh, Mr. Kearns, I-I-I keep kosher and well, uh... yes, I want the business... Yes, I understand you're extremely busy... I realize you're under a lot of pressure to assign the property to other agents, but please listen to me for a minute. I am willing to work with you but I'm afraid I simply cannot and will not compromise my religious beliefs and practices for your convenience! I hope you understand."

Goldie strained to hear what Mr. Kearns was saying, but he was talking too fast. A resigned Nate replied, "If that's the way you want it, that's the way it will have to be."

As Nathan Shapiro hung up, Goldie's heart sank to

her shoes. For over thirty years, she'd hoped, prayed, and waited for one deal that could make things a bit easier. Now it seemed that this deal was gone for good, and with it her dreams.

NATE PLOPPED DOWN on the overstuffed blue chair next to the phone and closed his eyes. Goldie looked at her husband. "Nate, why?" she said with a lump in her throat and a pool of tears in her eyes.

For a minute there was silence. Finally, Nathan explained: "Listen, Goldie... I can't pretend to be something I'm not. I'm not a big-time broker. I'm not a developer. I'm a Jew, a simple, run-of-the-mill Jew. But I know one thing: Hillel says, 'If I'm not for me, who will be?' And that's it."

The next day, Sol Shaffer was lying in wait for him at shul.

"What happened? I worked hard to give you this deal and you turn it down? I mean, how could you blow it? Do you have any idea what you just lost?" He was more than angry. He was hurt.

"Look, Sol, it just wasn't meant to be. I tried returning his calls. I tried finding a time when we could meet. What more could I do?"

"For once, you could bend! *Daven* a little faster. Or a little earlier. Or a little later. But at least do something!"

"It's too late. He said he was going to look for someone else."

Sol stalked off, leaving Nate unfolding his *tallis* and thinking to himself, "Maybe he was right. Maybe Hashem *wanted* me to bend this time. Maybe I really did blow it."

THAT MORNING Nathan Shapiro took his usual two hours *davening*. Then he carefully folded his *tallis*, cautiously locked the shul, and quietly walked the three blocks home.

The thirty-nine steps up to the landing were still there waiting. (He liked to call the climb "Mount Never-rest.") Today, they looked steeper than ever before. Finally, he reached the top. Goldie was waiting for him. He thought he detected the hint of a smile on her face. "Now what?" he muttered to himself.

"There's a man here to see you," she said simply.

"This is Mr. Raymond Kearns," she announced as he entered the living room.

"Mr. Kearns! It's a pleasure to meet you. Excuse me for a minute while I put away my things."

Before he could move, Goldie was right there, taking his coat, his hat and his *tallis* bag.

"Pardon me for asking, Mr. Kearns, but aren't you supposed to be in court this morning?"

"I was, but I postponed my appointment for a half-hour to come here."

"I see. Well, if it has anything to do with our conver..."

Before Nate could reiterate his position, Kearns interrupted. "Mr. Shapiro, I want you to handle the O'Hara estate for me."

"But I thought you told me yesterday that..."

"I know what I said yesterday. Please let me explain. When Sol first spoke to me, he mentioned that you were a good real estate man but that your first priority was your lifestyle."

"It still is," Nate said, wondering what the lawyer was getting at.

"Forgive me, but frankly, I was a little skeptical. After all, a person could make a great deal of money on this project. And to be honest, I thought that you would compromise your values rather than lose this opportunity. So I purposely called at 8:30. I also tried to meet you at times I knew to be inconvenient. However, during our conversation I began mistaking your sincerity for stubbornness. And in the heat of the moment I may have said some things that were inappropriate. So I want to apologize."

"Mr. Kearns, you don't have to apologize... I understand."

"Perhaps, Mr. Shapiro, but I still want to clarify something. At the time, I told you I would look for someone else, and I really intended to. I'm sure you know what that would have meant..."

Nate nodded, still not believing his ears.

"Well, let me put it this way. I have been a lawyer for quite a number of years. During that time, I have seen what money and power can do to a person and his values. It was inconceivable to me that you would be any different. But after I cooled down, I realized that you were. And that's when I decided that instead of your rearranging your schedule to meet me, I should rearrange mine to meet you."

Still in shock, Nate mumbled, "That's very nice of you."

"Now, if you are still interested in handling the estate, I would like to find a time when we can get together to go over the papers."

NATHAN SHAPIRO peered at the lawyer. He was as unaccustomed to hearing confessions as Ray Kearns was to making them. Fortunately, now that the uncomfortable part of the conversation was over, Nate could concentrate on business.

"Thank you very much for your confidence, Mr. Kearns," Nate said. "Needless to say, I would be happy to work with you on the O'Hara property. As to when we can get together, anytime is really fine." Then Nate added automatically, "At your convenience, of course."

"No, Nathan," Kearns replied with a smile. "At yours!"

Heard from: Grand Rabbi Levi Yitzhak Horowitz

Above Board

HIGH ABOVE Trans Am's terminal at JFK Airport in New York, the executive board was called into special session. Word was out that the chairman was in a fury and the axe was poised to strike. The board members could be assured that this meeting would not deal with a prosaic agenda consisting of rating club facilities, selecting the attendant of the month, and skirting FAA regulations. They sensed that something major was, pardon the pun, in the air.

The conference room was surrounded by large glass panes providing an observation-tower view of the airport. The plush, deep-pile carpet almost had to be waded through, whereupon it emitted enough static electricity to illuminate the runways. The book-matched rosewood conference table bore witness to the felling of a major forest, while the leather-upholstered chairs, coordinated to match the elaborate fixtures, contributed to the atmosphere of total elegance, luxury, and power.

Nonetheless, simply by displaying a few figures and statements on the overhead projector the chairman successfully dispelled any aura of comfort. These deficit figures, accompanied by his growls, were enough to make any executive feel like melting into his exquisite leather upholstery. Gifted in the art of making everyone feel directly responsible and thoroughly guilty for any loss the company suffered, Ernest Kolodny was a terror.

Kolodny was a nattily dressed CEO who resembled nothing so much as a leprechaun, with oversized eyeglasses like a Jeff MacNelly caricature. His mercurial temper seemed to fluctuate with the Dow Jones average, yet as some of his executives wryly observed, when he's on a down even a bull market couldn't get him to rally.

"**Q**UITE A JOB you overpaid muckeymucks have been doing," was Kolodny's gentle introduction. He shook his head in mock wonder and glared at his staff with disdain. Everyone present realized that their fears had been justified and they were in for the worst. The inchoate requiem had begun.

"We opened up service to Tel Aviv," he fumed, his eyes reconnoitering every corner of the room, "because it was supposed to be a big-buck endeavor. For the first quarter of this year all we've shown is a marginal profit. We don't have to pay for maximum security and antagonize the Arabs just to make a few paltry pennies. Do you get my drift?!"

Everyone at the table intoned, "Yes, E.K."

"How can twenty-one percent of a fully booked flight with three-month-advance reservations — and twelve percent overbooking — be cheap youth fares?! This has happened for the last two weeks on every flight coming out of Tel Aviv." Kolodny slammed a pile of printouts down on the table to corroborate his accusation.

"Furthermore, the flights are leaving outrageously late. I want this airline run like a flagship on the eve of a naval battle: military precision! I worked for six years to build up the reputation of this carrier, and no siesta-minded Israeli is going to destroy everything I've accomplished. A plane that doesn't come in on time can't leave on time. It fouls up the whole system, it's bad PR, and it costs me big bucks!"

"Yes, E.K.," they chanted in unison.

"I don't know who hired this mentally sterile, Mid-East, dim-wit manager, but I want him replaced and our act cleaned up at once! I don't care if we have to fly in our own staff, who no speaka de language, is that understood?"

The obedient "Yes, E.K."'s were more vigorous this time.

"Johnson," the CEO roared at the head of European operations, the victim's body snapping to attention. "You've got six days to show a complete turnaround, which gives you just two incoming flights. If I don't see figures in jet-black ink, you'll be four floors down punching tickets at the counter. You got me?"

This time only Johnson echoed, "Yes, E.K."

☙

I N A SMALL OFFICE in Ben-Gurion Airport, Gabi Miron, local manager and supervisor of Trans Am Airlines, was scratching his head. Stacks of computer printouts and piles of ticket coupons covered his desk, but there was no correlation between them. He had gone over the figures twenty times. He began for the twenty-first.

This was one of the busiest flight seasons of the year. From one week before Purim right up until Passover, all of his outbound flights, and most of his incoming ones, were booked to capacity.

Yet despite bookings and full-fare reservations made months in advance, hundreds of cheap three-day-in-advance student coupons were collected from boarding passengers. It just didn't make sense. The student standby was introduced to fill up flights during off-season periods. The rule was that eligible youth could travel for almost half-price if unsold seats were available three days before departure. The three-day clause virtually precluded the use of such tickets during peak seasons, but the carbon paper sprawled all over his desk confirmed that here were standby tickets aplenty.

Miron first became aware of the problem from a barrage of phone calls by disgruntled travel agents. Speaking (and shouting) on behalf of their clients, they wanted to know why passengers who had purchased Apex tickets well in advance were consistently being bumped off their flights. Trans Am certainly didn't engage in any favoritism; they bumped only the last passengers to arrive at the airport. True, they overbooked, but so did every other airline.

And now a threatening phone call from Miron's boss in New York had refreshed his memory. Hearing the tone in Johnson's voice, Miron knew it wasn't just his boss on the line — it was also his job. Johnson demanded to know how a flight booked so far in advance with full fares was packed with student cheapos. Miron wanted to know, too.

CLOSE TO TWENTY American students had gathered in a dorm room of an Israeli academic institution. They had convened to discuss an efficient and inexpensive means of getting to the airport for their return flight to the States during intersession. The mood in the room was already jovial in light of the approaching vacation and the students' imminent reunion with their families.

Suddenly the meeting was brought to an abrupt halt as Zev ran into the room clutching a crumpled aerogramme.

"Hey guys," he panted, smoothing out the letter (if not his furrowed brow). "Listen to this — it sounds like the three-day student-ticket gambit is over. My sister flew back to the States two weeks ago and her airline is putting a stop to it."

"They're what?" Mordechai's face, only minutes earlier wrinkled with laughter, was now a picture of concern. "What are we going to do?"

A gloomy cloud of silence descended over the dorm. It seemed like the good times were gone and the cunning conundrum that had enabled them to get cheap tickets home was no more.

The scam had been ingenious: the students flew *to* Israel when there were abundant seats available and their travel agents in America booked their return flights at the busiest times but didn't list them in the computer's P&R as student tickets. No one at the airport ever thought to verify the listings in the P&R against the ticket's fare basis.

By definition, these student tickets could not be booked more than three days in advance. And every student fare preempted the availability of a full fare. During this busy season, all flights were overbooked, but passengers holding student tickets knew enough to arrive at the airport well before those with expensive Apex tickets. Most of the assembled were distressed that their early arrival meant full-fare passengers would be bumped. But it was the thought of getting home that troubled the students now, as the distance between the dorm room and their families seemed greater than ever.

Finally David broke the silence. "Look on the bright side, fellas. That was just one airline — maybe Trans Am hasn't caught on yet. And anyway, I know for a fact — my father's a travel agent, don't forget — that the only foolproof way of detecting an illegitimate booking is by tracing the history of every passenger's reservation on screen. This would take ages, so there's no way they'd do that with hundreds of passengers waiting to board.

"The worst they can do is ask each person when he booked his return flight. And if they do that then... " David shrugged awkwardly, "then we may have to bend the truth a little."

The other students shifted uncomfortably in their seats. Telling an outright lie, i.e., saying they had made their booking in the last three days, seemed worse than anything they had done so far... but the alternative was losing the ticket. And everything seemed dependent upon their returning on schedule. Besides, some reasoned, perhaps the dreaded question would not be asked.

The mood in the dorm room grew heavy with

pragmatism. It was unanimously decided to arrive at the airport well before the flight. If they checked in early, reason dictated, by the time the airline realized what was flying, it would be too late. After all, they figured, if it came down to logic, no airline personnel would be able to outwit them.

YAAKOV BERNSTEIN was one passenger not yet aware of the reservation ruse. An extremely diligent yeshiva student and a budding scholar, he was blessed with the will to live what he learned. Not coincidentally, he had a strong aversion to "shtick."

Yaakov was just one of hundreds of American students due to return to the States at peak season. Without the three-day student discount, he could never have come to learn in Israel, since a full fare was way beyond his family's means.

His return flight was scheduled for the first week of intersession, and one of his closest friends was to be wed in New York the day after he arrived.

The Bernsteins' travel agent booked Yaakov's return flight with a fictitious but virtually standard procedure. Since he had not personally purchased the ticket — an errand run by his father — he was never informed of the stipulations of his fare. He was merely told that he was listed for Flight 421 and he should confirm his reservation in advance.

Yaakov's anticipation about returning home was heightened by his excitement over his friend's approaching nuptials. He knew nothing of the check-in contingencies arranged by other passengers his age. Dutifully following instructions, he arrived at the airport two hours before takeoff and found the lobby already mobbed with fellow travellers.

AT THE VERY HEAD of the check-in line, Gabi Miron conferred with his sales representative.

"And you still want to know if we're overbooked, Gabi?" the sales rep. demanded, sweeping his hand towards the sea of passengers and luggage. "A Hercules Transport couldn't carry this lot."

Miron shrugged in acquiescence.

"And not only that," the sales rep. continued, "it looks like it's 'youth night' on Trans Am today."

There was no denying that the majority of the passengers were in their teens, which did not jibe with the number of youth fares listed in the flight roster. Something was askew and the solution was painfully obvious: illegitimate passengers had to be weeded out without delaying the plane's takeoff.

TRANS AM'S sales rep. strode to the front of the line while Miron climbed on top of a table used for security checks and announced that anyone possessing a student ticket should have it ready for inspection. The proclamation sent shivers and quivers up and down the more youthful spines. Feverish consultation erupted among the passengers, all within easy earshot of Yaakov Bernstein:

"The ticket doesn't say a thing," whispered Doug to Steve. "If the guy asks you when you made your reservation, answer, 'Within the last three days.'"

"And they can't catch you?" Steve asked skeptically.

"That's what I just told you! The ticket doesn't say when you made the reservation, so they'll try and trip you up by asking when you booked."

"And what happens if you tell them the reservation was made more than three days ago?"

"Either they can deny you a seat on the plane since they are running short, or they can insist that you pay the difference between a student ticket and full fare."

"I don't like this," Steve muttered out loud, "I can't wait until it's over."

"Don't worry," Doug reassured his distraught companion, surveying the long line. "They don't seem to be having too much luck."

MIRON started with the rear of the line while the sales rep. worked his way down the front. Despite their suspicions and the obvious discrepancies, everyone questioned responded with the same formula: "Within the last three days."

There were over a hundred people on line with student tickets, but only a dozen of them appeared on the roster. With hopeless abandon, Miron realized that his failure to ferret out the frauds could mean the end of his career with Trans Am. On the other hand, rooting out deception by delaying the flight would be a Pyrrhic victory, for the hierarchy insisted upon punctuality — without excuses.

Frustration and anguish cacophonously collided in the manager's brain: frustration over the stalemate and anguish over the fact that despite his devotion and hard work, he might be fired because of a horde of kid fakers beyond his control. Revulsion and antipathy welled up within him toward the students waiting to board his plane.

The sales rep. managed to eliminate a few poorly briefed passengers from the line, which was good news for Trans Am, but not for its employees, for the culprits did not know how to graciously accept their lot. Some ranted and raved, others shouted and screamed — all several decibels above toleration — while yet others flailed their arms like evangelists preaching salvation.

The girls pulled out of the line began to wail and throw tantrums, blaming everything on their travel agents. They were innocent victims, they claimed, and they had to get home on *this* flight. Didn't the airline understand *anything*? The sales rep. was obviously not impressed. He was not prepared to lose his cool, his supervisor, or his company's money over a bunch of young con artists.

T O THE SENSITIVE HEART beating within Yaakov Bernstein, the scene was ineffably horrendous. In his opinion the shrieks and grousing were no less tasteful than the conniving that had precipitated them. But Yaakov was an island of conscience in a sea of self-absorption.

Most of the youth in line were preoccupied with the hope that they would not share the same fate of their unfortunate comrades. If this meant misleading the airline employees, so be it. By hook or by crook, they were determined to get on that flight.

Suddenly, the supervisor approached Yaakov and asked him when he had made his reservation. The yeshiva student just couldn't bring himself to supply the most patently prudent answer, which was his only guarantee of making it to his friend's *chassunah*. Numerous rationalizations raced through his head, justifying the "within-three-days" response — after all he really didn't know what his travel agent had arranged on his behalf — but Yaakov summarily dismissed them all.

What he *had* understood and what he was *led* to believe no longer corresponded to what he *now* knew. He could *drey* as well as anyone but although he might convince someone else, he wouldn't convince himself. To rephrase a response so that it was technically accurate was simply untenable. Furthermore, his desire to attend his friend's wedding robbed him of an unprejudiced perspective.

Fortunately his conscience was fortified by the loathsome scene taking place in the airport. The last thing he wanted, best friend's wedding and parental desires notwithstanding, was to be a party to a *chillul Hashem*.

"The departure date on this ticket was arranged long in advance," Yaakov related quietly. Gabi Miron was at first startled by the response and then visibly moved by the boy's honesty and composure. Those who heard the confession were utterly amazed, except for two of Yaakov's contemporaries, who smugly smirked and gestured to each other that he was nuts.

As if following his own cue Yaakov bent down, lifted up one suitcase, and moved to a vacant chair in the adjacent lounge. He quickly returned to shlep away his second piece of luggage but stopped abruptly, looked up at the manager, and said meekly, "I'm sorry."

BY THE TIME Miron and his assistant had finished their inspection the departure was still running on schedule with close to two dozen full-fare passengers bumped and scores of illegitimate passengers boarded.

Once all the seats were assigned and check-in was completed, Miron activated his walkie-talkie to verify his tally with the Gate. Occasionally the number of coupons collected did not match the number of seats, and it was standard procedure to double-check whenever there were standby passengers. The last thing Miron needed was for New York to pick up that aside from all the fraudulent fares, the plane left with an empty seat.

The distraught supervisor had little patience for his gadget to crackle back a response. After repeated attempts to make contact with the Gate Gabi stuffed the device into his jacket pocket and raced upstairs past passport control and boarding security.

Time was running out. Any minute flight control would radio clearance for takeoff, and Miron was still loathe to give the go-ahead. Darting through the terminal and practically vaulting over lounge chairs, the supervisor lunged toward Trans Am's departure gate, only to be greeted by a confounded ticket agent.

"Gabi," the clerk blurted out with total surprise, "the numbers don't add up; we're short one ticket!"

Barking into his walkie-talkie, Miron ordered the purser to take a head count immediately. This was no small endeavor considering that the subjects of the census had occupied every inch of the plane — except their seats. Instead of strapping themselves in in preparation for takeoff — as they had already been requested umpteen times — they were busy stashing parcels, backpacks, and cartons everywhere imaginable, making passing through the plane's narrow aisles all the more unlikely.

Since practically everyone on the flight knew each other, passengers felt compelled to introduce each other to the few individuals not known by all. Naturally this meant crossing rows, blocking aisles, and filling the galleys. The stewardesses pleaded, prodded and pressured the passengers to take their seats, but to no avail.

Even the veteran crew members had never witnessed such a spectacle. All flight attendants can attest that whenever anyone from a garage mechanic to a football tackle boards a plane, he is invariably transformed into a cooperative individual content to obey the crew's directives. But this flight's passengers were impervious, and utterly oblivious, to everything they were instructed.

The exasperated stewardesses were finally relieved by the authoritative voice of the captain, who threatened that if the flight were delayed any longer, they would be forced to make a stopover in Paris. The gimmick worked, and everyone took his seat.

A PASSENGER COUNT was conducted and one seat was indeed empty. The purser relayed the message to the supervisor, who contacted the sales rep. to check if there were any standby passengers left in the lobby. The answer was affirmative.

Miron rushed downstairs to the Trans Am counter. He glanced at the stranded passengers and then at his watch; they were half an hour behind schedule, but at least he would see to it that the last seat was a full fare.

Miron scanned the harried assemblage, and in seconds the crowd intuitively grasped that there was room on the plane. Pandemonium ensued. Passengers rushed the check-in counter like a fire-crazed mob fleeing toward an exit. They stormed the hostess, crashed the counter, and carried on with their carry-ons, begging for deliverance.

Gripped by incipient nausea, Miron skimmed over the pitiful crowd and one passenger stuck out: the one who wasn't demanding to be let on the plane because he understood that he wasn't entitled to fly. Understandably predisposed against young people after such a trying day, the supervisor kept searching for a worthy adult, but his sights continually refocused on the boy sitting and studying on the near side of the lounge.

All at once the frustration and tension of the day climaxed in a cathartic crescendo. Miron painfully realized that his superiors didn't care that he was trying his hardest to do a good job. His corporate dedication and sacrifice were irrelevant in the absence of a profit. He felt like a company man without a company, as alone as... as the yeshiva student lost in the crowd, resigned to his fate.

The yeshiva student, he meditated, was admirably forthright in admitting that he didn't belong on the flight, and honest enough not to change his tune now. Everyone fighting for his attention seemed to be a member of a group, a family, a couple... There were just a few single stragglers...

THE BOARDED PASSENGERS squirmed impatiently in their seats after the captain's last warning. The restlessness of the youthful passengers was tempered only by their relief that they made it on the flight.

"We'd never have made it otherwise..." Mordechai said, as if to justify the lie he had told the supervisor.

"It would have broken my mama's heart not to see me," David added with somewhat sincere emotion.

All the passengers looked up as the gangway backed off and the door sealed behind the last person to board. All looked up, that is, except a number of students, whose eyes fell to the floor in acute shame as Yaakov Bernstein walked down the aisle to take his seat.

Heard from: Sossie Abramowitz

Balance Sheet

Months	Chessed	Teshuvah	Torah	Tefillah	Tzeddakah	Aveiros
Tishrei						
Cheshvan						
Kislev						
Teves						
Shevat						
Adar						
Nissan						
Iyyar						
Sivan						
Tammuz						
Av						
Ellul						

Accruing Interest

Prepared by

Date

Index No.

✿

ואם נראה לנו אדם שהוא עושה עול
ומתקיים לו עשרו בודאי שהעושר שמור לו
לרעתו.

שפת תמים פרק ב'

*If we see someone who earns his
money through sin, and retains it,
this income is surely only being
maintained for his detriment.*

Sfas Tamim: 2

Wheels Within Wheels

REB MEIR declared his retirement at the age of sixty-four and moved his worldly possessions to the campus of Beth Midrash Govoha — the Lakewood Yeshiva. There, students served as his caretakers, and he, in turn, served as a fount of knowledge. Day and night for the final four years of his life, he graced Lakewood's thriving *beis midrash* with his presence.

And when this lofty soul was released from its paralytic prison, the entire yeshiva and hundreds of others came to bid their mentor farewell. Reb Meir Feist had taught them how to live an upright life devoted to serving the Almighty despite dreadful hardships.

At the rear of the funeral chapel stood a stranger, a tall, black man with a shiny *yarmulka*, courtesy of the chapel, perched incongruously on his thick, curly hair. Even more incongruous, however, was the fact that he was quivering helplessly and crying like a baby, cupping his grief-distorted face in his large hands. He was one of the very last to leave the chapel and he followed the bier until it disappeared from view.

The black man's appearance at the funeral generated a great deal of speculation. Who was he? What possible connection could a man like that have had with the revered Rabbi?

Two students could not contain their curiosity and mustered the courage to solve the mystery in the most direct way. "How did you know Rabbi Feist?" they asked him without preamble.

The man removed a large handkerchief from his pocket and dabbed at his eyes, white soppy pools shot with an intricate tracery of blood vessels.

"**I** AM WHO I AM," he responded in a hushed voice, "because of that Rabbi." He stopped to collect his thoughts, and other mourners and students from the yeshiva gathered around as he prepared to tell his tale:

"Many years ago I was nothing but a crook. I robbed and stole, and anyone who got in my way got mowed down. The police had a long rap sheet on me, but I pulled off lots more heists than I got nailed for.

"I had a beat," he continued, his resonant voice thickened by emotion, "which stretched for about three blocks in Morningside Heights, uptown Manhattan. We crooks arranged it so that none of us would mess with each other as long as we stayed on our own turf and didn't squeal to the cops.

"In the daytime I was breaking into cars belonging to doctors who worked in St. Luke's, and at night I would clean out apartments in the area. That's right near Morningside Park, and the cops would never respond to a call there unless they heard gunfire, or unless some hotshot got ripped off.

"**O**NE MORNING I'm making my way from place to place when I break into this joint on the ground floor. I didn't get very far in looting the closet when I hear a noise coming from the kitchen. I was sure that everything must be hid pretty good 'cause the apartment was practically bare. I grab the only valuable thing there, a tape recorder lying on the bed, and run out the door as fast as I can.

"Halfway down the hall I hear this voice shouting behind me. I take a peek over my shoulder and there, trying to wheel his way after me, is this old guy calling me to come back.

"The scene is so weird I stop in my tracks and walk back slow-like to the man in the wheelchair. When I'm close enough so he doesn't have to yell, he tells me that the tape recorder is worthless without its electrical cord. The dude tells me where I can find the cord in the house and begins to wheel himself back in. I figure, okay, so the guy is whacko, but what the heck?

"While I'm back in the apartment looking for the cord, he asks me — now get this — if I ate supper. This was the weirdest cat I ever seen. I shake my head 'no,' and then this guy starts wheeling all over the apartment, making me some lousy health kind of cereal.

"Over 'supper' he asks me why I steal. So I tell him the truth: I got kids to support and if I don't bring home enough dough my old lady'll move out on me. I don't mean no one no harm. He hears me out and then says, 'Well, if that's the case, I'll get you a job.'

"Before I know it, he's on the phone, and I can tell he isn't calling the cops. He starts mumbling Jew talk and, without understanding a word, I figure he's begging some chump to give me a chance. Then he hands me the receiver.

"This guy with an accent asks me if I ever worked in a warehouse before, so naturally I lie and say 'yeah, sure.' He tells me that he got work for me and that I should be at his place on Broadway and 40th at 8:30 in the morning."

The black man paused from his monologue and shook his head in disbelief as he relived the turning point in his life.

"I HANDED the old man back his tape recorder and made my way out of the building, not like a thief, but like a human being with self-respect. I told myself I was going to try out the job and make good. I never got a break before, and God knows I didn't want to blow it.

"The next morning I showed up at 'work' as excited as a kid on his first day of school. Heck, I was sitting on the pump across the street from the warehouse from 7:00 in the morning!

"The boss, this real religious Jewish guy, took me to the back and explained that I was supposed to empty cartons of clothing onto racks according to size, and do whatever the other guy in the warehouse told me to do.

Believe me, I followed orders like a good little soldier. It was the first time I had a job since I'd dropped out of high school eight years ago.

"This all happened sixteen years ago, and now I work as a salesman for the very same outfit, all thanks to Rabbi Feist. I'm going to miss that guy. I guess you will, too.

"A few weeks after I started working, I went to thank him for the job. From then on he would call me every once in a while. He always used to say that we have to try and overcome the trials we're given in life. He would tell me that he was trying, and that I should, too."

"**H**EY... HELLO? Is there anybody here?" demanded an out-of-town conductor clutching a bundle of sheet music.

"Over here," came the answer.

"Over where?" the conductor bellowed. He peered left and right until he caught sight of a bearded, elderly man in a wheelchair behind the counter.

"Oh, er... I'm sorry," the customer apologized weakly, "I didn't see you."

The man behind the counter was not offended. From childhood he'd been paralyzed from the waist down, and for more than a jubilee he had been confined to a wheelchair. He was accustomed to being humiliated, insulted and unnoticed.

SELLING SHEET MUSIC was the proprietor's occupation, but certainly not his vocation. It was merely a job that enabled him to devote his spare time to his true calling, the study of Torah. By design, his "spare time" constituted the lion's share of the day. Thus, Reb Meir Feist, a late starter in learning, had not only mastered the entire *Shas* and its commentaries, but earned the respect of some of the greatest Torah scholars in America.

The strain of maintaining the family business and the indignity of dealing with a callous public paled alongside Reb Meir's pathetic accommodations. His neighborhood in upper Manhattan, called "Morningside Heights," is a euphemism for South Harlem. Bleak by day and terrifying by night, the area could be the set for a "B"-movie about a nuclear apocalypse. The nightmarish tenements huddled together along filth-strewn sidewalks are habituated by local thugs, hardened drug addicts, and social deviants. In this kingdom of crime and muggings, the "Crack" capital of the world, innocence is hostage to violence and bystanders too often end up victims.

When darkness descends, law-abiding citizens cower behind locked doors. Shadowy gangs of toughs break-walk down the asphalt while police cruisers impotently roam the streets. For many, morning never comes to Morningside Heights.

DEEP IN THIS JUNGLE, on the ground floor of a mammoth apartment complex, resided Rabbi Meir Feist and his handicapped roommate, Reb Baruch. The two of them, devout Jews in a hostile world, tended to one another's needs. They seemed to have wheeled straight out of the generation of Rav Yehuda bar Ilaie, when six men could be covered by one *tallis* because, as Reb Chaim Shmuelevitz explained, each person pushed the garment upon his neighbor.

Reb Meir and Reb Baruch were right and left arms; they were two halves of one body. One held the door open while the other turned on the light; one tugged the clothesline while the other removed the pins. They helped each other into and out of the bed, the tub, and their clothing. They divided chores such as grocery shopping and cooking between themselves, each contributing the maximum that his disability allowed.

Inside their apartment they cared for each other, but against the crime that raged outside neither could offer his companion protection. They were utterly defenseless. The muggers and gangs that prowled the area were most discriminating in their choice of victims — all were fair game, but old ladies and cripples were prime targets.

BUT SOMEHOW, from the depths of that dreadful district, the sterling influence and remarkable erudition of the saintly Reb Meir shone forth. Jewish students from nearby Columbia University flocked to that dingy ground-floor apartment to learn from him, as did scholars from far greater distances. They would feast on Torah and bask in the glow of their teacher's wisdom. On a weekly basis, Reb Meir would endure tremendous hardships and grueling physical strain in order to lecture in synagogues in the metropolitan area, or to speak before audiences of *baalei battim*.

Those who came to Reb Meir were appalled by his dreadful living conditions — the fetid hallways, the rotting woodwork, the cracked and grime-streaked windows. They were equally confounded by the fact that Reb Meir neither complained nor appeared disconcerted by his surroundings. For Meir Feist, it must be assumed, was a product of his upbringing.

Because of his handicap he had not been able to attend yeshiva. He had to study by himself and grew accustomed to solitude. While other children his age went to school and frolicked on playgrounds, he was being examined by a series of physicians and specialists. Therapy session after therapy session, hospital ward after hospital ward — all the doctors' offices and clinics blurred into the same sterile, antiseptic environment. Fancy or plain, comfortable or displeasing, secure or hazardous, became insignificant contrasts for this humble, erudite man.

THUS IN ONE of the most unlikely and despicable places on earth, Reb Meir established his learning and *chessed* operation. Whoever visited apartment 1C was treated to a banquet of lovingkindness: a hot drink or a simple meal accompanied by a lively discussion and garnished with *divrei Torah* comprised the appetizer. The guests would invariably offer to fetch their own drink and provisions and not put their host to the trouble and physical exertion of wheeling himself back and forth. Reb Meir, however, would always dismiss their attempts, and insist on fulfilling his mitzva in its entirety.

Hachnassas orchim and *harbatzas Torah* were only the tip of Reb Meir's mitzva iceberg; his *gemilus chassadim* went far below the surface. It was not uncommon for those who braved the slums of South Harlem to become the unwitting beneficiaries of that *chessed*. When a destitute teacher cried bitterly over the loss of his employment, Reb Meir wheeled into action.

"How fortunate I am," exclaimed the scholar, who had plumbed the depths of the Talmud, "for I am in desperate need of a *chumash* tutor and you are available!" He insisted upon paying the teacher handsomely for his services and to further ensure that the pride of his new "tutor" would not be wounded, assured him that it was common for the disabled to hire a *melamed*.

Since Reb Meir's personal needs were modest — food, rent, and utilities — he saw no need to invest in savings plans. Each month he calculated how much money he needed and donated the remainder to charity. His very essence was one of sharing and giving.

ON ONE OCCASION Reb Meir found an excellent opportunity to help out when he learned of the plight of a shul custodian in the South Bronx. This simple Jew had labored tirelessly for many months, but the congregation, elderly Jews who themselves were in need, had failed to raise the funds to cover their custodian's salary. Reb Meir launched no investigation or inquiry: he simply reached into his pocket and surrendered its contents.

This gift cost Reb Meir dearly in terms of personal subsistence during the next few weeks, but for the man whose pride compelled him to consider it a loan, it meant survival — for himself and his large family. Soon thereafter, the shul went the way of so many Jewish institutions in the South Bronx. But its debt to the janitor remained. In lieu of cash, Congregation Anshei Emmes offered the only compensation it could afford: its no-longer-needed *tashmishei kedushah*.

THE COLLECTION WAS surprisingly large, having been amassed in the glory years of this now-impoverished *minyan*. Protected by decades of dust and tarnish, the religious articles remained bathed in an aura of sanctity. The custodian had since secured gainful employment elsewhere; now he sped downtown with the torn shopping bag full of *tashmishei kedushah*, eager to recompense his benefactor.

Reb Meir was in no hurry to exhume the earthly remains of a congregation that had died, and the bulky, tattered bag, filled with yellowed newspapers from a previous era, was relegated to the back of his closet while he attended to a more pressing need: hosting his guest. The janitor was treated to a cup of hot tea and the finest fare *chez* Feist could offer, with an inspiring *dvar Torah* for dessert.

Years might have passed before Reb Meir got around to examining the contents of that bag, but the very next day a tiny orphan kitten scurried into the apartment while Reb Meir was awkwardly maneuvering his chair through the narrow front doorway, and it sought refuge among Reb Meir's old coats and suits.

IN NO TIME at all, the kitten began mewling from hunger and Reb Meir, the embodiment of the *Mishna* — "Who is honored? He who honors his fellow creatures" — brought it a saucer of milk. To grant his diminutive guest easy access to its supper, he removed some of the debris that littered the bottom of the closet.

While the kitten contentedly lapped its milk, Reb Meir began to unwrap the items in the shopping bag with only the mildest sense of curiosity. One by one, he laid the pieces on his bed and gazed at them in awe, for there before his eyes was a treasure trove the likes of which Morningside Heights had never seen: three ornamental Torah crowns, two exquisite *attaros*, and one ornately-figured *yad*, all finely wrought from pure silver.

Reb Meir reached for an old shirt and began vigorously rubbing the shaft of the *yad*. Soon the mottled strata of tarnish parted to reveal a sight almost as wondrous as the silversmith's workmanship: the name of the original owner, Reb Shea (Rokeach) of Belz.

"The custodian did say these items had a long history," Reb Meir said aloud as he examined the *yad* in the light. "He did say they were from the *shtiebel* of the second Belzer Rebbe, but who would have be..."

"What's that, my friend?" Reb Baruch asked, wheeling into the bedroom. His roommate explained and the two passed the remainder of the evening huddled over the sacred *objets d'art*.

There is no doubt whatsoever that the resale of these few precious articles would have generated sufficient capital to raise Reb Meir — and his friend — up and out of the depths of his squalor, but the thought simply did not cross his mind.

It was as clear to him as Reb Shea's inscription itself that the *tashmishei kedushah* that had belonged to one of the foremost leaders of Galician *chassidim*, the forebear of the present Belzer Rebbe, had to be returned, either to the Rebbe's family or to the court of Belz.

REB MEIR carefully rewrapped the items in their crumbling, yellowed newspaper and replaced them in the torn shopping bag, determined one day to restore these very special ornaments to their rightful owner. He was certain that he was meant to serve as the conduit for their safe passage to *Eretz Yisrael*, although at the time he had neither plans to travel nor a reliable courier to send.

Many months later, one of Reb Meir's *talmidim*, a graduate student at Columbia University, announced that he was getting married. "She's a wonderful girl, Rebbe," he said, "and from a very fine family." Reb Meir listened with interest as the *talmid* described her "*yichus*" — like himself, his *kallah* was a "*Belzer ainekel*." The boy pronounced the word *ainekel* in typically Galician dialect, rather than the Lithuanian *einekel*, and Reb Meir smiled knowingly. Even before his *talmid* uttered the next sentence, the Rabbi wheeled his chair over to the closet and reached for the knob.

"With God's help, we're going to live in *Eretz Yisrael*," he concluded as Reb Meir hoisted the old shopping bag onto the bed.

REB MEIR carefully explained the mission he envisaged for his student. "I see the concern on your face, my son," he said. "You are worried lest these items be lost or stolen before you can safely deliver them. But you have nothing to fear. It is true they are of great value and here, hold this Torah crown in your hand." The young man gripped the work of art with both hands, and the tiny gilt bells tinkled delicately. "Do you not feel the *kedushah* in it? This crown has survived pogroms; it has survived the decimation of Galician Jewry; it has transversed oceans and continents. Do you believe it cannot withstand a mere jet flight to the Holy Land?"

Still the young man protested. It would be some time before he and his bride embarked on that flight, he said, and there had been many robberies in the neighborhood where they had rented an apartment.

Reb Meir dismissed the notion with a wave of his hand. "Quite recently, I myself was robbed," he said casually. "The thief, or should I say, would-be thief, took one look in that bag and rejected its contents in favor of an old tape recorder. Poor fellow! I had to chase him halfway down the hall to give him the electric cord he'd left behind, but that's another story. *Baruch Hashem*, he's out of the thieving business now and into something steadier, not to mention safer."

The student just shook his head in wonder and took his leave, the precious parcel clutched firmly in his arms. Weeks passed and the *talmid* learned of Reb Baruch's untimely demise. What would become of his beloved *Rebbe?* he wondered, greatly distressed. Who would take care of him? The young man called the Rabbi's number with trembling fingers, imagining the distraught, bewildered voice he would hear on the other end of the line. But once again, his *Rebbe* surprised him.

"You know, Baruch suffered far more than I ever did," he said philosophically, "because until he was twenty he stood on his own two feet. His disability was the result of a degenerative disease and, *nebbach*, each year he became more dependent, whereas I was born this way and learned to manage at a very early age. Baruch dreaded what the doctors confirmed would be the next manifestation of his illness — total paralysis. I am devastated by the loss of my companion but, at the same time, I'm relieved his suffering has ended. Did not *Amsa d'Rabbeinu haKadosh* pray that he endure no more?"

The *talmid* silently wished that his *Rebbe*'s prayers would also be answered, whatever they might be.

"**B**EFORE HIS *PETIRA*," Reb Meir continued, "Baruch told me something that helped me to cope with my loss. He said I had taught him by my example that one must never give up, that one must keep on trying, for if one does all he can, *HaKadosh Baruch Hu* will pay special attention. I never thought of myself as setting an example."

Of course not, the student agreed wordlessly. When did my *Rebbe* ever think about himself at all?

"But it is true that I have always tried very hard to do one thing: from the day I discovered Torah and realized that my handicap closed the doors of the yeshiva world to me, I have tried to create my own yeshiva, to immerse myself in learning, to surround myself with the holy words, in the hope that I might at long last come to understand them."

Would that we all understood as little as you, *Rebbe*, the student thought.

"And now, *Baruch Hashem*, my prayers have been answered." Reb Meir explained that he had been invited by Reb Shneur Kotler to join the scholars of the Lakewood Yeshiva. "Can you imagine, at my age, starting to attend yeshiva?" he gushed, his boyish exuberance belying his sixty-four years.

The student wished him well and bade his *Rebbe*

goodbye, but before he could hang up, Reb Meir had one more parting word. "Thank you, my son, for relieving me of the onus of the Belzer *tashmishei kedushah*. I have always preferred to travel light."

Heard from: Yacov Mordechai

Windfall

REUVEN WAGNER abruptly removed his hand from his pocket as he passed a soda machine in the departure terminal of Milwaukee's General Mitchell Field Airport. Normally he would buy himself a can — out of habit more than thirst — but this time he could not afford such a luxury. Every penny was precious.

His excursion to New York was a business trip and his insolvent Judaica store was footing the bill. The social calls and sightseeing, part and parcel of every visit to New York, would be conspicuously absent from this trip. Rubie had a mission to accomplish, and failure would mean dire consequences for his struggling household. Simply put, he had to find bargains; he would hunt them and stalk them in the name of turning his fledgling shop into a profitable venture.

"Wagner's Kol Bo" had opened its modest doors eleven lean months ago. From the very beginning it merited neither a "grand opening" nor a grand continuance. The local impression was that Wagner's prices were too high and the truth was that he was too small and too new in the business to really be competitive. Those in need of religious articles had managed without a shop before the Wagners came to town, went the reasoning and excuse for non-patronage, and they could manage in its absence. Such thinking was anything but welcome for the Wagners, a family of five.

THE YOUNG FAMILY had set up shop in Milwaukee under the assumption that they would be providing an important service. In fact it hadn't even been their idea; but those rabbis, community leaders and residents who had initially encouraged them had suddenly made themselves scarce. Rubie felt very betrayed.

The townsfolk were willing to drive more than an hour to Chicago to save $1.50 on two record albums and a *siddur*. No one was prepared to pay a few extra pennies for the convenience of a local store. The logic escaped him.

Rubie tried cajoling potential customers. His prices weren't high, he argued; why, his profit margin was lower than that of the Judaica stores in the major cities. As soon as he could attract enough customers to place large orders, the New York dealers would give him the same discounts they gave the larger outlets. But his reasoning was wasted on unreasonable people. Irony of ironies, the very shoppers who failed to buy from him couldn't possibly justify driving sixty miles and spending more on gasoline than the amount they saved on their out-of-town purchases.

Logic aside, the harsh reality of an unprofitable

endeavor weighed heavily on the dwindling Wagner budget. After almost a year in the red, Rubie Wagner had to make a decision: either cut his losses and close the business, or discover some way to reverse the downturn.

Rubie opted for the latter. He would have to find a way to buy stock at reduced prices. His previous attempts to do so had been unsuccessful, but this time he would rely not on impassioned pleas but on personal appeals.

The round trip airfare to New York was a whopping $320. The ancillary expenses of room and board, phone calls, car, etc., would have to be covered by mooching and borrowing.

The plane landed in the early afternoon and Rubie got straight to work. His first stop was Brooklyn, where he was able to borrow a station wagon from his ex-neighbor. It was too late in the day to go shopping in Manhattan, so Rubie made a barrage of calls in search of Brooklyn *metziahs*, but all for naught. Everyone he spoke to about bargains directed him to New York's Lower East Side. "That is," they always added, "if you don't mind the hassle." But Rubie could live with temporary frustration and aggravation, as long as his efforts paid off.

THE NEXT MORNING, Rubie and millions of others crawled their way into the "melting pot" theory's greatest refutation: New York, New York. The ethnic enclaves on that island had grown more and more diverse with time, and the Lower East Side had become home to almost as many peoples as there are nations.

Crossing Delancey Street, Rubie rapidly awoke from his Midwest stupor, born of mile after mile of unchanging scenery and populace. Here, every avenue was a cornucopia, a potpourri of multi-ethnic ingredients: Chinese merchants hawked their wares from pushcarts, Sikhs manned their Brazilian-Malaysian-Philippine produce stands, Jamaican junkies hustled customers for their contraband, Puerto Ricans shot craps and played three-card monte on the sidewalk, and black youth break-danced in the gutter. The detritus of their activities littered the dingy streets.

The sprinkling of Caucasian Americans looked oddly out of place, but even more conspicuous were New York's Finest, pounding their beat. They sauntered down the block, their burly figures bulging slightly at the belt, their holstered guns sagging heavy at the hips, and their arms akimbo like Sumi wrestlers about to begin a championship match.

Rubie headed down Essex Street, where the first indication of a Jewish presence emerged. Signs in Yiddish could be discerned on windows and above storefronts, and numerous men scurrying to and fro were clad in the attire indigenous to the devoutly religious. Soon he knew he would reach the corner of Essex and Canal, the heart of the wholesale and retail Judaica market.

In his attempt to acquire favorable terms, Rubie had personally met or phoned almost every merchant on this block. He backed into a parking space, locked the car, and then reached for a quarter to feed the meter. But in a stroke of good fortune, Rubie had pulled up in front of a truncated meter decapitated by vandals. He interpreted the free spot as an auspicious harbinger of greater bargains.

RUBIE ENTERED the first shop and asked to speak to the proprietor privately. Carefully and deliberately, Rubie explained his situation to the sympathetic merchant. In the end, however, instead of low-cost merchandise, the obliging shop owner offered some cheap advice:

"Just lest night, mebbe night before," the merchant said, "I'm hearing two stores is making whaddayacallit, a moiger first of the month. I figure they not gonna moige all the stock — what for? Then you gotta lotta whaddayacallit, duplicates. Better they should unload the soiplus for peanuts. I would.

"One of these here partners, he's the brother from my wife's sister's husband, he told me about the moiger. You want I should call him up, see mebbe they wanna make a deal with you?"

Rubie nodded incredulously, not trusting his voice. This was the break he needed, the chance he had prayed for: a windfall.

The call the proprietor placed on his behalf resulted in two meetings that day to buy up the excess stock of both stores.

The businessmen who were merging, Horowitz and Langer, were practically household words in religious articles. They carried everything: from Israeli Judaica to Soviet Jewry posters, from esoteric *sefarim* to designer *tallis* clips.

Horowitz offered the Midwesterner *yarmulkas* for half price. He was willing to unload popular *chumashim* sets at a similar discount. All his English books he made available at cost, which was 22% less than Rubie usually paid to the same publishers. And he let his music cassettes go for a song.

Later that afternoon, Langer presented Rubie with rock-bottom prices and special deals on gifts imported from Israel. He also gave him an exceptional discount on woolen *talleisim* and terylene *challah* covers. The plethora of bargains presented Rubie with a painful dilemma: he couldn't afford to buy all the *metziahs*, but then again, he couldn't afford not to.

The station wagon was three-quarters full of merchandise and his checking account was three-quarters empty of cash by the time he finished with Horowitz. Rubie dreaded the thought of borrowing more money, but Langer's willingness to accept a head check was an offer he could not refuse.

The thought of the kind of money he was risking for a debilitated business was reducing Rubie to jelly, but he reminded himself that the trip itself had been a gamble. Having decided to make this last-ditch effort, he was committed to carrying it through to completion. The items he had just purchased and the prices he had paid could conceivably turn his business around.

W ITH AN AIR of confidence that was almost genuine, Rubie stuffed every carton from Langer's into his borrowed station wagon. Thank God, the trip had been a complete success, he told himself. He couldn't get over his *mazel*. Now he had just one more stop before heading back to Brooklyn to arrange shipment of the goods he wouldn't be able to take with him on the plane.

Rubie drove to the other end of the Lower East Side's Jewish section to pick up a few unstocked items that customers had specifically requested and even paid for in advance. Ironically, Horowitz and Langer didn't carry these things, either.

He found a parking space not too far from a Judaica store. Then like the entrepreneur he had suddenly become, he felt himself glide into the shop, a heady feeling of satisfaction pervading every fiber of his body. He glanced at the figures marked above each item and a broad smile spread across his face. Here he was on the Lower East Side of New York — America's bargain basement for religious articles, the cradle of cut-throat price wars — and the list prices seemed outrageous in comparison to what he had just paid.

WHILE RUBIE patiently awaited his turn, he fantasized about the advertising spreads he would splash in the local Jewish newspaper. "Bonanza Blitz," he would call it, and present "The Wagner Challenge": "Quote lower prices in a two-hundred-mile radius, and the item is yours free!" By the time he was next in line, he had already imagined the crowds fighting to get into his store and his wife begging him at ten o'clock at night to come home despite the dozen customers he still hadn't served.

When Rubie's turn finally came, he understood why the wait had been so long. The clerk was a Galapagos tortoise in disguise — nearly as old but not nearly as fleet-footed. Record breaking achievements in inertia were taking place — in slo-mo — before his eyes. With a glance at his watch, Rubie discovered that he'd been in the shop for more than half an hour. He grabbed the purchases the clerk had finally assembled, mumbled a "thank you," and darted out of the store toward the parking meter.

Breaking some records of his own he flew to the car, but when he came to a screeching halt at the curb, the sight that greeted him was far more devastating than a metermaid: The station wagon was looted clean, and all his *metziahs* were gone without a trace.

Rubie pounded his fist against the hood of the car, tears of fury and frustration stinging his eyes. He felt like screaming, but what was the use? He cursed New York soundly under his breath. For every crime committed in that city there are a hundred apathetic witnesses, and robbers and thieves are free to carry out their deeds with impunity.

It was as if his entire future had been stuffed into that car. Now, all that was left of that glorious tomorrow was a debt of over $600, payment due in four weeks.

BY RIGHTS he should have reported the robbery to the police, but he sensed intuitively that the time spent crying was better invested. He could just see himself attempting to explain to a detective exactly what was stolen. Why subject himself to the additional aggravation when it would not lead to the retrieval of his property? He was sure that in a city plagued by so many murders and other heinous crimes, the only purpose of filing a theft report was to collect insurance.

No doubt the perpetrators would try to sell the goods, Rubie figured, so he decided to inform the local store owners of his loss. Maybe he would recoup some of his money; at least he would feel that he'd tried.

His grim trek from shopkeeper to shopkeeper became cathartic. Each one had words of empathy, and they all shared their own robbery experiences; it was a sort of neighborhood initiation rite. Merchant after merchant took his phone number and promised to keep a vigilant eye out for Rubie's goods.

DEJECTED, Rubie drove back to Brooklyn, his head bowed on his slumped shoulders. The vexation that had welled up within him knew no bounds. How could he explain to his wife — who had begged him not to overspend — that their borrowed money had been stolen?

The more Rubie contemplated his situation, the bleaker it seemed. His wife was expecting their fourth child; there were mortgage payments to be met on his house; and even their modest Midwestern living expenses soared. Rubie worked his way through the traffic to Brooklyn, grateful that night had fallen. Had the sun still been shining, fellow motorists would have spotted his dripping tears.

Rubie returned the borrowed car, related his tale of woe and bade farewell to his kind neighbor of long ago. It was obvious that he was not in a loquacious mood and wished to return to Milwaukee as soon as possible to reassess his situation.

BUT WHILE RUBIE had despaired, others had not. The Jewish merchants of the Lower East Side maintained a watchful eye for Wagner's stolen goods. Beyond the ambit of their vigilance, however, a lanky Hispanic entered a Jewish bookstore just three blocks away from the scene of the crime. With no irony intended, the glassy-eyed tough asked the proprietor if he was interested in a real "steal".

The youth led the shopkeeper outside, where three cartons brimming with brand new *talleisim*, Jewish books, *yarmulkas*, etc., were piled on the sidewalk.

The owner of the store, Akiva Yosef Weissbraun, stared at the heaps of merchandise and blinked hard. It was a windfall; an answer to his prayers. Times were rough for this merchant and he had been wondering when he would get his break. His eldest daughter was to be wed in eight weeks, but he still didn't know how he would meet the financial commitments of the *chassunah*.

In between visits by his sporadic customers, Akiva Yosef had plenty of time to review his calculations. But there was no need to agonize over them yet again: he simply didn't have the cash to mount a proper wedding. His *mechutanim* had assumed that because he owned a shop in Manhattan he was a man of means, but nothing was farther from the truth. For the past three years he had barely turned a profit.

AKIVA YOSEF'S WORK-WORN HANDS rummaged through the merchandise and verified that outside his store stood a veritable fortune in mint condition. There was no mistaking the value of the goods. Or their source: the stuff was hot. It was very clear to him, however, that before grappling with the moral issue of trafficking in stolen goods, he had to redeem them from the impure hands of the thief — no matter what.

"I'll give you $50 for the whole lot," Akiva Yosef offered. "Take it or leave it."

The youth didn't hesitate a minute. He grabbed the fifty and vanished.

Akiva Yosef hauled the three overflowing boxes into his store and immediately began erecting mental castles and elaborate *chupahs*. He knew he was shlepping thousands of dollars worth of merchandise.

Weissbraun's *yetzer hara* commenced a brutal, unremitting assault. Within moments his conscience was neutralized and he was at the mercy of an evil inclination garbed in the specious cloak of virtue. Like a zombie, he perfunctorily emptied the cartons onto his shelves, racks, and counters, rationalizing that he was thus safeguarding their good condition. After all, the cloth items musn't get wrinkled, the *siddurim* torn or the *bechers* bent.

Akiva Yosef closed his shop early that evening. Some days business was so slow that he couldn't bear to leave for home until he made one more sale, however meager, to justify his coming to work in the first place. But tonight he wasn't waiting around for that one last customer. His fortune had changed.

AKIVA YOSEF boarded a Williamsburg-bound subway train and spotted a neighbor of his who also owned a Judaica shop on the East Side. He sat down next to his friend and, despite his hesitations, found himself unable to contain his secret.

The neighbor seemed dazed by the story. "I can't believe it," he blurted out. "I think I know whose stuff it is." The man then fumbled through his pockets until he found a business card with an out-of-state phone number scribbled on the back in pencil.

Akiva Yosef tried to look interested, but inside he was overcome with deep regret at having related the day's events. "Please call him as soon as you can," the neighbor insisted. "The *Yid* is so heartbroken. He was betting his entire future on that carload."

Akiva Yosef duly copied the phone number and mumbled a thanks of sorts to his friend, but the matter was far from resolved in his head. His conscience afforded the subject some space on a back burner, but in his heart of hearts he hoped the flame would burn out.

THE NEXT DAY Akiva Yosef assiduously busied himself straightening up his shop and keeping the telephone well out of sight. To his great relief, several customers also kept him occupied that morning.

But in the mid-afternoon, when things quieted down and he had nothing at all to do, he somberly pondered his dilemma. He hadn't gotten very far in his thinking when the phone rang.

It was his old friend Sam from up in the Bronx, boasting that he had the best news imaginable. His shul was holding a gala weekend event in honor of a donor who had just contributed half-a-million dollars. In the donor's name the shul was going to purchase significant quantities of religious articles, including an entire Judaica library, two dozen new *talleisim*, a hundred *yarmulkas*, two hundred and fifty *siddurim*, and lots more.

"Listen, Akiva Yosef," Sam implored, "if you can fill this order immediately, it's yours. Otherwise we'll have to turn to a larger outlet. Usually our shul buys from that big place up on Essex, but since I'm now on the shul board I can throw this your way. But most important, you have to ship out the goods this week at the latest, because the weekend is only eleven days off.

"Akiva Yosef, if you pull this off, you can count on a steady account as long as I'm sitting on the board."

AKIVA'S HEART POUNDED. Normally his inventory was never large enough to fill such an order, but the items the shul sought were precisely what he had ransomed from the hoodlum. His daughter would have a beautiful wedding after all. "Don't worry, Sam," Akiva Yosef assured his friend, "I won't let you down."

Opportunity had knocked and he didn't want to waste any time opening the door. But as the elderly merchant eagerly rose to consolidate the shipment, the small voice of his conscience rose to a resounding crescendo, and he was haunted by the image of a poor shop owner somewhere in the boondocks tearing out his hair.

Akiva Yosef slumped down at his counter and fished the phone number out of his pocket. "Who says these are the things that were stolen from this guy, anyway?" he consoled himself. He picked up the phone and punched in the number.

"Hello? Is this Wagner? I'm calling from New York, and I want to know if you're missing some religious articles in large quantities."

"Yes, yes! Have you found them?"

"Maybe. Can you tell me what you had?"

"About eight dozen *yarmulkas*, three hundred *bentchers*, at least twenty *challah* covers..."

"All right, all right,"Akiva Yosef grumbled, letting the

truth sink in. "It sounds like the stuff is yours. Come in to my shop — I'll hold the merchandise for you for another week. My name is..."

"Just a second," Rubie broke in. "First of all, I don't know how to thank you for what you are doing. You could never imagine how important this merchandise is to me. But to tell the truth, I can't afford to make a return trip to New York.

"I'm not going to go into a sob story on your dime — and of course I will pay you back for this phone call — but the travel expenses are simply beyond my budget. Please, I... I know I have no right to ask this of you, but could you possibly send it UPS collect? I'll reimburse you for your trouble as well. Tell me what your phone number is and I'll call you right back with my address..."

"You don't need my number. Just give me your address, and we can settle our account afterwards."

Rubie obligingly dictated the information.

"All right," the distant voice acknowledged, and the line went dead in Rubie's hand.

AKIVA YOSEF WEISSBRAUN had some serious soul-searching to do. He had a large order at top dollar for practically everything that Wagner claimed was his. And while Wagner could present a long-distance song and dance about how much he needed the money, no one knew as well as Akiva Yosef how badly he himself needed the extra income right now. It would enable him to meet his commitment to his *mechutanim*, and to his daughter.

Maybe, Weissbraun thought to himself, the fact that the

thief chose to enter my shop was an indication from Above that the merchandise was meant to be mine. Maybe...

He had half a dozen "maybe"s and even more rationalizations for holding on to the goods. After all, he did pay for them, sort of...

One thing was clear: Wagner would not be making any more trips to New York in the near future to investigate the whereabouts of his goods. And even if he did, all the evidence could swiftly disappear in one large shipment to the Bronx.

But against all of these factors was pitted one slight problem: deep down, Akiva Yosef knew the merchandise rightfully belonged to Wagner. It didn't matter if Wagner were a millionaire and Weissbraun had seven daughters to marry off — it was still *gezel*.

"Akiva Yosef," he involuntarily addressed himself, "you know you can't do it. You can't make a wedding out of *treifa gelt*."

He placed his UPS book on the counter but he couldn't start writing. "Wasn't there some way to compromise?" he asked himself judiciously. "Maybe I can ship out the goods and then pad the bill to compensate for my trouble. Maybe I should write him a letter describing the hardships I've undergone to secure the items from the thief and locate their true owner, forfeiting time and energy in the process. Such a saga might at least morally compel Wagner to make all his future purchases exclusively from me..."

EIGHT DAYS LATER, Rubie Wagner received four neatly wrapped boxes filled with the goods that were stolen from him, exactly as he remembered them. Everything that should have been there was — except the bill. The UPS charges had been paid in New York but none of the boxes contained a bill for the shipping, the phone call, or the handling. Rubie scrutinized the packages several times but he couldn't even find a return address. All he discovered, scribbled on one of the boxes, was a message: "Sorry for the delay, A. Y. W."

Seven weeks later, Akiva Yosef Weissbraun's eldest daughter was married. The affair was very *balabatish* — although by far not the fanciest — and the celebrants were all very happy. Within the year, Akiva Yosef became a grandfather for the first time. Despite frequent gentle reminders from his daughter and son-in-law that the child's name was Nachman, Akiva Yosef persisted in calling his grandson "*Oitzer'l*" ("my little treasure"), for when all is said and done, a healthy grandchild is truly the greatest "windfall" of all.

Heard from: Aryeh Zak

To Teach a Lesson

AS FAR AS the Jewish community was concerned, Seattle turned into Sadville the day Shmuli Katz decided to leave town. He had accepted a job as vice-principal of a prestigious Day School on the East Coast. According to his contract he had to give only three months' notice before departing — an imprudent clause, Katz's employer now conceded.

Shmuli Katz was not merely a Jewish-studies teacher in the Day School; he was a *mechanech* par excellence, and embodied the loftiest goals and values of the Jewish-studies department. His absence would create an absolute, unmistakable vacuum.

The vacancy, like any other problem directly or remotely connected to Jewish education in Seattle, fell squarely on the shoulders of Seattle Hebrew Academy's principal, Mr. Dennis Silver. Silver was a competent, well-respected man dreadfully overburdened just by maintaining the school's budget. Nonetheless, he was also responsible for the school's academic standards and the education of each and every child.

Finding a teacher on such short notice — especially one to replace the popular Shmuli Katz — was a formidable task, and it was made no easier by the constant inquiries about his successor.

Silver wished he could interpret the enormous outpouring of solicitude as reflecting a genuine interest in Jewish education, but he knew otherwise. The sad fact was that very few parents in his community were concerned with Jewish studies altogether, and most tolerated the handful of Hebrew classes as one does a useless college requirement.

Like so many other Jewish Day Schools across America, the Seattle Hebrew Academy attracted most of its students by default. Rather than out of a desire to place their children in a Jewish environment, most of the parents enrolled their children in the Academy merely to spare them the execrable influences and elements prevalent in the public-school system.

It was no secret that the overwhelming majority of the Academy's parent body would not have protested had no Jewish studies been offered at all. On numerous occasions they requested that more time be devoted to computer courses and crafts, implying that the extra hours could be expropriated from "less relevant" subjects. Only grudgingly had they come to accept Torah-related classes as part of the curriculum.

Their sudden interest and enthusiasm, Silver understood only too well, was triggered by their fear of who would replace Katz. Shmuli was the first religious teacher everyone really seemed to have appreciated. The kids adored his youthful charisma, and their parents respected his sincerity and conviction. Even the P.T.A., which was traditionally hostile to the school's Hebrew staff, had a special affinity for Rabbi Katz and expressed it with seasonal bonuses.

The long line of teachers that had preceded Shmuli Katz were poignant reminders of the *mechanech*'s lonely lot. Underpaid and unrespected, they were viewed as parasites feeding off the school's budget. And if, God forbid, they had an idiosyncrasy or shortcoming, it would never be forgiven or forgotten.

All along Silver realized that Shmuli wouldn't stay forever; he only wished that this favorite teacher's tenure would last a little bit longer. The principal was confident that just a few more years of Katz's positive influence would erase the harm caused by his predecessors and alter the acrimonious attitude toward Jewish studies. But that was not to be.

THREE MONTHS was precious little time to find the likes of a Shmuli Katz, but Silver would have to try his hardest. Unfortunately, geography was not on his side. He had yet to figure out why Seattle sounds thousands of miles farther from New York than Los Angeles, but that was the mindset he confronted every time he courted a candidate.

After nine weeks of searching, running advertisements, conducting interviews, and evaluating model lessons, the Seattle Hebrew Academy was no closer to finding a replacement than it had been two months earlier. Time was running out.

In ten days, the Day-School Teachers' Network was holding its midwestern convention, and Silver was staking everything on landing a Jewish-studies instructor during the proceedings. Teachers seeking new positions flocked to these events, and the other attendees were always fonts of information regarding available talent.

Meanwhile, pressure had been mounting on the principal to teach the Jewish subjects himself. After all, went the reasoning, why import new blood when capable personnel were already on staff? Of course, even without a teaching burden, Dennis Silver worked overtime to finance and run the school, but that never occurred to these voices of dissention.

Dennis understood that he wasn't looking for just a "teacher" but for a replacement of the school's biggest asset. If he failed to find the right man at the convention, then everything he had accomplished over the previous eight years would unceremoniously dissolve into oblivion. Despite his demanding criteria, however, he knew he could not offer a large enough salary to tempt an experienced instructor to make the big move.

DENNIS SILVER arrived at the conclave and got straight to work. He had barely dropped his suitcase at the check-in desk when he abandoned registration to join a huddle of principals conferring in the lobby.

Normally teachers look forward to their conventions as a vacation and a means of unwinding after months of frustration. Funny and not-so-funny stories abound about stubborn school boards, pedantic P.T.A.s, and didactic dilemmas. But Silver had no time to shmooze or socialize; he had to find a miracle worker to save his Jewish-studies department.

None of the candidates he spied roaming the lobby and snoozing through the sessions readily appealed to him. He recognized many of them from past years, and the fact that they were still looking for employment wasn't exactly a point in their favor.

From the very outset two major constituencies of contenders were disqualified from the position: those with large families and those still single. For the patresfamilias the salary was insufficient and the local *chinuch* was below par; for the singles, Seattle was no place to look for one's match.

But Dennis Silver considered anyone outside these two categories. He followed up on leads, canvassed his colleagues, and picked any brain worth picking. Late Saturday night, three grueling, depressing days culminated in a resounding fulfillment of the talmudic adage, *"Yagata umatzasa, ta'amin."*

Finally, a *Rosh Yeshiva* from Detroit who addressed the gathering informed Dennis that a *yungermann* in his city was looking to teach. The fellow was very learned, and since he was just beginning in *chinuch*, he was prepared to forgo the major Jewish centers and settle for a modest income, his eight children notwithstanding.

Anyone and everyone Dennis spoke to from Detroit confirmed that this *yungermann* was exceptionally nice and as dedicated as they come. Actually he had planned to attend the convention, but his wife had contracted mono just one week before.

WITH A PRAYER on his lips Dennis excitedly phoned the candidate. And just as everyone had attested, Zvi Mandel was friendly, forthcoming, and very "yeshivish." He wasn't intimidated by moving to Seattle, for he and his wife felt they had already traversed half the world the day they left Lakewood for Detroit. "A couple of hundred miles this way or that wouldn't make a difference at this point," he assured the apprehensive principal. Furthermore Mandel knew that the position wasn't permanent, and he was anxious to break into *chinuch*.

Dennis just hoped *chinuch* wouldn't break him. But the experienced administrator consoled himself by recalling that usually the young and the eager were the most determined not to let impediments stand in their way.

Since he could pay only a pitiful salary, Dennis offered to find a house for Mandel's growing family, thereby saving him the expense of a pilot trip. The Mandels accepted gratefully but emphasized that Silver should keep the price down, even if it meant their living in a run-down area a mile from shul.

"Leave it to me," he promised. "I will try, God willing, to get you the most for your money."

DENNIS SILVER returned to Seattle triumphant but tremulous. On the one hand he was anxious to spread the good news of his "mission accomplished" in order to quell the rumors of failure. But on the other hand, he was embarrassed to admit that he hadn't even met the new teacher, much less interviewed him. He didn't even know what he looked like although it was easy to imagine.

Dennis feared that he was about to provide his detractors with fresh ammunition. Indeed, he often mused that he could write a book — co-authored by dozens of other Day-School principals — about what it means to be employed in a thankless job.

Silver tried hard and was undeniably well-educated, articulate, devout and sincere. But for all his self-sacrifice and dedication to Jewish education there was always a critic at every turn. He couldn't afford a major faux pas like hiring the wrong teacher. Every child in the small community would be affected, and he would be blamed. In the face of this grim scenario, Dennis Silver banished the thought that Zvi Mandel would not work out.

DENNIS BLINKED hard as the motley Mandel clan emerged enthusiastically from the airport terminal. They might just as well have walked straight out of the shtetl. But appearances aren't everything, he kept reminding himself as he loaded the Mandels and their baggage into the two vans he had hired to take them to their new home.

To his relief, the Mandels, all ten of them, turned out to be the most agreeable people imaginable. Dennis' informants had not let him down.

But Zvi was very much the Lakewood Yeshiva graduate. Apparently his sojourn in the midwest had altered neither his garb, his demeanor, nor his manner of speech. Kids always appreciate sincerity, Dennis tried to reassure himself.

THE SCHOOL YEAR would begin in three days and Dennis recommended that Zvi come into school beforehand to get acquainted with the building and the curriculum. He looked forward to the opportunity to prime the neophyte about the nature of the student body, and to offer some teaching tips.

Dennis patiently outlined the organization of the school and its particular problems. Religious life in Seattle, he explained, was different than anything this Lakewood graduate had ever seen, and it was important to relate to the students on their level. Gradually inroads could be made if the lessons were made to seem interesting and relevant. Certainly this was the plan.

But things did not quite work out according to plan. In the better classes the children were merely disobedient. In the worse ones, it didn't take the pupils long — about four seconds — to realize they were sharing the classroom with a greenhorn, and they felt duty-bound to offer him a stark initiation into the world of bratty children.

Zvi weathered the unabating storm philosophically, but the same could not be said for the students or their parents. They demanded his resignation. To their chagrin, the principal was unwilling to comply, and he begged the parents to give Mandel a chance.

Week after week they badgered Silver until they finally presented him with a veiled ultimatum:

"Mr. Silver," the delegation pressed, "we have given your teacher ample time to prove himself. But instead of improving every day he gets more and more obscure. Our children are bored in his classes and want to avoid school altogether because of him. He just doesn't speak their language.

"We understand that he has a large family and is not a man of means, but these are not valid considerations if you value the education of your students. We all know you have a big heart, but misplaced pity in a situation like this is detrimental. Surely you know the Yiddish expression, 'You must provide to eat, but children may not be the meal.' We will not put up with this any longer!"

Dennis was crushed, for he knew they spoke the truth. Zvi Mandel, for all his scholarship and sincerity, was simply not cut out to teach non-religious, disaffected children. The principal had taken a gamble and lost.

THE WORLD seemed to be crashing in on Dennis Silver. He would have to fire Zvi Mandel and look for a replacement all over again. But he had no choice. He was paying Zvi with communal money, an expenditure he could no longer justify. The Mandels' predicament could not figure in his decision; he had to do what was right for the school.

Dennis agonized over the task of breaking the news to Zvi. In one sentence he would inform him that he was fired and effectively stranded in the northwest corner of the United States.

"Tonight," Dennis resigned himself, "I'll do the grievous deed." *Derech eretz* mandated that he inform Zvi at home rather than in school. At least this way Zvi and his wife would understand that he was trying to be as amicable as possible, and that the decision had not been easy for him.

SILVER had personally found the Mandels their house, but the area suddenly seemed inexplicably foreign — and more impoverished — to him now. Maybe it was the Mandels' beat-up station wagon parked awkwardly in the driveway.

He made his way up the stairs to the house and waded through the pitiful array of dolls and decapitated toys littering the front porch. It was hard to imagine that these playthings were ever new.

Dennis took a deep breath and knocked on the door, but the noise emanating from the children inside drowned him out. He knocked harder, but still there was no response.

Dennis Silver, the father of three — the youngest of whom was nine — stood at the doorstep in awe. There was as much of a racket inside the Mandel home as there was on the elementary-school playground during recess. With quivering fingers he rang the doorbell.

Mrs. Mandel, accompanied by three half-dressed children clinging to her skirt, opened the door.

"Oh, Mr. Silver...," she said with a look of complete astonishment, "what a nice surprise, what an honor. Please come in. Zvi is taking someone around the neighborhood. He should be back right away. I hope you'll stay for supper," she added, clearing a chair for him to sit down.

"Oh, no," Dennis demurred, taking in the cyclone of a household in one quick glance. "I only wanted to speak to your husband for a few minutes, but I see this is a bad time for you."

"Why, no," Mrs. Mandel insisted. *"Bli eyen hara,"* she said, directing her eyes to the seemingly infinite number of children — all under the age of twelve — dangling from every conceivable projection in the house, "it's always like this, but after supper it will quiet down a bit. Please have a seat."

WHATEVER APPETITE Dennis Silver might have had dwindled from the time he entered the Mandel residence. He hastily concluded that there was no point in his remaining now, especially if they were having company. Just as he reached for the door, he caught sight of Zvi Mandel and another man heading up the steps.

"Mr. Silver! What a treat!" Mandel exclaimed, his eyes dancing with delight. "Please meet Barry Winter. Mr. Silver," he continued, now addressing his guest, "is the principal of our Day School, not to mention the most respected Jew in town."

Dennis extended his limp hand with a profound sense of discomfort and angst. The Mandels had become attached to him.

"I'm glad to meet you," Mr. Silver responded. "What brings you here?"

"Not the best of reasons," Barry replied with a slight shrug of his shoulders. "My son will be undergoing extensive medical treatment in Seattle, and I am looking for a place to rent. Zvi was just showing me some of the possibilities."

"How do you know each other?" Silver asked.

"We just met. He's not here very long, but Zvi's pretty famous. Everybody knows to stay at his house."

As if on cue, two *meshulachim* emerged from a bedroom. One of them had appeared on his doorstep the day before. He was sure the man had caught the last flight out of town.

Zvi hurried over to his guests and launched into more introductions. Dennis tried to interrupt him by indicating that they'd already met, but it was too late. He realized the second introduction would cost him money: the other *meshulach* was a Yemenite from Israel collecting for youth-group activities.

In broken Hebrew, English, and body language, Zvi invited everyone to the dinner table. Dennis had no gracious way of declining and by now his ears had grown accustomed to the constant crying and occasional bickering of the children in the background... and foreground.

The older kids joined the adults at the table while the younger ones continued taking apart the worn-out couch.

Z VI SEATED DENNIS at his side in what was meant to be a gesture of esteem. In actuality, however, Silver was struck by the reverent honor and respect Zvi accorded each of his guests. It was awe-inspiring to watch the way the Mandels catered to those assembled around their table. Indeed, Zvi was so engrossed in entertaining his company and sharing *divrei Torah* that it never even occurred to him to inquire why his principal had come to visit.

The faded, grimy plastic tablecloth was set with badly cracked and chipped Melmac plates that apparently doubled as pot covers or trivets. The glasses were a ragtag assortment collected no doubt from various filling stations over the years. The silverware, Dennis hypothesized, had been an incentive offered by a bank for opening an account.

The frozen condition of the bread suggested that it had been imported in bulk from the East Coast, and the meal itself resembled lunch in the dining room of a yeshiva on the verge of financial collapse. Colonies of peas rolled all over the plate before lodging in the mashed potatoes, while the ersatz meat loaf's main ingredient seemed to be coagulated catsup. Water and ice cubes were also provided.

Mrs. Mandel apologized for not attending the meal but she was busy getting her brood into bed. Dennis, in an effort to be sociable, struck up a conversation with Barry Winter, an exceptionally normal, wholesome-looking fellow. He was convinced that the visitor would have lodged in a hotel were he not trying to save his money for his looming medical expenses.

DENNIS LEARNED that Winter had attended a well-known yeshiva on the East Coast and held both a bachelor's and a master's degree from Johns Hopkins University. As the meal progressed, Winter revealed that he had been involved in *chinuch* for the past three years and had found tremendous satisfaction in it.

Light bulbs and alarms suddenly exploded in Dennis' head. He took an immediate liking to Winter, who was both articulate and on the ball.

"What will happen with your job while you're away?" the principal inquired delicately.

"They are looking for a replacement for me," Barry answered. "I've already told them they can count on my being gone for at least five months, but frankly I believe it could stretch out longer than a year. I pray that the Seattle Medical Center staff will be God's proper emissaries.

"Strange I should meet you here," Barry said in a low tone, mustering his courage, "for Zvi advised me to contact you while I'm in town. I just can't get over how providential it is that you came over this evening. I had intended to speak to you about schooling for my children when we move here but I was afraid I wouldn't get around to it since my flight back is early tomorrow.

"Aside from my children," Barry continued awkwardly, "I hope I'm not being too forward but I also wanted to ask if you have any teaching openings." Winter looked at his host as if to acquire permission to proceed. Zvi eagerly urged him ahead.

"As I mentioned, I have three years of experience teaching *limudei kodesh* at the grade-school level, and I have been trained in the field."

DENNIS couldn't get over his good fortune, nor over Zvi's incredible magnanimity — and naiveté. He seemed blissfully unaware of or at least unconcerned with the fact that any position which would be offered in the realm of *limudei kodesh* would be at his own expense. After experiencing the Mandel abode it was patently obvious that Zvi desperately needed a raise, not a cut in salary.

"Yes, I think I just may be able to offer you something," Dennis responded. "I'll speak to you after supper, after I discuss some school matters with Zvi."

Everything was perfectly clear to Dennis now. God had sent Barry Winter to be Zvi's replacement. With such a qualified teacher, the principal's own reputation would not suffer, nor would the children of his school.

Now that he had solved Seattle Hebrew Academy's dilemma, he was left with the thorny problem of firing Zvi. He had been dreading this task all along, but now that he saw how Zvi lived, and how giving he was in spite of it, he couldn't just throw him out into the street. But then again, there was no way whatsoever that his P.T.A. or board would agree to hold onto him.

Regardless, Dennis made up his vacillating mind. He would not dismiss Zvi until Barry moved to town... and he hoped that the move would be soon.

"Mr. Silver," Zvi interrupted his pensive principal, "Rachamim is here collecting for an important youth group in his town in Israel. Maybe you could help recommend potential donors?"

At first, Dennis was annoyed at being put on the spot. The request, however, was in complete consonance with Zvi's personality and very being. Having essentially never left yeshiva, he lacked the rudimentary polish and tact necessary to relate to uncommitted Jews and their assimilated progeny.

NO ONE had informed Silver of this failing at the convention, for no one knew. True, Zvi Mandel was an exceedingly kind and very learned fellow, but he was also the product of his cloistered upbringing. Those who had recommended him had mistakenly assumed that as yeshivish as he was, he could adapt himself to those with dissimilar backgrounds. Zvi's sterling qualities and gilt-edged attributes rendered him an excellent example, but not a qualified teacher.

Silver's contemplative reverie was interrupted by Zvi's next question: "Do you think Mr. Morgan would be interested in giving?"

"Er, maybe," the startled principal responded

unconvincingly. "How would Rachamim get to see him?"

"I would take him over," Zvi answered matter-of-factly. "I would hate to see Rachamim leave town with so little to show for his efforts in this community. After all, I only gave him a few dollars, and even that was a head check."

Suddenly remorse shot through Dennis like a live wire. Here *he* was known as the charitable, devout Jewish role model in town, and nothing he ever did even came close to the *chessed* of the Mandels. Their overcrowded house was filled with strange freeloaders but they weren't complaining. On the contrary, Zvi appeared genuinely grateful for the opportunity to help those Providence had placed in his path.

"**L**ET ME LEARN a lesson from what I have witnessed this evening," Dennis vowed to himself. "I will not allow this righteous couple to worry about their next meal, which they will most likely share with others. I shall not let Mandel's shortcomings as a teacher blind me to the man's remarkable character.

"I will personally undertake to support him for one year's time. I don't care if he has to check the *sifrei Torah* in town or give my son bar-mitzva lessons. And if he finds time to teach me as well — so much the better. In a year from now, the problem will be academic. By then he will have to move on his own volition to accommodate his older children's educational needs."

Dennis realized he had taken upon himself an onerous responsibility, but he felt so relieved about his decision that he was sure he had committed himself to the right course. A heady sense of satisfaction overcame him and he sought to channel it into even loftier pursuits. Fortunately, they weren't hard to find:

Dennis Silver reached into his wallet and presented a bill to Rachamim and a calling card to Barry. "Mrs. Mandel," he called from his seat, "thank you for a most delicious meal. It has satisfied a lot more than just my hunger."

Heard from: Rabbi Heshy and Chavi Dachs

Balance Sheet

Months	Chessed	Teshuvah	Torah	Tefillah	Tzeddakah	Aveiros
Tishrei						
Cheshvan						
Kislev						
Teves						
Shevat						
Adar						
Nissan						
Iyyar						
Sivan						
Tammuz						
Av						
Ellul						

A Positive Balance

Prepared by

Date

Index No

שאלו המעות הבא לו בדרך שקר ומרמה יכלו
גם את מעותיו הכשרות שיש לו מכבר
וכדאיתא במס' ד"א זוטא אם נטלת את
שאינו שלך את שלך יטלו ממך ולא נשאר
בידו כ"א עון השקר והמרמה לבד.
שפת תמים פרק ב'

*Income derived from lying and
fraud will consume money acquired
honestly, as it says in* Derech Eretz
Zuta, *"If you take that which does
not belong to you, what is yours will
be taken from you." All the sinner
will be left with will be the crime of
falsification and deception.*

Sfas Tamim: 2

Holy Smoke!

AVON PARK is an island of white in a sea of black.

The neighborhood's thirty square blocks in the heart of Brooklyn are jammed with two-family apartments filled with jumping, yelling, running, screaming Jewish kids. All are Rostover chassidim.

Forty years ago, the neighborhood was very different. At that time, the stately houses that linked Kent, Avon, Berkshire and the other impressive boulevards belonged to affluent Jews who could afford the very best life had to offer.

These families were catered to by a collection of dress shops, milliners, shoe emporia, and other sundry retailers. Most of these establishments disappeared along with their Jewish patrons during the '50s and '60s. Many were burned out, bought out, or broken into during the social unrest of the '70s and virtually all were closed by the '80s.

In their place came two distinct types of stores. One

kind served Haitians, Hispanics, and blacks; the other kind served the chassidim. In Avon Park, you could easily determine which stores served which customers without ever seeing the clientele. Depending on the block, you could find "Salem Liquor Store," "New Wave Hair," and "Reggae City," or "Sholom's Books," "Spiegel's Fish," and "Triple Tov Clothes for Men and Boys" ("Boys' Shabbos suits our specialty!").

T HERE WAS ONE EXCEPTION to this rule of "East is East and West is West and Never the Twain Shall Meet." It was a holdover from the bygone era when men and women used to parade up and down Kensington Parkway in a long and leisurely display of the latest styles. The store was "Fishman's Fashion Palace," specializing in draperies, slipcovers and window shades.

Fishman's Fashion Palace was set in a two-story building that took up the entire block between Kent and Berkshire Streets. At one time, this venerable building housed a number of other shops. Now most of the storefronts were empty; only the Abazz barber shop at one end and Fishman's at the other prevented the structure from being another casualty of "white flight."

For years, Fishman's Fashion Palace was the only place in Avon Park where both black and white women mingled. Together, they valiantly searched for ways to make their respective homes a little nicer, and a little more elegant. It was a difficult, almost impossible task.

Virtually all the homes in the Avon Park section of Brooklyn had seen better days. The concrete steps were beveled by the incessant pounding of countless feet.

The weathered walls and doors appeared beaten into submission by years of sun, wind, snow, and stickball. The once-gracious rooms wore layer upon layer of cheap paint. And the plumbing had more leaks than a political convention. In fact, dripping taps, burst pipes, and little or no water pressure were practically a way of life in Avon Park. So were cockroaches and other denizens of the night.

Why did anyone stay? Because the Rostover Rebbe said "Jews don't run!" And what the Rebbe said went (especially since no one could afford to leave even if he wanted to). So the only thing to do was to make the best of the situation. And for many people, that meant frequenting Fishman's Fashion Palace.

MAX FISHMAN once carried the finest imported materials. He still claimed to. But instead of hand-stitched brocades from Italy, France, and England, he sold machine-manufactured polyester from India, Korea, and Taiwan. Besides his current stock, Max had collected mounds and mounds of manufacturers' samples, overruns, remnants, close-outs, and other miscellaneous textile orphans. Assorted lined and unlined draperies hung everywhere. Bedspreads were heaped on long tables. The effect was total, unadulterated visual chaos.

Nonetheless, for between three and seven dollars a yard, you could make any room look different. And for a lot of Max's customers, that was exactly the objective.

For his part, Max Fishman accepted the change in his neighborhood, fabrics, and clientele as he accepted the change in seasons. "Is complaining gonna help?" he would ask. *Baruch Hashem*, he had sent his five kids to yeshiva, watched them grow up and get married, and played with his grandchildren. There was just one thing left in life he wanted to do: live in *Eretz Yisrael*.

THE LAND OF ISRAEL was the focus of Max's every thought and dream. He read every book, poured over every map, and interrogated every person who ever set foot on its holy soil. "One day," he would muse wistfully, "I'm gonna move to Jerusalem. Then I'm gonna relax and spend all day in a yeshiva!"

The fact that relaxing and studying were antithetical never bothered Max or anyone else he talked to. He was sure they could coexist.

"Better take advantage of my store while you can," he would tell his customers. "I'm going to sell out soon."

The only person who didn't encourage Max was Rabbi Cohen, the spiritual leader of Congregation Anshei Sfard, one of the last non-Rostover shuls in Avon Park. "You just can't leave for *Eretz Yisrael*," the Rabbi said. "We need you for the *minyan*. And besides, a Jew has the power to make himself and his domain almost as holy as *Eretz Yisrael*."

While Rabbi Cohen took Max seriously, his customers did not. Still, they were a loyal bunch, and no one would ever dare let a little reality intrude on his hopes for the future. "Will you write us?" they asked. "Have you decided where you're going to live?" "When will you have your going-out-of-business sale?" These were the questions of the day, every day for years.

Max Fishman lived the dream of closing his store and moving to the Land of the Jewish People. One night in the summer of 1985, that dream turned into a raging nightmare.

HOW IT HAPPENED, people still don't know. The best guess is that the wiring blew in the Abazz barber shop. That would explain why the fire rose to the second story instead of spreading through the empty stores to Fishman's Fashion Palace.

When Roberto Avila, age seventeen, spotted the smoke it was early Saturday night. The people in the street stared at the first strands of gray, wispy smoke. But in Avon Park, one soon learned to mind his own business and hope for the best.

"——!" he exclaimed as he spotted the source of the smoke. "That buildin's on fire!"

"So what?" said a black man, casually taking a sip of something in a brown paper bag.

Roberto ran to the corner fire alarm box, ripped open the cover and tried to contact the nearest Fire Department. But he couldn't. The Fire Box had been vandalized years ago and no one bothered to report it.

Next, he ran to Reggae City. "Hey, man!" he yelled. "There's a fire down the block. Yo'r store could be next if you don' get no fire trucks down he in a hurry!"

Manuel Rodriguez was behind the register. In the twelve years since he had come to the United States from Puerto Rico, he had seen all sorts of scams. Getting salespeople distracted was one of the oldest. And the best.

"Go on man, ain't no fire roun' here!"

"I ain't lyin'. It's over Abazz!"

Manuel Rodriguez eyed the messenger suspiciously.

Roberto started shouting, fear and anger burning inside him. "Man, I'm tellin' you! There's a fire! Don't you hea' me?"

Slowly, without ever taking his eyes off the seventeen-year-old standing in front of him, the manager picked up the phone and called the fire department. While he didn't trust this kid, his life savings were tied up in Reggae City. And he didn't want to risk them any more than he already had.

T HE CALL WAS REFERRED to Company 232. It was just one of the network of batallions and divisions that make up the New York Fire Department. In fact, the NYFD is the nation's largest firefighting organization, with more than 13,000 firemen, 369 engine companies, and 282 firehouses. Not coincidentally, New York's fire department is not only the biggest in the nation, it is also the busiest.

"Avon Park, 497 Kent Ave. Fire in abandoned building." The dispatcher's voice was cold and mechanical. But it did the trick.

In seconds, hook and ladder No. 4 from NYFD Engine Company 232 was racing to the scene. The four men under Captain Martin Henley were veterans. All of them knew that a fire in a deserted building was especially dangerous because you never knew what you were up against; they were prepared for the worst.

The red Mack hook and ladder rammed its way

through the streets of Brooklyn, its siren screaming at any traffic in the way. Finally, Captain Henley's fire truck reached its destination. As soon as it pulled to a halt, the Captain began barking orders. "Malone, get your airpack and see what we've got! Carey, start loading those lines. O'Shea, as soon as he's ready, hose down everything in sight."

Like clockwork, the men of Company 232 attended their jobs. After five minutes, Malone returned with an initial report. "The fire's based in a barber shop. There's only one other store that's occupied. The rest of the stores are filled with combustibles... old pallets, boxes, paper, wood... If we don't work fast, the whole thing's gonna go!"

"Wilson!" Captain Henley yelled. "Start ventilating this thing!" Instantly, one of his firemen scrambled up a ladder and began smashing a hole in the roof with his ten-pound axe, letting heat and smoke out and water in.

Meanwhile, several other firemen were busy connecting hoses to fire hydrants several hundred yards away. Before long, the bloated lines were pumping 300 gallons a minute into the flames.

THE SIGHT of a blazing yellow fire, the sound of sirens, and the stench of acrid black smoke, soot and charcoal brought out the spectators. Some watched intently, others laughed and gabbed with their friends, and still others were looking for ways to cash in on the situation. But the vendors hawking cold beer, hot wrist watches, and newspapers on the street lost out to the spectacle.

The night was muggy and murky. And the men in their heavy yellow turnout suits, helmets and boots produced rivers of greasy, salty sweat. It ran down their faces, matted their hair and made their clothes stick to their skin. As the fire raged, it seemed to take on its own personality, challenging the firemen like a chess player responding to the moves of his opponent.

For three hours, the men of Company 232 battled the blaze, shifting winds, low water pressure and the occasional interference of the hundreds of people on the street. Finally, the last sparks drowned in the drenched building.

MAX FISHMAN was sleeping when the word came. "Max, there's a fire on Kent." It was Rabbi Cohen. "I think it reached your store."

"*Gevald!* I'll be there in a minute!" Max's heart was pounding like a jackhammer. "A fire? How could it be? There's nothing in that building but busted chairs, cardboard boxes, and the old barber shop! No. It can't be. There must be a mistake."

Jumping into his clothes, Max ran down to his car, turned the key and gunned the motor. The old Chevy seemed to spew a little more smoke and oil all over the neighborhood than usual. "C'mon, don't quit now!" Max urged.

As if hearing his plea, the Chevy settled down to a noisy idle. Max maneuvered the car into reverse, jammed it into drive, and set off for his store. "It can't be. It just can't be," he repeated to himself. Max kept expecting to wake up from this nightmare. But a block or two from the store, he saw and smelled that the nightmare was no dream.

The odor of burnt wood and smoke was ubiquitous, and tongues and eyes smarted. By the time he reached the building, there was little doubt that Max's Fashion Palace was no more.

I N THE FIRST RAYS OF DAWN, a devastated Max Fishman could discern the shell of the building. There was rubble and water everywhere. Straining his burning eyes, he assessed the damage.

As the light diffused, it revealed an astonishing sight for his sore eyes: out of five storefronts, three were gutted and two were saved. Fishman's Fashion Palace was one of the survivors.

"Are you Mr. Fishman?" a tired voice called out from one of the fire trucks.

"Y-y-yes," Max said numbly.

"My name is Henley. I just wanted you to know we fought like crazy to save it. As far as I can tell, we were pretty successful."

"What about the building? Is it safe?" Max queried.

"I believe so. We were able to confine the fire to the three units. The City Building Inspector will know for sure. But you were lucky. The brick walls between the stores slowed down the fire."

Max left Captain Henley and entered his parched Palace. The fumes of polluted water and smoke filled his lungs. Water dripped from the ceiling and flooded the floor, but all in all, the damage wasn't as extensive as he'd dreaded.

Fishman proceeded with his inspection through the wreckage until he reached the back of the store, where he kept his *sefarim*. One little kabbalistic *sefer*, *Raziel HaMalach*, seemed to stand out proudly on the shelf. Max planted a gentle kiss on the *sefer* — known to protect against fire — and resumed his tour.

T HE REST OF THE EARLY MORNING, Max cleaned up the store. "I've got to get the smoky smell out of here," he thought. "Later, I'll call Irving Feldman, my insurance agent. My policy should pay for dry-cleaning most of this stuff."

Starving and thoroughly exhausted, Max eventually went home to *daven* and rest. He didn't return to Fishman's Fashion Palace until a little after twelve-thirty. By then, the entire neighborhood knew about the fire and the miracle. All his customers crowded into the store to congratulate him on his *mezuzos* and his *mazel*. But when they left, not one piece of material had been sold.

"It must be the smell," Max told Irving Feldman. "My insurance will cover that, right?"

"Max, I don't know how to tell you this, but... "

"But what?" Max said suspiciously.

"The policy. It covers fire, water, and smoke damage. But there's nothing in here for smell."

"You mean, I'm not covered?"

"That's right."

Max felt like he'd been run over by a truck, a fire truck to be precise. "B-b-b-but what about the store? How can I sell stuff that smells like burnt wood?"

Irving answered Max's questions with one of his own. "What can I tell you? It's not in your policy."

"I can't afford to dry-clean everything. And even if I did, I'd have to pass the expenditure on to my customers. And they'd never pay it! Do you know what this means?"

Irving Feldman nodded his bald head. "It means you're out of business."

FOR THE NEXT FEW MINUTES both men were silent. "Listen, Max," Irving suggested with sudden inspiration. "I've got an idea. Late tonight, we'll come in, smear charcoal on the walls, and douse everything with water. The adjuster on the case is a friend of mine. If we slip him a couple hundred bucks, he'll take pictures and report that the place is a complete write-off because of smoke and water. What do you say?"

"I couldn't do that. It's fraud."

"No it isn't. You've paid your premiums all these years. Now you're getting them back. I mean, it's not gonna cost the insurance company extra. If anything, they should be happy to settle."

"No, Irv. I just can't... "

"Listen to me. You can take the money and *go to Israel*. You've always wanted to go to Israel, right? Well, here's your chance. I'll tell you what — you don't even have to do a thing. Let me take care of it. I'll hire a couple of kids and no one will ever know."

"I'll know."

"You'll know that you'll finally be going to Israel instead of selling *shmattes* till you drop!"

"Forget that idea," Max said firmly. "I'll salvage what I can and dump the rest. God willing, I'll still be able to make enough to retire in Israel."

"Don't be foolish. You can't sell this stuff. It stinks. Chances are, even dry cleaning won't take out the smell. Listen to me. It's your only chance."

"Lemme think it over."

"Think it over. But do it fast, because I won't be able to put my adjuster off forever. And once he's seen the store like it is, it will be too late."

IRVING FELDMAN was a good agent. In fact, he was living proof of the adage "There's no one with endurance like the man who sells insurance." As such, he was not about to give up without a fight.

Leaving Max to ponder the fate of Fishman's Fashion Palace, Irving called Rabbi Cohen.

"Rabbi, listen, you've got to help Max. As it stands now, his insurance policy won't cover the damage to the store. I told him what I want to do, but he refuses to listen. Talk to him. *It's a mitzva.*"

"What do you want to do?"

"Nothing bad. Just soak everything and put a little charcoal on the walls. Then he'll be covered. It's not like we're lying. There *was* water damage. And there *was* smoke. We're just making sure Max gets what he's owed. What do you say? Will you talk to him?"

"Let me think about it, Irv."

Rabbi Cohen put down the phone. But no sooner had he hung up than Max was on the line.

"Rabbi, I've got a problem... "

"I heard. Irv just spoke to me."

"Listen, I can't go along with him. It's not right. I don't care if I lose everything — I couldn't live with myself if I did it his way."

"What are you going to do now?"

"I don't know. It's really funny, you know? I mean the store's not ruined. But I am."

Rabbi Cohen listened to the weary voice of a man too sad to be depressed, and too depressed to be sad.

"I guess I'll just have to start over. I just don't know how. I sure won't be able to save the stuff I have. Maybe my suppliers will lend me on credit, but at this point in my life, I just don't know."

"What about retiring?" Rabbi Cohen suggested cautiously. "You've always wanted to go to Israel."

"I can't afford it now. And I won't go with funny money I didn't earn."

RABBI COHEN had seen a lot of people face trouble over the years. But to have a way out, a way to save his store, his livelihood, and maybe even his dream of going to *Eretz Yisrael* and to turn it down, knowing that the future may not be as bright as the past — this was something special.

"Rabbi, let me ask you something."

"Yes, Max...?"

"You always said that a person can make wherever he is almost as holy as the Land of Israel. Do you think I could ever do that?"

Rabbi Cohen caught himself choking with emotion. In a barely audible voice he finally responded, "Max, my friend, you just did. You just did."

Heard from: Rabbi Yehuda Parnes

All Wrapped Up

FOUNDER of Merkaz Shomrei Sta"m and renowned tefillin expert Moish Ungar has become, since the day he opened his tefillin workshop in Meah Shearim, Jerusalem, the primary address for all related inquiries and activities. He never intended it to be that way. He figured he could open a shop to buy, sell, and repair tefillin, provide a respectable *parnassah* for his family, and still have plenty of time left for learning.

His shop filled such a vital need, however, that it was transformed into a veritable factory, and today the services and expertise of his organization are sought the world over.

Neither Moish nor his partners in M.S.S. have any regrets. They opened up the Center to improve the maintenance and consumer awareness of tefillin, *sifrei Torah*, and *mezuzos*, and their booming volume attests to the fact that they are achieving their goal.

With all the Center's success, the one thing Ungar

had not anticipated was the plethora of inquiries and investigations that inevitably landed in his lap. Some of them might be considered material for a book, some for a documentary; this one is for a comedy:

It all started on a Tuesday afternoon when a fellow we'll call "Shnook" entered Moish's shop carrying a large attaché case. Shnook warmly greeted Moish and his partner Tuvia, lifted his case onto the counter, and informed the proprietors that this was their lucky day.

"I have here brand-new tefillin," he began, "the finest that money can buy, but I am prepared to unload the entire lot for a steal."

Moish and Tuvia looked at each other. "Unload" was hardly an expression one would apply to tefillin. But before they could utter a peep of protest, Shnook had arrayed his wares on the counter: fourteen pairs of tefillin in all, each appearing to be in excellent condition but certainly not new.

THE PARTNERS examined the goods and instantly discovered the telltale signs of wear that any observant Jew would immediately detect. In addition, labels inscribed with the name, address, and telephone number of the owners were affixed to the bottom of several of the *battim*.

Tuvia deferred to his senior partner to handle the negotiations with the charlatan, and resumed his repair work. To give the impression that he was genuinely interested in the merchandise, Moish scrutinized a few pairs and scribbled some figures on a scrap of paper. Then he asked Shnook how much he wanted for the tefillin.

"Two thousand five hundred shekels."

"Sounds fair enough," Moish replied, "but I'll need a little time to open them up and determine if the insides are as nice as the outsides."

The customer raised no objections. Moish asked him to return in one week's time, when he hoped they'd be able to conclude the deal. Shnook agreed and exited, and Tuvia and Moish entered into a heated discussion.

"This is no ordinary pilferer," Moish exclaimed. "It's one thing to steal, it's another thing to steal tefillin, and quite another to steal fourteen pairs of them!"

"What're we supposed to do now?"

"It's very simple. We're not going to let this guy get away with it."

"Hey, now watch it, Moish. He could be dangerous."

"Tuvia," Moish said, taking in all three hundred twenty pounds of him, "don't tell me you're frightened."

"Well, I mean... eh... er..."

"We have just been confronted with a big mitzva so there's nothing to be afraid of. The Top Cop," he said, raising his eyes skyward, "is on our side."

"So what should I do?" his oversized partner inquired. "Sit on him the next time he comes in?"

"I don't want to *squash* him," Moish emended with the voice of authority, "I want to *quash* him."

"Huh?"

"You know — police, the courts, jail — the works. Listen, I'm going to ask a *shailah* to find out if I may turn over a fellow Jew to the police. In the meantime, I want you to look up all the addresses on the tefillin — from what I can see they're all from one neighborhood. Call up the owners and try to get the story."

MOISH CONSULTED with one of Jerusalem's foremost *posekim* and was advised in this case to involve the police. Meanwhile, Tuvia discovered that not only were all the tefillin taken from the same shul on the same day, but many of them had long histories or special stories attached to them. The most moving concerned the pair that was one man's sole inheritance from his father. He had never told his mother they were stolen, knowing what anguish it would cause her.

The owners of the pairs bearing address labels were able to provide information about other tefillin thefts in the neighborhood. By the time Ungar returned to his shop, two of the owners had arrived and others were phoning for verifications.

The men who had come to collect their tefillin were incredulous when Moish refused to return them. He assured them that he would restore their tefillin as soon as possible, but first and foremost he was interested in apprehending the criminal so that a crime like this would never happen again. And he needed the tefillin as evidence.

But even when Moish assured the distraught victims that he had the backing of a *poseik*, many remained skeptical and some even cast aspersions on his integrity, insinuating that he was planning to sell the stolen goods as used tefillin.

MOISH PAID THEM NO HEED. He carefully locked the evidence in his shop and left for Jerusalem's police headquarters. The scene that greeted him inside this run-down, aging edifice was pure pandemonium. In a city holy to three faiths and dozens of Peoples, it is perhaps not surprising that the police and the courts are housed in part of the former Greek Orthodox basilica in the "Russian Compound." Previously the headquarters of the British Mandatory regime, *Migrash Harusim* is an immense and extraordinarily confusing place.

Moish was among the early arrivals that day; only a few hundred assorted souls were ahead of him. Long, single-file lines snaked throughout the station in intricate patterns until they neared any one of the department doors, where all order collapsed and they took on the aggressive chaos of a rugby scrum. The lighting was scarce, the noise terrific.

A stranger entering the police station would think he'd stumbled upon a disaster area in mid-evacuation. A powerful last-chopper-out-of-Saigon feeling pervaded the premises. It was hard to imagine that this same scene was reenacted daily.

Moish started off at the Complaint Department, then tried his luck at Fraud, and was finally referred to a detective of sorts. The officer, a tall, scrawny fellow wearing the round, mirror-lensed sunglasses a Yale undergrad might wear to the beach, gazed down at the concerned citizen in disbelief, as though seeing a religious Jew for the first time. It was evident from his expression that he doubted every word Ungar uttered.

Moish couldn't tell if that attitude was part of his job, if the detective hailed from Missouri (the remotest of possibilities), or if he had chanced upon one of the less astute members of Jerusalem's Finest (less remote). In due time he concluded that the third option was the correct one.

SERGEANT SEGEV had an enormously difficult time grasping what had occurred. He removed the pen suspended from a buttonhole at the top of his shirt and began to transcribe: "You say you stole the tefillin this morning?"

"No!"

"Yesterday?"

"No!"

"This afternoon?"

"No, no! I didn't steal the tefillin."

"Why not?"

"I'm not a thief. I didn't steal the tefillin. A thief who stole the tefillin tried to sell them to me."

"Did you buy them?"

"Please let me finish. I didn't buy them, but I do have them. He thinks I took them in order to inspect the contents, but actually I want to use them as bait in order to catch him in the act of selling stolen goods. Then *you* can arrest him and *I* can return the tefillin to their rightful owners."

"Oh, I got it. Now, just sign here and keep this form so you can collect insurance."

If someone at that moment had suggested to Moish Ungar that the salaries of the Jerusalem police force were paid by the Walt Disney Studios, he would not have found the idea so preposterous. In exasperation he demanded to speak to the detective's superior officer.

"Well, the Chief of Detectives is standing right behind you," Segev said condescendingly.

Moish leaped up from his seat and tried to position his slender frame to attract the chief's attention. How he wished that Tuvia had accompanied him; his larger-than-life partner was eminently more noticeable. At last, the chief caught sight of Moish's frantic arm-waving and turned to hear him out. "Go to the squadroom at the end of the corridor," the chief said when Moish completed his recitation, "and ask for Erez and Alon. Tell them I'm assigning them to this case." Although this seemed a bit irregular even to Moish, who was unfamiliar with police procedure, alongside all the other irregularities that transpired at headquarters, it was downright formal.

MOISH TROOPED to the other end of the station, entered the specified door, and swallowed hard. He spun around to check the sign outside again, but there was no mistake about it. The door plaque read "Detective Squad" and he had indeed followed the directions he'd been given.

Without ever really thinking about it, Moish had imagined a detective squadroom to be entirely, colossally different from the environs in which he now found himself. The long room bore a distinct resemblance to a Nautilus health club. About half a dozen sweat-slicked men were pumping iron while a few more were skimming body-building and weapons magazines and chug-a-lugging orange juice.

"What are you doing here?" an Arnold Schwartzenegger clone bellowed as soon as he noticed the intruder.

"The Chief of Detectives said I should speak to Erez and Alon," Ungar replied.

Mr. Middle East aimed a muscular finger in the direction of a brawny athlete who was working out on a mock heavy bag. "Alon," he said.

ALON was circling the bag rapidly, throwing short lefts and rights with the speed of rotor blades, and wearing only a pair of baby-blue shorts. They looked about the way baby-blue shorts would look on a jeep.

Alon grabbed a towel and jogged over to the slender scribe. Close up, the man's gladiatorial physique appeared even more imposing and Moish had considerable trouble finding his tongue. Even Tuvia, he told himself, would feel dwarfed by this mountain of a man.

Moish regained his composure. "Is Erez here, too?" he asked. Alon whistled to his companion, a wiry rope-jumper who turned and jumped over towards them without missing a beat, maintaining his rhythm as the scribe spoke.

Ungar related his story in detail, and suggested that the police ambush the thief in his shop the following Tuesday. The two detectives agreed, but pointed out that the perpetrator had to be caught in the actual act of receiving money for the stolen goods. "It's the only way we'll get a conviction," Alon said with a shrug.

The detectives proposed that they follow the thief into the shop and offer to buy the tefillin directly from him. Moish readily approved the plan. "But we'll need a signal," he said, "so you'll know the items he's selling are the stolen tefillin."

UNGAR RELATED that since many of the tefillin had labels affixed to the bottom of the tefillin housing, these stickers could serve as the signal. "Shnook must think those are put on by the 'manufacturers,'" he chuckled. Erez and Alon looked at him blankly. "Skip it," Moish said, rather than going into a lengthy explanation. "When I point out the names and addresses on the tefillin, you close in. Got it?"

It was arranged that the detectives would arrive in an unmarked car and park down the block from the shop. As soon as Shnook entered the store, Tuvia would slip outside and signal to the officers by wiping his brow with a handkerchief.

The three men reviewed the plan a second time to ensure that every detail was understood, and Erez skipped over to the desk to fetch his cigarettes. He flipped open the box, slipped out the foil lining and scribbled the appointment on the reverse side. Then he carefully rolled up this scrap and tucked it behind his ear. Moish shook their hands, then hurried outside to breathe some fresh air.

MOISH FILLED TUVIA IN on their scheme and every day they rehearsed their roles. Meanwhile the owners of the stolen goods repeatedly phoned to ask when they would get back their tefillin. Moish begged them to wait until the thief was brought to justice, explaining that a "sting" operation was under way to catch him and that the tefillin were needed as evidence. Eventually everyone became resigned to the situation, except the fellow whose tefillin were his sole heirloom. He lodged an emotional appeal:

He and his wife had only one son, a *ben zekunim*, who would reach bar mitzva in a few weeks. The father intended to present these tefillin to his son for that occasion. "Yanky is the only one to carry on my father's name," the man implored. Moish assured him that he would make every effort to retrieve the tefillin before the bar mitzva.

S HNOOK entered the shop Tuesday afternoon, as prearranged. On cue Tuvia told his partner that he was stepping out to pick up some cigarettes, and as soon as he reached the sidewalk, he whipped out a huge, white handkerchief and began mopping his brow with great vigor. His eyes darted up and down the street, but no police activity was to be seen. After cautiously peering into the shop to make sure Shnook was distracted, Tuvia galloped over to an unmarked car with two occupants and paused to pant for breath. He wiped his forehead feverishly, but still his signal was ignored. Finally, with one great heave he hoisted himself up onto the hood of the vehicle, at last making an impression on both it and its passengers.

The two officers of the law leaped from their sedan to inspect the damage inflicted by the corpulent signaller. Checking and assessing and examining the Japanese compact — which had suddenly been rendered significantly more compact — they might never have curtailed their investigation had Tuvia not informed them in plain Hebrew that a robbery was taking place in the tefillin workshop down the block.

That seemed to jog their memories, and they jogged their bodies into the store, with Tuvia at their heels. Behind the counter, Moish apparently had the situation well in hand... until the cops walked in. "These aren't my cops," he whispered to Tuvia out of the side of his mouth. Tuvia rolled his eyes and jiggled his eyebrows expressively until Moish understood: they had to work with what they had.

Playing for time, Moish spread the stolen tefillin out on the counter and turned to the newcomers. One of them, he noticed, was obviously the senior partner. He had curly gray hair and an air of confidence his associate lacked.

"You know, you two look like my friends Erez and Alon," he said, hoping to elicit a sign of recognition.

"Oh, we know them," the older of the two replied, picking up the hint. "They were going to come here today, but Erez's daughter was having a birthday party in school. He couldn't miss that. And Alon had to finish his calisthenics." Moish and Tuvia exchanged an exasperated look. "They sent us instead," the detective went on, "to buy some tefillin."

"Well, you've come to the right place," Moish assured him.

S HNOOK WAS REMARKABLY UNINTERESTED in this exchange and paid no attention to the goings-on. The junior officer drew nearer to the counter and asked if they had any tefillin on sale, "You know what I mean — a really good buy."

"Sorry," Moish told him. "We haven't got any bargain tefillin in stock now."

"Then what are all these on the counter?" the senior officer demanded to know.

"Oh, these? They're not mine," Moish replied.

"You mean we can't buy them?" Junior questioned.

"I didn't say that. I said that *I* can't sell them because they're not *mine*. But Mr. Shnook here might agree to sell them to you. He's offered them to me but I don't mind if you buy them from him directly."

Shnook perked up at the sound of his name and displayed keen interest, handing each officer a pair. "How much do you want?" Senior asked.

Before Shnook could respond, Moish interjected that the buyers should first inspect the tefillin carefully. "Didn't Erez and Alon tell you to check the tefillin before you purchase them?"

"Oh, yeah," Junior reflected, rubbing his chin. "They did mention something about it, but I can't remember what it was."

Tuvia strategically positioned his bulk to block Shnook's view as Moish madly gesticulated to Senior to look at the bottom of the tefillin casing. But the message did not get across.

"It looks okay to me," Senior commented, hoping to get on with the bust.

"I know a good piece of leather when I see one," Junior added, trying to sound knowledgeable.

"Hey, look at this," Senior said, pointing to the *shin* on the *shel rosh*. "That's my initial."

Moish and Tuvia frantically began to examine the bottoms of the tefillin — in the most demonstrative way — and then passed them to the officers, urging them to do the same.

Attracting the detectives' attention without arousing Shnook's suspicions was no mean feat. Shnook was as anxious to close the deal as the officers were to get back to the Nautilus, but it was obvious that their briefing had been too brief and they knew nothing of the incriminating name labels.

I N DESPERATION, Moish went out on a limb: "Tuvia," he asked, "can you make out the inscription on the bottom of these tefillin which this gentleman wishes to sell?"

Tuvia removed his glasses and held up a case for close scrutiny. After protracted squinting and gawking and half-mouthing names and addresses, he declared himself unable to read the writing. He asked the senior officer if he could decipher it. Intrigued by the challenge, Senior read the name to himself and finally grasped the ruse. "Can't see a thing," he apologized. Holding that very pair in his hand he turned to Shnook and asked him how much he wanted for it.

Shnook quoted a figure and was immediately handed a large-denomination bill, which he pocketed. In a flash, the cops flashed their tins and busted the crook for selling stolen goods. "Cuff 'em, Oren," Senior said, and Junior snagged the bracelets on Tuvia and Moish. "We've got you now," he declared proudly over their protests. For good measure, his partner handcuffed himself to Shnook.

"What's going on here?" Tuvia demanded, quite beside himself at the predicament in which they'd been placed. But Moish was quick to calm him down. "This way we won't appear to be police collaborators," he explained in Yiddish, "so Shnook's cohorts won't come after us."

THE THREE OF THEM (despite his gargantuan girth, Tuvia only counted as one) were escorted to the tiny unmarked car and a reenactment of a Keystone Kops routine ensued:

Since Moish and Tuvia were joined at the wrist, Senior instructed them to get into the back and Shnook to get in front. Junior pointed out that Senior would then have to drive since he was cuffed to Shnook, but then Shnook was liable to grab the wheel. "I'm not handcuffed to anyone," he said, "so I have to drive."

"If you drive," Senior said, "where will I sit — on the stick shift?"

"How about you and Shnook sit in the back?" Oren suggested. The five men turned to the Daihatsu and sized one another up. They had reached an impasse.

"Moish and I could take a cab," Tuvia offered magnanimously.

"All right, all right!" Senior said with both hands. "Enough! Oren — you drive. You two — in the back. Shnook, sit next to them and I'll go in the front and hang my arm over the seat."

Four pairs of shoulders shrugged, and captors and captives embarked on their Mission Impossible. There was no way Man-Mountain Tuvia was going to fit through the rear door of a subcompact.

"Hold your breath," Senior commanded, but to no avail. The top half of Tuvia could fit, and so could the bottom half — but not at the same time.

"I got it," Junior said, raising his index finger skyward. "Put the big guy in first, in the front, and then squeeze the little fella onto his lap." The "partners in crime" did not take this sitting down; "contorted" would be a more accurate description. Pushing and shoving and thrusting and poking, moaning and groaning and howling and squawking, all five men were compressed into the undersized auto.

A roaring dirge poured forth from the Daihatsu in stereo as it ground its way to the police station. When they arrived, neither Senior nor Junior nor any of their clever colleagues could figure out a way of extricating themselves. Junior was wrapped around the steering wheel and the others were so firmly implanted in the upholstery that they appeared to be welded in place. Every movement one of them made evoked a shrill yelp of pain from the others and locked them tighter together. Removing the roof seemed the best solution until a more resourceful cop happened by and obligingly removed first the steering column and then the front seat. The extra half-foot of space did the trick.

THE THREE DETAINEES were brought directly to the lockup, where the police were confronted with the problem of how to separate the innocent from the guilty without making Shnook suspicious. This resulted in a lot of stalling.

Just to pass the time Tuvia went into his "A fine mess you've gotten us into this time" routine, which provided the warden with a brainstorm. "So," he accused, "you're conspiring with each other! We'd better separate the three of you."

The crook was led into an available cell and Moish and Tuvia were directed outside, where Junior set them free.

"But what about the tefillin?" Moish protested.

"That's evidence," the detective responded matter-of-factly. "It can't be released until after the trial."

Moish and Tuvia gaped at each other. "When will that be?" they asked.

"At least six weeks," Junior replied.

"But the owners need the tefillin today!" Moish protested.

"Police regulations," Junior countered. "Nothing can be done about it."

T HE TWO REMORSEFUL SCRIBES limped their way out of the police station. "So how come no one told us about this before?" Tuvia asked Moish.

"So how come Alon and Erez turned into Senior and Junior?" Moish snapped back. "I write parchments, not police procedure scripts. We're going to have a lot of explaining to do to fourteen residents of this city."

"Don't worry, Moish," Tuvia consoled his partner. "We'll tell them the truth. What else can we do? God knows we tried our hardest. My legs will probably ache for a decade. If I ever walk straight again, I'll still never be tempted to take a ride in a Japanese compact."

They returned to their shop to find several notes stuck under the door and the phone ringing off the hook. Everyone, without exception, demanded his tefillin back. The fellow making the bar mitzva was heartbroken to learn that his tefillin were impounded. "But you gave your word," he whimpered before the line went dead. Moish wanted to cry. Instead he sent a heartfelt prayer Heavenward that the evidence would be released swiftly.

Six weeks passed and Moish's name had gone from mud to worse. There was still no word on the tefillin. "I'm going back to the police," he declared resolutely, putting on his hat and jacket. Tuvia was incredulous. "You've got to be out of your mind," he sneered. "Who do you think you're going to reason with? Senior? Junior? They'll probably stuff you into another little car just for being so brazen as to ask for their assistance. Do you realize how much business we have already lost over this affair? Think of the *bitul Torah*..."

"*Bitul Torah*? This *is* Torah. I have a responsibility to the owners, and I'm not absolved of it just because of some inept cops. Whatever it takes, I must redeem those tefillin." And with those words he stomped out the door.

MOISH RETRACED HIS STEPS of six weeks earlier and encountered the exact same scene, but with new characters. It was as if time had stood still. From door to door, department to department, line to line, he was referred to a different clerk, each venue providing yet another taste of police efficiency. It didn't take long for Moish to conclude that he was getting nowhere fast. "Maybe my old pals Erez and Alon could be of help," he thought hopefully.

He worked his way over to the squadroom, but the two he-men weren't there. "Don't tell me," Moish said to the cop still perusing the same sports pages. "This time *Alon's* kid is having the birthday party and both he *and* Erez went to celebrate."

"Na," the cop responded, looking up from the tabloid for but a split second. "They both went to the market and should be back at five o'clock. You're not allowed to wait for them here. You gotta go to the main entrance and come back at five."

Moish thanked him and went back where he had already vowed twice never to return. Time passed very slowly.

A LL OF A SUDDEN a big commotion was heard outside and a brigade of cops shunted a handful of *charedim** into the station. Moish soon learned that they had been arrested for protesting the excavation of a holy site.

The cops were in a rush to lock up their catch, and in their hustle and bustle they mistakenly snatched Moish from among the onlookers, assuming that he was one of the busted *charedim.* Ungar's protests fell on professionally deaf ears and he was thrown into Cell Two of the police compound.

In accord with regulations he was held incommunicado and denied permission to make a call or speak to counsel. By law he could be held this way for forty-eight hours.

---

* A term used to describe devout Jews.

But even this setback didn't dampen Moish's eagerness to accomplish his mission. Somehow, he prayed, he'd figure out a solution.

&

"Hello? Is anybody there?"

"Quiet in Cell Two! It's ten to six in the morning."

"I SAID, IS ANYBODY THERE?"

"Quiet already! You're waking everybody up."

Moish grabbed the tin cup from the floor and banged it against the bars. By this time all the prisoners in the adjoining cells were yelling at him to cool his jets, but he kept on banging.

Finally the warden appeared rubbing his eyes and asked public enemy number one what he wanted. Moish calmly requested a pair of tefillin for the morning prayers.

"Tefillin?! Here?" the warden fumed. "What do you think this is, the Great Synagogue? I'm working here fourteen years and none of the prisoners never asked for no tefillin. And even if they would have, there ain't none here." The warden invested the last line with all the factual finality of "The sun rises in the east." The cop turned on his heels and sleepwalked back to his desk.

NOT EASILY DEFEATED, Moish rattled the bars with all his strength. His cacophonous clatter was soon drowned out by a chorus of jailbirds shouting for the nut to quiet down.

"You, in Cell Two, SILENCE!" the warden snarled. "Or you'll end up in Ramla for an extra six months."

But Moish Ungar was incorrigible and banged louder than ever.

"O.K., all right," the cop sighed in resignation, "if tefillin will keep you quiet, I'll take a look." The man disappeared and returned ten minutes later emptyhanded. "Listen, fella," he cajoled, "I looked all over and I couldn't find any tefillin. Nobody's got any. Now go back to sleep like everybody else."

Moish remained unconvinced. Keeping time with his trusty tin cup, he began chanting that he be given a pair of tefillin "right now!"

"Sorry, mister," the warden apologized weakly, his expressionless features betokening a man accustomed to dealing with a disappointed clientele. "That's the breaks," he concluded as if reading from a script. "So today you won't have tefillin."

Moish indignantly thrust his arms through the bars and grabbed the warden's rumpled lapels. "I have a legal right to be provided with tefillin," he asserted. "Israeli law protects my right to observe Torah commandments and anti-religious coercion is a felony. Watch out, buster, or you'll end up on the inside."

"O.K., O.K.! But what can I do? There ain't no tefillin here."

"Check the evidence locker," Moish suggested.

Extricating himself from Moish's clutches, the warden ambled down the hall. Along the way he stopped in front of the lavatory, removed the key from the lock, and inserted it into the locker door. One entire shelf was crammed with tefillin. The warden removed a pair, relocked the locker, replaced the key in the bathroom door, and headed back to Cell Two.

S UDDENLY the light bulb in Moish's head flashed in incandescent brilliance. He realized that he had the cop just where he wanted him. Moish grabbed the tefillin and immediately verified that they were one of the famous fourteen. "These are too small," he complained and reached for the tin cup.

"O.K., all right, just be quiet now." The warden shuffled back down the corridor, removed the bathroom key, unlocked the locker, and pulled out a second pair. He handed them to Moish, who received them with a look of disdain. He eyed the warden as if the man were suffering from latent dementia. "Can't you see that these are for a lefty?"

The warden, who obviously didn't know the difference, offered an embarrassed smile, revealing a row and a half of teeth like broken rocks. "Sorry," he apologized and retreated once again down the hall. Only this time he returned with his arms full of all the tefillin contained in the locker.

"Take your pick," he said. "If nothing fits, you can complain to the management later in the morning. You're lucky they're not here now 'cause they wouldn't let *nothing* out of that locker without signing a heap of forms."

Moish had achieved his aim! Now he had to make sure the tefillin would stay with him and not end up back in the locker.

"Eh... er, I'll leave them all here for my friends when they wake up," Moish offered.

"Do whatever you want," the cop said with a wave of dismissal. "They're all yours."

"Are you sure?" Moish questioned in disbelief.

"Of course I'm sure. See the red tag on each one? It means they've already been used as evidence. We got no use for 'em and nobody's claimed 'em, so..."

Moish nodded wisely and rolled up his sleeve in preparation for *davening*, overwhelmed by the realization that he had a lot to give thanks for. God had clearly entrusted him with an important mission, and he was close to carrying it out. A small matter like getting out of jail wouldn't stand in his way now.

He cradled the priceless tefillin that were the Jew's only inheritance from his father. Moish's trained eye examined the workmanship with esteem. Despite their age, they were in perfect condition. Suddenly Moish remembered with a jolt that today was the bar mitzva! He prayed that somehow he would manage to get these tefillin to their rightful owners.

TWENTY SECONDS HADN'T ELAPSED from the time that Moish finished *davening* when he heard his name being called out. "Ungar, Moshe. Ungar, Moshe."

Moish stuck his hands out of his cell and waved. "I'm over here in Cell Two."

A new warden who had obviously just begun his shift came down the hall and unlocked the cell. He instructed Moish to follow him and the scribe quickly gathered his haul. The warden escorted him along the corridor, out the security door and back to the main entrance, where Moish's partner was waiting.

Tuvia's arms were folded across his big chest, and a "Now look what you've done" expression adorned his face.

"What's the matter, Moish?" Tuvia said at last, a smile twitching his lips. "Couldn't find anywhere else to sleep?"

Heard from: Chaim Kass

Matzos Mitzva

AT A DISTANCE OF one highway, two expressways, and fourteen congested city blocks from his home in Far Rockaway, New York, Sheldon Lefkowitz conducts a thriving medical practice. From early morning until late at night his office is always bumper-to-bumper with patients. Considering that the ear, nose and throat specialist is internationally known for curing countless individuals of hearing impairments, breathing obstructions, crippling infections, and a host of other disorders, it is no wonder that he should be so popular. What is unusual is the homogeneity of Lefkowitz's patients.

Almost all are religious Jews, and the lion's share are chassidim, devout disciples of a famous Rebbe in Williamsburg (who himself is a patient of Dr. Lefkowitz). Walking into his waiting room is almost like entering a chassidic court. By mid-afternoon, the crowd *davening mincha* is as thick as the stack of medical journals in the corner.

Among the thirty or so patients gathered one wintry Tuesday evening was Aharon Deitch and his six-year-old, Yoel. When father and son stepped into the examination room, the doctor dispensed with his usual social graces. A *talmid chacham* of note, Lefkowitz is known to *farheir* his young patients on what they are learning. In this particular instance, however, he diagnosed that the situation called for exclusively medical questions.

"He has frequent nose bleeds," the father began in Yiddish. "His nose is stuffed, and everything he says sounds nasal. At first we thought it was allergies. We gave him some medicine, but it didn't get better."

Dr. Lefkowitz motioned for the boy to climb onto the examination table. He placed two tweezer-like clamps, specula, into both nostrils, flipped the aperture of his physician's mirror over his eye, and looked into Yoel Deitch's nose. Without leaving his stool, he reached for his otoscope, peered through the lens, and jotted down some notes.

With a flick of the wrist, he unclasped each speculum and repositioned the mirror above his headband. "He has something in there," he said to the father.

"What kind of something?" Aharon Deitch asked with concern.

"Your son has a tumor in his nose," Lefkowitz responded matter-of-factly, gently placing one hand on the boy's shoulder. "How extensive it is an x-ray will reveal, but it requires immediate medical attention. Tomorrow morning you must have x-rays taken — I don't believe a CAT scan will be necessary — and report right back to me with the results."

Before Lefkowitz finished the last sentence, he started

scribbling notes and authorizations on a set of forms. "There's a group of radiologists near here," the doctor continued, handing Deitch the papers. "If you're there first thing in the morning, you won't need an appointment. I begin tomorrow at eleven o'clock, and I would like to see the x-rays as soon as possible."

"What does this tumor mean?" Deitch questioned, sensing the severity of the situation but not comprehending the implications.

"It means that your son will need an operation to remove it, but until I see the x-rays I cannot tell how far the tumor has spread."

A T TEN AFTER EIGHT the next morning, Aharon and Yoel Deitch were waiting outside the doors of Palmer and Ross, Radiologists. At least fifteen anxious minutes elapsed before they were admitted by a laboratory technician, who could tell by their distinctive garb that they had been referred by Dr. Lefkowitz.

Aharon accompanied his son into the x-ray room and helped position him on a table above the channel holding the x-ray cassette. The procedure was simple, painless, and very quick. In a matter of minutes they were handed a large envelope of x-rays addressed to Dr. Lefkowitz.

Aharon dropped his son off at *cheder* and then headed back to the doctor's office to show him the pictures. For the second time that morning, he was the first to arrive at a clinic. Unaccustomed to being prompt, and certainly never early, he was gratified to know that he would be the first to get Dr. Lefkowitz's attention.

Deitch followed the specialist into his office anxious to

hear the prognosis. Lefkowitz emptied the large envelope, affixed the two x-rays to the view box, and scrutinized the pictures carefully. The doctor was so visibly relieved that Deitch ventured to verbalize his wishful thinking. "So, it was just a stuffed nose after all?"

Lefkowitz shook his head. "Oh," Deitch reconsidered as if he understood, "but this tumor has disappeared since yesterday?"

"No, no," Dr. Lefkowitz responded, realizing that he had overestimated his patient's father. "Your son definitely has a tumor in his nose. Come look." With the tip of a pencil, he outlined the growth in Yoel's x-rays. "We have a lot to be grateful for that the growth has not spread to the brain. That would require a far more complicated operation involving a neurosurgeon.

"As you can see," Lefkowitz continued, "although the tumor has not yet reached the brain, it isn't far away. The operation must therefore be performed very soon."

Deitch remained silent, grasping only that his son would have to undergo a serious operation.

Lefkowitz depressed the intercom switch and asked his receptionist to reserve the O.R. at Isaakie Hospital for the middle of next week.

"Next week?!" Deitch protested. "This is a dangerous situation, you said, so something must be done right away!"

"Just a second," Lefkowitz said firmly, motioning for the distraught man to calm down. He turned away from the papers on his desk and directed his full attention to Aharon Deitch. "The operation cannot and need not be done immediately. A number of preliminary tests must be taken first. Then, a day or two more is needed to prep the patient."

Lefkowitz looked into the panic-stricken eyes of the chassid and understood at once that he was overwhelmed. The physician hoped the father would not inadvertently alarm his son.

F ROM THE DAY Sheldon Lefkowitz opened his practice, he realized that his task of serving patients extended past the examination table and beyond the operating theater. He had to do everything necessary to support them psychologically and help them cope emotionally with their medical problems.

Just as some families insist on knowing every single detail so they can make an informed decision, others are better off being left in the dark as much as possible. It was manifestly clear that the less Deitch knew the better he, and in turn Yoel, was. Everyone required a personal approach tailored to his needs.

The doctor buzzed the intercom again and asked for the roster of anesthesiologists on duty this month at Isaakie Hospital. As he waited for the list, the ENT specialist asked the chassid how he planned to pay for the operation. Deitch shrugged his shoulders; he had no medical coverage. Lefkowitz expected as much. "Another standard operating procedure," the doctor quipped to himself, all-too-familiar with performing surgery free of charge for countless patients. Many of the chassidim recommended by the Rebbe to Lefkowitz were poor individuals whose budgets could not cover the staggering costs of an operation in a proper hospital.

Surgeon's fees aside, Lefkowitz's altruism didn't solve the problem of the anesthesiologist, who most likely was looking for remuneration rather than benefaction. The roster arrived, and Lefkowitz leafed through the pages with a *krechtz*. No one scheduled for the next two weeks was either Jewish or unusually sympathetic. The doctor apprised Deitch of the dilemma and offered, "Let me see what I can do. If it's possible, I'll try and work something out."

THURSDAY MORNING Sheldon Lefkowitz drove out to Isaakie Hospital in the Bronx to request a favor from one of the resident anesthesiologists. He entered the doctors' lounge and approached Lho Chung Hee, a Korean physician in his mid-thirties. They had operated together several times in the past and Lefkowitz felt he was a decent man. Soon he would know for sure.

The ENT specialist explained the whole situation to Dr. Lho and made a personal appeal. For the respected doctor the request was demeaning and Lho couldn't help but admire the man's courage and sincerity. It was obvious that Lefkowitz had nothing personal to gain from the favor, which made his plea all the more compelling.

The anesthesiologist thought about it for a moment and responded, "I'll tell you what I'll do. I did my residency at Brookdale, where there were a lot of religious Jewish doctors like you doing their internship. During one of their holidays they showed up every day with these large, oval crackers instead of bread. These crackers really intrigued me, and I asked one of my associates if he would mind if I tasted it. He assured me that I wouldn't like it — that it tasted like cardboard — but I persisted. And you know? I really liked it. It reminded me of something we used to eat with fish in my native village in Korea.

"I went to Waldbaum's the next day, to the Jewish-food section, and bought a box of the holiday crackers. But they weren't the same as what I had tasted in the hospital.

"I'll perform the operation with you for no charge, but I would like some of those crackers in return, the oval kind you can't find in the supermarket."

Dr. Lefkowitz was very relieved. "I will see to it that you get your 'crackers,'" the ENT specialist assured him. They shook hands and Lefkowitz descended to the surgical ward.

Since he was already in the hospital he decided to arrange the scheduling of Yoel's operation personally. This way he could ensure that it take place first thing in the morning, without affecting his day at the clinic.

Lefkowitz's preference was honored, and the operation was scheduled for 8:00 Tuesday morning. Beaming over the morning's accomplishments, he returned to his office thoroughly satisfied. He knew how relieved the Deitches would be to learn of the anesthesiologist's peculiar but prosaic request. He therefore asked his receptionist to mention it when she called them with the details of the surgery schedule.

ABOUT AN HOUR LATER the receptionist burst into the doctor's office explaining that Deitch was on the phone and was hysterically insistent upon speaking directly to him. He would neither reveal the matter he wished to discuss nor wait for his call to be returned. Lefkowitz blanched with concern and lifted the receiver.

"Dr. Lefkowitz," Aharon Deitch demanded with great emotion. "Where am I going to get *shmura matzah* now?"

The surgeon couldn't help but smile. "Not *now*, Reb Aharon," he comforted the chassid. "Later on, before Pesach. I will tell the anesthesiologist that you will bring the matzahs to the hospital. You must admit it is quite a bargain. Just make sure you carry out your part of the deal, since I have given him my word that he will get hand matzahs. All the best," he concluded, and resumed his work.

At 7:45 Tuesday morning, Sheldon Lefkowitz walked down the corridor outside the operating theater. He scrubbed his hands as a resident briefed him about the patient. The ENT specialist rinsed off the suds, lifting his hands to prevent water from running down. He then pushed open the door to the O.R. with his hip, and heard the conversation in the room trail off into silence. The surgeon accepted a towel from the scrub nurse and methodically dried his hands while checking the patient's vital signs. And then, like a general reviewing his troops, he briskly moved around the table, nodding to the surgical assistant and the anesthesiologist.

Lefkowitz disposed of the towel and slipped on his sterile gown. He turned to the patient and simultaneously thrust his hands into rubber gloves, and, as if on cue, the senior surgical fellow looked up from the operative field.

With a prayer on his lips, Dr. Lefkowitz articulated the instructions he knew God had enjoined him to command: "Forceps and scalpel." Swiftly but without undue haste, he began to work. Lefkowitz's operative technique was deliberate and absent of wasted motion; each incision was precise, every moment counted. His knowledge of anatomy was encyclopedic, his feel for tissue extraordinary.

Two hours and twelve minutes after he began, Sheldon Lefkowitz had successfully completed the excision of the tumor. He left exact instructions regarding post-operative care, and orders to contact him immediately if any blood was noticeable on the nasal packing or gauze. Then he exited the O.R. and went to greet the Deitch family with the good news.

THE NATURE of Dr. Lefkowitz's work and clientele left little time for himself and his family. Even when he finally closes his office and returns home, there is always a plethora of messages awaiting him and non-stop phone calls from people seeking his medical opinion. Few Jews could match his devotion to his People; few physicians could match his devotion to his profession.

Although most of the calls he receives are only minimally related to the field of medicine, he awards each one an attentive ear. Admittedly there are too many midnight callers with high blood pressure and too many sure-I've-got-hypoglycemia cases; it is tough to pick out the insulinomas, the Addison's diseases, and even the ruptured spleens from among all the walking worried. For this reason Dr. Lefkowitz responds to every call and investigates even remote possibilities.

Only a few times a year does he heed the voice of his wife and spend time at home. One of these rare occasions is *erev Pesach*, when the surgeon lends his expertise to the clean-up operation.

It was Passover eve 1987 when the doctor's pre-Pesach activity ground to a complete halt. It all started with an innocent phone call:

"Hello, Dr. Lefkowitz? This is Dr. Lho Chung Hee."

"Why yes, doctor. How can I help you?"

"You remember four months ago when I assisted you in a tumor resection, gratis... At the time I requested Passover crackers in lieu of payment. Well, I don't have to tell you that the holiday is about to begin — it's in all the papers and alternate-side-of-the-street parking has been suspended — and I still haven't received my crackers."

"I see," Dr. Lefkowitz stalled, more than disconcerted.

1987 was the year of the great *shmura matzah* shortage in America, and he considered himself fortunate to have just enough hand matzahs for the mandatory *seder* eating requirements. "I will look into it right away," Dr. Lefkowitz added, not knowing what else to say. "Just give me your address, and I will try and arrange for the matzahs to be delivered before the holiday begins."

Lho told him his address and Lefkowitz jotted it down.

"All right, I've got it. And I'm very, very sorry."

THE DOCTOR replaced the phone on the hook and continued to fret. "I gave this man my word," he thought to himself. "He was magnanimous enough to waive a four-digit fee for a few matzahs and my patient was too irresponsible to hold up his end of the bargain. Now I'm left in the lurch."

At first Lefkowitz felt like getting Deitch on the line and giving him a tongue-lashing for his lack of gratitude, and for causing such an execrable *chillul Hashem*. He even started paging through the phone book for his number when he caught himself.

"What's the point?" he rationalized. "If he neglected

to take care of the matter until now, he's not about to suddenly comply so close to Pesach. I must assume that with the matzah shortage he was barely able to get enough for his own family. He must have figured that the anesthesiologist could manage without his 'crackers'. By calling him I could vent my anger, but all that would do is destroy his *Yom Tov.*

"But that doesn't resolve my dilemma," the doctor fumed. "Lho is waiting for his matzahs. He doesn't know about the shortage and it's not his problem. No doubt he thinks we've taken advantage of him.

"**Y**OSSI!" Dr. Lefkowitz called upstairs to his son. A youthful face appeared at the top of the stairs.

"I need you to run a quick errand for me."

Yossi flashed his father the "minute" sign, and in a matter of seconds he was downstairs, clutching a jangle of car keys.

Dr. Lefkowitz carefully handed a parcel of *shmura matzah* to his son, and instructed him where to deliver it. "This is for a gentile colleague of mine who is infatuated with our customs. It's a long story, but please just apologize to the man for the delay. You see, he was expecting this a while ago."

As the father watched his son pull away, he froze. Vexation engulfed him and his temples throbbed in annoyance. "What have I done?" he chastised himself.

Scenes of his grandfather's *seder* flashed in his mind. He vividly recalled that the high point of the night was seeing, holding, smelling, and finally eating the crisp, oval matzahs. Square matzahs out of a shrink-wrapped box off a supermarket shelf, aside from their halachic problems, could never evoke that special Pesach aura.

Furthermore, he recalled with a shudder, their *seder* was to be attended by Yossi's *kallah*. What would she think of the family she was about to marry into when she saw machine matzahs on the *seder* plate? How could he possibly explain that he wasn't being stingy or succumbing to mass-produced ritual?

Holding onto the door for support, Sheldon Lefkowitz seemed to enter a trance-like state of contrition. His melancholy and tortuous thoughts were suddenly interrupted by the chime of the doorbell. "Could it be that I didn't give Yossi clear directions?" his father wondered. He looked through the peephole and saw a young chassid waiting outside.

"There goes tonight's *seder*," he worried to himself, as he opened the door to what he feared might be the harbinger of a medical emergency.

"**H**ERR DOKTOR LEFKOWITZ," the young man respectfully began, "I bring you greetings from the Rebbe. He sent this for *Yom Tov* with his best wishes, deep appreciation, and blessings for a kosher and happy Pesach." The chassid handed the surprised doctor a box, wished him a "Gutte Yontiff," and disappeared.

Sheldon Lefkowitz placed the white box on his dining-room table and peered inside. There before his eyes was a stack of freshly baked, still-fragrant hand matzahs.

Heard from: Dvora Goldstein

Balance Sheet

Months	Chessed	Teshuvah	Torah	Tefillah	Tzeddakah	Aveiros
Tishrei						
Cheshvan						
Kislev						
Teves						
Shevat						
Adar						
Nissan						
Iyyar						
Sivan						
Tammuz						
Av						
Ellul						

Money Matters

Prepared by

Date

Index No.

אמרו חז״ל ארבעה נקראו רשעים ואחד מהם
לוה ואינו משלם שנאמר לוה רשע ולא ישלם
וכמה יש לו לאדם להתבייש מעצמו כשיודע
שהיכולת בידו לפרוע והוא מונע עצמו מזה
ומביא על עצמו שם רשע.

אהבת חסד פרק י״ד

Chazal *have taught that four people
are called "evil." One of these is a
person who does not repay his loan,
as it says, "Evil is the borrower who
does not repay." How ashamed one
must be if he has the wherewithal to
repay a loan and refrains from doing
so, incurring upon himself the name
"evil."*

Ahavas Chessed: 14

A Gem of a Mitzva

IT WAS just after Rosh Hashanah when Zalman Klein concluded that in order to properly fulfill his obligation of living in a sukkah, the land beneath it had to belong to him. This thought occurred to him when he noticed his gentile landlord's distress over the scrap-wood shanties being erected in the courtyard of his Chicago apartment building.

Zalman discussed what he viewed as a serious dilemma with his co-religionists, but they were unconcerned. "We're legally entitled to erect a sukkah here," they argued. "There's even a city ordinance protecting our rights. And with the exorbitant rent Skinner is gouging, and the way he bills us for every little nothing, we've already more than paid him for the privilege."

Zal, however, disagreed. He had spent several years learning in the Brisker Yeshiva in Jerusalem, which had a profound impact on his character. Serious and kind-hearted, high strung and easily excitable, Zal exudes a naive wholesomeness and exuberance that would do any mother proud. But among his friends, this young *kollel* member is best known for his conscientiousness.

From early youth, Zalman's performance of the *mitzvos* between man and God — and between man and his fellow man — was remarkably meticulous. Just after his bar mitzva, he opened his first bank account; later that month, he returned three cents to the teller for interest credited over a bank holiday. He routinely peels off and saves uncancelled postage stamps, as many people do, only Zal returns them to the post office. To say that he is careful in his observance of Hashem's laws would be a gross understatement; to imagine that his friends' rationalization might allay his concerns about his sukkah would be folly.

ZALMAN didn't like disputes, especially when the outcome could hinder the fulfillment of a mitzva, but the circumstances clearly bore all the earmarks of incipient controversy. He understood his neighbors' sentiments, yet there was no justification for antagonizing the landlord. Zal feared that Skinner's displeasure might have halachic ramifications, and no Brisker graduate worth his salt would consider performing a mitzva under such conditions.

Zal applied his talmudically honed mind to the problem and after some lengthy cogitation, he came up with an ideal, albeit cumbersome, solution: if he were to erect his sukkah on the roof, no one would be the wiser. Thus he could exercise his rights without incurring the landlord's wrath.

But Zal operates under different rules than those that govern other mortals. He would not undertake such a project without first securing his landlord's consent, and Skinner, detecting an opportunity for easy profit, was not about to acquiesce without an incentive.

Avaricious Ernie Skinner knew very well that his tenants viewed the roof as an integral part of their own property. Indeed, he had never challenged their access to it and if the truth be known, he couldn't care less what they did there. This, of course, did not deter him from taking advantage of Klein's naiveté.

Still Zal was determined. Somehow he would get his landlord to grant him exclusive rights to the roof for the week before and during Sukkos — even if it meant offering an "incentive". Skinner's reluctance quickly evaporated in light of his tenant's exploitability. Zal insisted, however, on getting this privilege, known as an "easement," formalized in writing. Only when he had the official contract in hand did he commence his construction project.

CHICAGO is a city familiar with contracts of one form or another. Once the headquarters for underworld operations throughout the United States, Chicago's Syndicate not only controlled local crime, it controlled the city. The beleaguered citizenry was somewhat consoled by the knowledge that the Mob performed at least one public service: since the days of Al "Scarface" Capone, it had provided the police with ample bribery opportunities; the man on the street, therefore, was less likely to be subjected to a shakedown by one of Chicago's Finest.

Graft was a way of life in Chicago. The city had the best government that money could buy — literally. Even outside government echelons, honesty was relative: an "honest inspector" was someone who would "stay bought" once the payoff was made without requiring further inducements to turn a blind eye to improprieties committed under his jurisdiction. "Honest graft" was not a contradiction in terms; it meant the kind of graft that fell one's way, as opposed to the kind one aggressively sought.

Fanning the flames of corruption was the Syndicate, with the Police Department in its pocket. From the day Joseph DiLeonardi was promoted from homicide chief to superintendent in 1980, the number of arrests made in the Mob's preserves fell from negligible to nil, a statistic Zalman Klein never imagined would affect him.

Without devoting a moment's thought to the Mob-inspired extortion he had just been a party to, nor to his meager budget, Zal proceeded with his sukkah preparations.

EVIDENCE of the tenants' conception of their inalienable right to the roof was lavishly displayed all over Zal's intended construction site. Across the length and breadth of the roof, decades worth of stinking, rotting refuse were heaped several feet deep, reduced by the elements and the ravages of time to an almost unrecognizable agglomerate of decay.

Zal was struck dumb by the awesome sight. In addition to the enormous task of clearing the area, he knew he would have to spend weeks restoring the property to the same pristine condition in which he'd received it. The low railing surrounding the roof precluded the possibility of stacking the debris into one monumental pile, as that would present a serious hazard to passersby below. Zal was stymied, but only for a moment.

Upon closer scrutiny, he observed that everything on the roof was clearly ownerless. The eclectic array of suitcase sides, contorted baby-carriage frames, defoliated evergreen trees (sans tinsel), rusting beer cans, etc., radiated an aura of abandonment. The mess was eminently disposable.

A RMFUL BY HEAPING ARMFUL, Zal began to make inroads in the trash piles. Repeatedly he trudged down the stairs to the incinerator room and back up again. Only after dozens of descents and ascents, however, did the first traces of tarpaper become discernible. It was a Pyrrhic victory at best.

When the young rabbi-*cum*-garbage collector's removal operation was two-thirds done, he uncovered the first of four sacks filled with what Zal at first imagined to be marbles. In fact, to his utter astonishment, they were crammed with glittering, exquisitely crafted jewelry.

"How could they possibly have gotten here?" he wondered uncomfortably. "Maybe the wind brought them — after all, this was the windy city, and the wind from the west and north blows across a thousand miles of unbroken prairies," or so his fourth-grade geography teacher had claimed.

"Perhaps someone left them here by mistake," he

said aloud, but he quickly rejected the idea. People don't "forget" thousands and thousands of dollars worth of jewelry. "Maybe they're fake," he hoped — until he saw the dainty four-digit price tags attached to each ornament. "Maybe..." There were no other "maybes". He knew perfectly well what the sacks concealed under an old tire and sections of a swing set were doing on the roof.

This was one time Zal almost wished he were not so conscientious. If not for his zeal, he wouldn't have been up on the roof in the first place; if he hadn't coveted the roof, he wouldn't have stumbled upon the jewels and he wouldn't have gotten into the hot water in which he now found himself.

Quivering with fear, Zal carefully collected the sacks, heaved them over his shoulder, and made for the stairs. His heart pounded in terror that he might bump into a claimant for the jewels on his way down the steps. Bounding down the stairwell like a sneak thief-mountain goat, he scraped his knuckles, sprained an ankle, and barked his shins.

Zal burst into his apartment with such force that he nearly took the door off. A dining room table and two chairs along the way arrested his progress and brought him to a dead halt. "Don't touch those bags!" he screamed at his wife, who had no intention of even approaching the filthy sacks.

ZAL HAD NO INTEREST whatsoever in "finders keepers"; his main concern was the weeping losers. The possibility of the goods' disgruntled owners shattering the tranquility of his Sukkos, not to mention the bone structure of his face, was not Zal's idea of a memorable *Yom Tov*.

He hopped over to the telephone on his good foot and dialed 911 with his less-bruised hand. "Hello!" he shouted into the mouthpiece, "I need a taxi right away, it's an emergency!"

"Mistuh," the dispatcher replied, "I cain't tell if I'z hearin' ya over de phone lines or tru' de winduh! Will ya stop shoutin', I got sensitive ears. Can't take nuttin' louder dan a sonic boom."

Zal realized how foolish he must have sounded and prayed that he would be able to execute his *hashavas aveida* in sound body and mind.

A CAB ARRIVED a few minutes later, but to the manic-depressive waiting at the curb and clutching four sacks tightly enough to burst the veins in the back of his hands, it felt like an eternity — at least. Zal leaped into a cab decorated with banner warnings: "DON'T slam the door! DON'T litter! DON'T stick your head out the window! Don't SLAM the door! DON'T get out on the left side! DON'T put luggage on the back seat! Don't slam the DOOR!!" Even one of the gewgaws dangling from the rearview mirror read "DON'T SLAM THE DOOR!" Already a nervous wreck, Zal threw his booty onto the back seat and slammed the door, bringing out the worst in an unfriendly cabbie.

"Whatcha got dere," the driver, who seemed to be a mixed ethnic group unto himself, inquired sarcastically, "hot ice?"

"Hot ice?!" Zal challenged defiantly, "How could I be carrying hot ice?"

"Genius!" the cabbie sneered. "Dat means stolen jools."

"How'd you know?" Zal almost blurted out, but he caught himself in time to rephrase. "How'd you know... it's so dark?"

"How'd ah knows it's so dark? What are ya', conductin' a poll or sometin'? Ah knows it's so dark acause ah got me a psycho in de back seat who's rushin' to get somewheres afo' he turns hisself into a werewolf. Now jus' tell me, bustuh, where ya headed?"

After the cabbie's invective, Zal was almost afraid to respond, "The closest police station."

"Well, Mistuh," the Afro-Jamaican-Polynesian-Arab growled, "de clock's tickin' and it's burnin' yo' dime. Now, ya mind tellin' me where ya's headed, or ya wants me to play '21 Questions?'"

"Eh... Uh..." Zal mumbled. "Take me near the main police station downtown."

"Near?" the cabbie mimicked, his voice oozing contempt. "Dat mean ya wants de fire hydran' 'cross de street, or de litta basket at de corner?"

EVENTUALLY, they arrived at police headquarters, Zal paid his fare, and the cabbie issued a final warning: "Slam da door agin and ya won't be needin' no po-lice station — ya be needin' da morgue!" Needless to say, in his agitated state Zal unwittingly slammed the door. With barely a glance at the snarling driver, he ran for his life into the police station.

His dramatic entrance caused a bit of a stir and several rookies leaped up from their crossword puzzles and comic books to stop the suspicious intruder. "You looking for someone?" asked a youthful cop, posting himself in Zal's path.

"Er, yes," Zal stammered, "I have, er... a lost item."

"Sorry, fella," the officer responded, "Lost 'n Found's closed now. Come back tomorra."

"Maybe I can speak to a detective," Zal offered meekly.

"What are you, a reporter or what?" the cop snapped.

"No, no," Zal protested, "just a law-abiding citizen, and I'd appreciate a little cooperation."

"Okay," the policeman agreed magnanimously. "Since you akst so nicely, folla me."

The cop led Zal down a corridor to the bullpen. "Take ya pick," the officer shouted over his shoulder, abandoning the innocent *yeshiva bachur* to the wolves.

Zal's jaw dropped at the sight of the squadroom, a scene straight out of bedlam. There were six desks with once-gray linoleum desktops positioned on a once-brown linoleum floor; the air was hazy with cigarette smoke, the air was redolent with the scent of rancid coffee and dirty feet.

At the first desk sat a detective perfunctorily taking dictation from an aging bleached blonde crowned with a hive of rollers. The second desk was graced by a girl of nineteen or twenty with a shaved head and a tattoo on her scalp which looked like a long, sutured gash.

"I could use one of those right over my heart," the detective joked, in an attempt to get her to complete her story. The gimmick worked and she continued in a voice that sounded like the Portuguese National Anthem played through an electric shaver.

At the third desk, a detective was trying to interrogate a black teenager who sat with his elbows on the table, twisting his bead-trimmed braid between his fingers, head cocked to one side as if he were listening for voices on the wind. The officer snapped his fingers repeatedly to rouse the meditating interviewee, but his efforts were in vain.

At the fourth desk, three policemen were subduing a menacing-looking Oriental youth clad in black leather and heavy metal who screamed a slew of obscenities in fluent polyglot. And at the fifth desk, a uniformed cop sat unperturbed, sipping coffee and listening to a basketball game on the radio, oblivious to the metallic voice of the dispatcher squawking robberies, murder, and mayhem over the police band on the shortwave receiver. Zal headed straight for the sports fan, whose nameplate read: "Carl Nunzio, detective second/grade."

"**O**FFICER," Klein began, toying with the sacks on his lap, "you see, I just found these sacks..." His deposition earned about as much attention from the detective as the braided black youth was giving his interviewer.

Zal raised his voice, and Nunzio raised the volume of his radio. Zal raised his voice louder still, but Magic Johnson was dribbling his way across the court en route to a slam-dunk and the crowd roared in anticipation.

Resigned, Zal rose to leave. "Try the lieutenant," the man behind the desk suddenly suggested, hooking a thumb in the direction of a glass-partitioned cubicle where a cop in shirtsleeves was sitting in a swivel chair. Zal followed the thumb.

The swiveller's label read: "Paul E. Gielli, Lieutenant of Detectives," and Zal thought this one at least looked the part. Beneath his bald pate, the lieutenant's face was creased with the first signs of age and battered with the sure signs of experience; the whites of his beady eyes were yellow and rheumy. Behind him, the wall was plastered with citations and pictures of his hand being pumped by various municipal officials and dignitaries. But most important, the cubicle was nearly soundproof. When Zal closed the door, he thought he'd momentarily gone deaf.

"Yeah?" the detective asked not impolitely. "What is it?"

Zal placed the four sacks of jewels on the scarred oak desk with a clatter that piqued Gielli's interest. He peeked into one of the bags, then quickly drew back as though he'd been stung.

"Er, could I get yer name, please?" he asked, suddenly all vigilance and officialdom.

"Zalman Klein. That's Z-A-L-M-A-N Klein, E-I. Now, this afternoon I was cleaning up the roof of my building, clearing away all of the junk, that is... Well, it's a long story... in any event, I uncovered these four bags and I looked inside and saw they were full of jewelry, and I knew right away that they couldn't have been abandoned there, so they must have been... uh, stashed!"

Everything came out in a rush, not at all the way Zal had rehearsed it, but now that he had someone's attention, he wasn't about to lose it.

Gielli gingerly opened each of the bags and began to inspect the merchandise. He pulled a wad of forms out of a desk drawer and licked the end of his pencil. "Exactly what time of day did this happen, sir?" he asked.

Zal took note of the new respect the gems had gained him and the lieutenant took note of every gem that passed his lips. Gielli was transformed into a stenographer, taking meticulous dictation from the black-clad citizen's every word.

ZAL WAS INTRIGUED by the police procedure. After answering a battery of basic questions, he realized the detective was trying to determine if he had stolen the jewels — a reasonable assumption from Gielli's point of view. But Zal continued to reply innocently until the lieutenant was convinced that he was clean.

It was apparent that Gielli had a special interest in the jewelry; he practically came out and said so. He thanked Zal profusely and sincerely for his honesty and for taking the trouble to come down to the station with the stolen items. Then he clasped Zal's hand firmly, looking like a modern-day Diogenes whose lifelong search had ended. "Yer don't gotta worry about no reprisals or nothin'," he said in that curious blend of street talk and legalese that forms a policeman's patois. "Dis stuff's from a major heist, not d'loot some two-bit punk or junkie ripped off an ol' lady. When de perps go lookin' for de stash an' it ain't dere, they'll do a disappearin' act for sure."

With that reassurance, Zal's blood pressure plunged down to normal. As he opened the cubicle door, the pandemonium of the squadroom renewed its assault on his tender eardrums. Eyes darting left and right, taking in the scene from Dante's Inferno arranged before his disbelieving eyes, Zal made a swift getaway.

A SATISFIED SMIRK adorned Gielli's untidy face. This just might be the evidence he had tried so hard to obtain. And yet... and yet... The lieutenant carefully straightened the papers on his desk and buzzed the file clerk on the intercom. "Bring me de print-out on dem Bijeaux heists, will ya?" he barked.

While he waited, Gielli tagged all four bags, called the police photographer, and told the lab to send over a technician. Serendipitous Zalman Klein had brought Lieutenant Gielli the key to closing the file on a case that had haunted and tormented him.

Six months ago, the Bijeaux Brothers jewelry-store robberies had dominated the local news for weeks and seriously undermined the public's minimal trust in law enforcement officials. The case broke just as Gielli was coming up for promotion to "captain" and he was placed in charge of the investigation.

Each of the four thefts bore the distinctive m.o. of Mob involvement: no alarms were triggered; the thieves knew exactly what they were after; every heist totalled at least a half-million dollars in goods; and — most telling of all — the police never arrived, even though the stores were in areas that enjoyed better-than-average surveillance and frequent patrols.

G IELLI'S INVESTIGATION and detective work were impeccable. He arrested suspects and put a tail on their associates; he interrogated witnesses and ran a complete check on the owners and employees. But for all the evidence he gathered, confessions he extracted, and alibis he refuted, he still couldn't nail down a conviction.

Police corruption was so widespread that Gielli didn't have a hope of wiping it out. But the bent cops were small fry; he was after the big fish. Without the stolen jewels, or any way of connecting the suspects to them, the case would be laughed out of court.

Gielli marshalled all the manpower and resources at his command to comb the city for the goods. Every clue was followed up and dozens of search warrants were issued, but to no avail.

Paul E. Gielli became a laughingstock. The lieutenant's failure to solve a series of major robberies within the same franchise caused many to insinuate that he was in league with the Syndicate. With a name like his, no one would give him the benefit of the doubt; it was automatically assumed that he wouldn't work against the Family. The Bijeaux case, therefore, constituted a double affront: not only was Gielli unjustly denied advancement — and the attendant salary increase — but he was pigeonholed with those of Italian descent on the other side of the law.

A S IT HAPPENED, this particular cop was straight. He had worked his way up through the ranks without ever once succumbing to the abundant temptations of corruption. But his spotless record failed to impress anyone. The only way Gielli could clear his name and prove that although he was Italian, he intended to enforce the law was by putting the lawbreakers — organized or not — behind bars.

And now, thought Gielli, this incredibly, almost laughably honest Joe — what was his name? oh, yeah, Zalman Klein — had provided him with the missing link, the crucial ingredient that could land convictions at last.

Gielli compared the photos in the Bijeaux file with the sacks' contents. There was no doubt about it; these were the Bijeaux jewels. He instructed the photographer to shoot the goods and the technician to dust the evidence for latents and suck up all the microscopic lint particles with his mini-vac. Gielli was going to hand the case to the D.A. all tied up in a neat ribbon.

Zal's evidence did eventually lead to several indictments and convictions, and for once a shiver ran up and down the Syndicate's spine. Gratified, the Chicago D.A. recommended to the police commissioner that Lieutenant Gielli be issued a citation for his outstanding detective work.

"**H**EY, Loo-ie," a rookie cop called out.

Without looking up from his report, Gielli returned fire with a face-saving reprimand. "Since when d'yer refer to yer superior as Loo-ie? It's 'Lieutenant,' if you don't mind."

"Sorry, Loo-, I mean, er... Lieutenant." The rookie's sincerity seemed rather doubtful, since he, too, never stopped skimming his newspaper as he addressed his boss.

"I'm tryin' t' clean up dis file on de By-jox robberies and we still gotta ton o' jools in de safe from dis case. What am I suppose t' do wit dem?"

"Dat's Bijeaux, flea brain," Gielli said, looking up from the endless pile of paperwork. "An' get yer big, smelly feet off de desk. De rocks go back to the jewelry store. Take care of it first ting in de morning. And don' forget — you gotta get 'em to sign a form."

"But Loo-ie," the rookie protested, "By-jox been closed down half a year now."

"All de branch stores?"

"Yeah, every single one."

"So den de stuff goes to de owner."

"Loo-ie..."

"Lieutenant!"

"I mean Lieutenant, sir, don' you read de paper? By-jox himself kicked de bucket six months ago. He left a fortune to de state."

"What?!" Gielli snapped to attention. "He didn't got no heirs... An dat's Bijeaux, lummox."

"Right, Loo. Bee-Joe's only heir was his cat."

"Well, den," the lieutenant pondered, "dere's gotta be a statute dat covers dat. Let me tink on it a second. Yeah, right — it goes to, eh... de finder. I remember de guy: black suit, fuzzy beard, kinda noivous. His name's gotta be in de file..."

"I got it right here, Loo-ie," the rookie replied, replacing his feet on the desk.

SEVENTEEN MONTHS after four sacks of precious jewels stolen from a chain of Bijeaux stores were handed in to the police, they were transferred to Zal and Mimmi Klein, in what may be the biggest windfall ever presented to a struggling *kollel* couple. Everyone was happy for them...except a certain money-grubbing landlord.

Making haste to correct what he deemed a legal error, Ernie Skinner filed a civil suit against Zalman Klein. True, Skinner conceded, the tenant was the finder; nonetheless, the jewels were found on his property, thereby rendering them rightfully his. Convinced that he had an open-and-shut case, the landlord was not even willing to discuss the issue with Klein. He was bent on suing and would settle for nothing less than every last gem.

Zal soon found himself in court, pitted against a very self-righteous landlord. Feeling small and defenseless in the face of the unremitting barrage of legal terms, citations, and precedents hurled at him by the lawyer for the plaintiff, Zal cowered behind the one and only document he had brought with him to the courthouse.

When it came time for Zal to present his side of the story, the easement was offered for the bench's scrutiny. The judge avidly read the contract and then asked if there had been a monetary component to this transaction. The answer was affirmative.

When the judge asked how much Zal had laid out for the privilege of having exclusive rights to the roof for a two-week period, the figure the defendant quoted (and the plaintiff confirmed) elevated his eyebrows just below his hairline and sent his reading glasses careening down his nose.

Hizzoner delivered a brief but biting reprimand to Skinner for wasting the court's precious time. "Court finds for the defendant, Mr. Zalman Klein, and orders the plaintiff to pay the defendant's legal fees, case dismissed."

And with a resounding BANG! of the judge's gavel, and a silent, unseen nod from the Judge of Judges, Zalman Klein became a wealthy man.

But, truth to tell, Zal has always been a man of means, affluent in learning and rich in *middos*.

Heard from: Eli Moshe Gross

A Match Made in Heaven

"WHAT DOES GOD DO EVERY DAY?" a Roman noblewoman once asked Rabbi Yose bar Chalafta. "He makes *shidduchim*," the scholar replied, "matches between couples."

"What?" she laughed in amazement. "I could do that, too! Why, I could marry off my hundreds of servants with no trouble at all."

Rabbi Yose smiled. "It's not as easy as it looks. In fact, it's as difficult as splitting the Red Sea!"

But the noblewoman was unimpressed. "I'll show him and his Torah!" she thought to herself. She summoned her servants, lined them up in separate rows of men and women, and paired them off. Within hours she had married them all.

The next morning, the noblewoman was confronted by an awesome site. Masses of servants were camped outside the palace. "What happened?" she cried.

"I don't want this woman!" shouted one servant.

"This man beat me!" "Find me another wife!" "Give me a different husband!" howled another.

The yelling, screaming, and bickering were tumultuous.

Above the din of the fracas, the noblewoman conceded to Rabbi Yose: "There is no Torah like your Torah!"

Others engaged in matchmaking — for themselves or for others — readily echo the noblewoman's sentiments. Actually the Almighty plies His profession not just between husband and wife, but between business partners, and between mitzva partners. This is the story of one such match — a partnership no less miraculous than a conventional *shidduch*.

REB FISHEL was a peddler. What he peddled wasn't important, but where he peddled it was. He lived in the Land of Israel. Every day he would walk the streets of Jerusalem, breathe its special air, and thank God for the privilege of living like a Jew in a Jewish land.

Like other residents of the holy city, Reb Fishel lived a humble life. His home was a basement rental in the Beis Yisrael section of Jerusalem. To say his apartment was small is as much of an understatement as was the dwelling itself. It was originally advertised as having two bedrooms, meaning that you could fit two beds in each room, and that was all. But Reb Fishel didn't mind. Even though his abode was underground, it was still a roof over his head.

Reb Fishel lived there with his 19-year-old daughter, Elishevah, his pride and joy. Both father and daughter were blessed with a gentle sense of humor that meshed their two souls into one. They teased each other as best friends might and shared each other's joys, sorrows and dreams. One day, Elishevah came home with news that was to change her father's life forever.

"Father, my best friend Rivkie wants me to meet her brother, Pinchas."

"Don't you know him already? After all, you spend a lot of time in her house."

"Father! You know what I mean."

"Yes, I know what you mean. But what does he mean? What kind of boy is he?"

"He's a *lamdan* and a *sofer*. I heard he writes beautiful tefillin!"

"I'm not interested. I already have a pair," Reb Fishel quipped. "But if *you're* interested, go ahead!"

Under the watchful eyes of her father and his sister, Elishevah and Pinchas met, courted, and became engaged. It was three weeks before Purim. Four months later, after Shavuous, they wanted to get married.

THERE WAS just one problem. Reb Fishel could barely afford to pay the rent, much less underwrite a *chassunah*. And while a Jerusalem wedding is not as expensive as the "made in America" model, it was still way beyond Reb Fishel's means. Still, it was his only child and he was determined to raise the capital. He just wasn't sure how.

Day after day, Reb Fishel thought long and hard. A proud man, he did not want to rely on the local free-loan organizations. "They're for poor people," he said. "*Baruch Hashem*, I am rich... in blessings. Besides, if I borrow money, what will be left for the person truly in need?"

Days turned into weeks, and weeks into months. Passover came and went, and so did the little money he earned. As proud as Reb Fishel was, he was also practical, and he realized something had to be done. "To understand how much I really need," he reasoned, "I first have to get a better idea of what everything costs."

So one *motzei Shabbos*, father and daughter sat down and calculated the cost of clothing, a second-hand refrigerator and stove, used furniture, dishes and silverware, linens, invitations, and the wedding itself. The sum was a whopping 11,260 shekels. By their reckoning, it would take Reb Fishel approximately seventy-two years to save up that kind of money.

"What are we going to do?" Elishevah moaned.

"Don't worry," Reb Fishel replied. "God provided you with a *chassan*, and He'll provide you with a *chassunah*." But he sounded much more confident than he felt.

So Reb Fishel contemplated and ruminated until he came up with a plan: "Elishevah, I'm going to sell my *sefarim*. I'm sure they're worth something."

"Oh Father, you can't!" she said. "They've been in the family for years!"

"Believe me, Elishevah, that doesn't bother me," he lied. "I'm not losing *sefarim*, I'm gaining a potential grandson!"

THE NEXT DAY, Reb Fishel lovingly packed about two dozen old and battered books into a cloth sack. Among his private treasures were his grandfather's tear-stained *machzor*, which had come all the way from Poland; a set of gilt-edged *Mishnayos* from Vienna circa 1869; a copy of *Toras Cohanim* published in Slavita in 1810; his late wife's *techina*; and an ancient, undated *Midrash Rabbah*.

With a lump in his throat, he placed the *sefarim* in his cart and made his way to "Eagle Eye Antiquities," located in the lobby of the Jerusalem Ritz Carlton.

As Reb Fishel entered the shop, the owner eyed him suspiciously. "Probably a *shnorrer*," Robert (né Reuven) Esterhazi thought. "Can I help you?" he asked somewhat solicitously.

"Yes," Reb Fishel answered. "I was wondering if you'd be interested in buying some old *sefarim*. I'm sure they're very rare."

"Let me take a look at them," Robert replied to his eminently dupable "salesman". With the eagle eye for which his establishment was named, Robert quickly examined the lot.

"They're only worth about 150 shekels," he sniffed, "but since you could probably use the money, I'll give you 200."

"What?" Reb Fishel asked incredulously. "I need at least fifty times that for my daughter's wedding! Are you sure? After all, they're quite old."

"Yes, but they're also quite used."

"Aren't holy books supposed to be used?" Reb Fishel asked naively.

"I'm sure they are. But if my customers want to buy incunabula, they want them to look like new. I can go up to 225 shekels, but that's it," the proprietor said dismissively.

"Thank you, but no thank you," Reb Fishel replied politely, as he began packing up his books. The father of the bride was crushed. In his mind, he was not only counting on that money, he had already spent it.

REB FISHEL felt like the fabled Leib Blecher — without a *niggun*. Leib Blecher was another father in another time — a penniless Breslover chassid and tinsmith who lived in the late 1700s. He, too, had no dowry for his daughter.

As the nuptials drew closer, it became painfully obvious that Leib Blecher's daughter would have not a wedding fit for a princess, but one fit for a pauper.

"Please, Father," his daughter begged. "If you can't afford a proper wedding, at least get me a wedding dress."

The chassid sadly shook his head. "With all my heart, I wish I could, but I cannot. I have no money."

She turned away with tears in her eyes. Suddenly the words of *Eishes Chayil* (Woman of Valor) drifted into Leib Blecher's mind. Softly and gently he sang to his daughter the ancient *niggun*: *Oz v'hadar l'vusha, v'tischak l'yom acharon* — "Strength and dignity are her garments; she looks joyously to the future."

Leib Blecher's *niggun* became his daughter's wedding gown. And for almost two hundred years that *niggun* and those words have continued to grace the weddings of the Jewish People.

As Reb Fishel compared his plight with Leib Blecher's, he began to feel that somehow, with only seven weeks left until the wedding, he, too, would find a solution.

S EVEN THOUSAND miles away and worlds apart, Peretz Weiss was facing the crisis of his life. His *eishes chayil*, Etta, had been diagnosed as suffering from a medical condition he couldn't even pronounce, much less understand. The doctors at the Cleveland Clinic said hers was a serious kidney disorder, and even a transplant wouldn't help. They had done all they could, apparently without success. The only thing left to do was pray.

Shattered, Peretz groped his way out of the quiet, climate-controlled atmosphere of the Clinic and returned home to Cleveland Heights to take stock. For years, this section of Cleveland had been as much a part of his life as the house they lived in. Peretz knew every shop and shopkeeper in the area, and they knew him. But now he could not bask in the warm, friendly atmosphere of the neighborhood; for the first time in his life he felt all alone.

Peretz telephoned his son in Detroit. "I'm afraid there's no news."

"Can't the doctors do something?" his son implored.

"They claim they've tried everything."

"What do we do now?"

"Pray."

BACK IN JERUSALEM, Reb Fishel's predicament had also gone from bad to worse. During the last few weeks, he had attempted to take on a second job as a tour guide for religious Americans. But his poor command of both the language and the city made it difficult, if not impossible, to attract business. So when he wasn't peddling, he spent hours saying *Tehillim* and waiting for tourists who never came.

Once this sideline bottomed out, so did his pride. In desperation, he approached his friends, hoping against hope that they could lend him the money he needed. But he got nowhere:

"I'm sorry, Fishel. But my daughter is also engaged."

"Try me after *Yom Tov*."

"Fishel, please take 10 shekels. Believe me, if I had money, so would you. But I'm afraid this is the most I can offer and still be able to put food on my table."

So many friends. So many excuses. "There must be a connection between *nissuin* [marriage] and *nissayon* [trial] even though they're spelled differently," Reb Fishel thought to himself with renewed determination.

ONE DAY, as Reb Fishel was dragging his pushcart down Rechov Malchei Yisrael, he passed the tall, formidable building that housed the Radiner Yeshiva. He surveyed the tinted glass windows, the inlaid wood doors, and the bright, metallic lettering. Closer up he noticed a plaque. THIS BUILDING DONATED IN MEMORY OF ROSE AND HERSHEL KRAMER, BY ALAN AND ELAINE KRAMER, LOS ANGELES, CALIFORNIA, 1981.

Reb Fishel was impressed. "Those Americans sure must have a lot of money if they can afford to give so much away," he mumbled. Then it struck him. "If *yeshivos* can get so much money long-distance, why can't I?"

Reb Fishel boldly strode into the Radiner Yeshiva. Its modern halls and clean classrooms were a far cry from the *cheder* he had known as a child. Just after the stairs he found the administrative offices. They were crammed with papers, files, typewriters, desks, and behind them all, one administrative secretary who looked busy.

"Excuse me," Reb Fishel began apologetically. "I have a problem. Maybe your yeshiva could help me."

"We have night classes open to the public," the secretary replied officiously. "But as for room, I'm afraid our dormitories are full."

"No, no. You see, my daughter is getting married and I heard that America is the land of the rich!"

"Actually, I think it's the 'land of the free.'"

"Well, in any case, I thought perhaps I could, um, write to some of your supporters. Maybe they would like to share in the mitzva of *hachnassas kallah*."

SEEING FISHEL'S earnest expression, the secretary quickly swallowed her smile. Now, she thought, she had heard and seen everything.

She marvelled at the simple peddler and his simplistic ideas. How could he understand that despite its apparent vitality, the yeshiva was still hundreds of thousands of shekels in debt? To make ends come close (if not actually meet), a sophisticated public relations agency was hired, extensive mailing lists were generated, hundreds of people were called. Yet donations still fell dishearteningly short of expenses. *Nebbach*, this shlepper thought a few letters was all it took to pay for a wedding!

"I'm sorry," she said, returning to the matter at hand. "I can't give out that information."

"But you must help," he implored. "My daughter wants to get married in a month. If I could just have the names of a few donors, I'm sure it wouldn't take away from the yeshiva. PLEASE!"

But rules were rules. The secretary looked around her cluttered cubbyhole for a way to get rid of the aspiring fundraiser. Suddenly, she spotted a receipt to be mailed that day to Peretz Weiss for the sum of $5. Every year, she remembered with disdain, she sent the same thank-you letter to this Weiss fellow for the same measly $5. A mischievous idea flashed in her head.

"Listen," she said, scribbling Weiss' address on a scrap of paper, "I'll give you the name of one of our primary benefactors. But please don't mention our yeshiva or I could get in trouble."

"Thank you! Thank you!" Reb Fishel was overcome with gratitude. He clutched the paper in his hand, confident that Hashem had answered his prayers. This was going to work. It had to.

That evening, Reb Fishel wrote a letter sure to solve his problem:

ב״ה

Dear Mister Weiss,

I be pedlar very humbel Jerusalemi. If God wants my dawter only, gets marryed next mont. To pay for a weding simpel, and help her make hous, I need shegel 11,260. Bless God with saving I have shegel 584. So far.

With Honor,

Fishel ben Zev Chaim

If you come Jerusalem, you should come.

Bais Yakov Hayashan

Bais Yisroel, Jerusalem
Tuesday, 6:00, 21 Sivan

PERETZ WEISS was desperate. The next forty-eight hours would reveal whether the doctor's grim prognosis was accurate. As he nervously paced back and forth, first in his wife's room, then in the crowded corridors outside, he lost all touch with reality. His only focus was Etta and her health.

"Ribbono Shel Olam!" he prayed, "Master of Creation! My wife and I have tried to fulfill the *mitzvos*. We have raised our two sons to follow Your Torah. We have endeavored to help others wherever we could. Please grant us Your blessings so we can continue to serve You in good health. Without my wife, I am nothing. Please, please, the doctors have done all they can. Now it is Your turn!"

As an incentive, so to speak, he made a vow: "If the Almighty will heal my wife, I will personally perform the next mitzva that comes my way, no matter what!"

Over and over again, Peretz sent his silent prayer aloft with whatever *Tehillim* he knew by heart. But his wife's condition remained critical.

In the wee hours of the morning he finally left Etta's bedside and drove home. Too tense to sleep and too exhausted to stay awake, he nervously rifled through the mail. There among the newspapers, bills, and supermarket flyers was a personal letter from Israel. "What could this be?" he thought.

Peretz ripped open the envelope and stared at its handwritten contents. The spelling was atrocious, the handwriting even worse. But Reb Fishel's message came across loud and clear: "Send *gelt*, and plenty of it."

Peretz made some quick mental calculations. "10,676 shekels is around $6,200. Who in his right mind would ask a total stranger for that kind of money?"

He put the letter down, only to pick it up once more. "It must be some sort of joke. I certainly don't have that kind of cash... although I could take out a loan on my house. Nah, this con artist probably sent out hundreds of letters. I'll just throw it out, with the rest of the garbage."

Then it hit him. All day long, he'd been asking God for a chance to save his wife. Maybe this was it. But how could he tell?

Again and again, he examined the letter. He looked at the return address, but didn't recognize the street. He studied the writing. It certainly didn't look like any professional solicitation mail he had ever received before. Finally, he read the postscript scrawled on the bottom: "If you come Jerusalem, you should come." No one says that unless he means it.

The next morning, Peretz ran to the hospital to see if there had been any change. There hadn't. Pulling a chair up close beside her bed Peretz quietly told his wife about his solemn promise and the strange letter.

She smiled weakly. "His timing was good. But I don't think we can afford it."

"You're probably right. It was just interesting, that's all."

REB FISHEL was also doing some praying of his own. Ten days had passed, and still no reply to his letter. Elishevah was more nervous than, appropriately enough, a bride on her wedding day.

"What are we going to do?" she demanded of her father. "People keep asking me about the wedding."

"It took four hundred years to get the Jews out of Egypt; it took forty years to get them out of the desert. From a historical perspective I don't think it's asking too much to wait a few more days. If we don't get an answer by the tenth of Sivan, we'll just have to postpone the wedding."

"Postpone it? We can't do that! I've already told people."

"So? You can tell them again. I won't spend money I don't have! I wrote this man in America exactly how much I need. He's probably just looking for his checkbook, that's all."

"I hope he finds it quickly and doesn't have to start looking for a pen."

PERETZ WEISS stood on line in his bank, waiting to meet with the loan manager. "It doesn't cost anything to apply," he rationalized to himself. "Who knows? Maybe I'm not even eligible."

When the manager heard Peretz's story, he offered his unsolicited professional opinion. "Don't be a fool! How do you know the letter is real? And even if it is, why give him everything? The guy probably mailed the same letter to a hundred people. If I were you, I'd send him a couple of bucks and be done with it!"

"You're probably right. But give me the loan, and I'll decide later."

Two days later, Peretz received a bank check. His wife's condition hadn't changed. That was the good news. The bad news was that Reb Fishel's wedding was getting closer and closer. Peretz was gripped with fear. "What if the manager was right? What if someone else sends him the money first? Then I'll miss out. I'd better hurry!"

With trembling fingers he made out a personal check; then he tore it up. "How can I do this?" he asked himself in disbelief. "I'm mailing $6,200 to a man I don't even know!"

Peretz paced around the house trying to think clearly, but the image of his ailing wife kept running through his mind. He stopped in his tracks, came to a decision and wrote out a check. As he was sealing the envelope the telephone rang.

"Mr. Weiss?" It was Etta's doctor. "Mr. Weiss, do you believe in miracles?"

"I don't know. Why? Has something happened?"

"According to the latest x-rays, your wife's enlarged kidney shows marked improvement. She's not out of the woods yet, but you could say we've seen a miracle!"

THE TENTH OF SIVAN dawned bright and sunny over the Jerusalem hills. This was the day Reb Fishel had decided was the deadline. No money, no wedding.

Anxious Elishevah and her frantic father thought the mail would never come. And when it finally did, bringing only a telephone bill and an appeal for a local orphanage, they were heartbroken.

"Well, at least we know what the Lord wants," Reb Fishel said quietly. "You'd better tell your *chassan* there's been a change in plans. Then we have a lot more people to inform. If Pinchas is willing to wait, well and good. If not..."

Elishevah left the apartment in tears. As she slowly walked up Rechov Chaim Ozer, a messenger stopped her.

"Do you know where Fishel Lifshitz lives?"

"Yes... why do you need to know?"

"I've been walking up and down this street for ten minutes. How's anybody supposed to find this place? Is it underground?"

"As a matter of fact..." Elishevah began. "What's the problem?"

"I have a mailgram for Fishel Lifshitz."

"I'm his daughter. I'll take it."

With shaking hands, she brought home the envelope, bearing a money order for exactly $6,200.

Heard from: Rabbi Aharon Feld

Diamond in the Rough

LEIBISH GOTTESMAN and Solomon Friedman walked out of the Diamond Dealer's Club at 30 West 47th Street and headed up the block to a modest restaurant. Along the way they exchanged tidbits in the *lingua franca* of the diamond trade.

The two prosperous dealers took their seats and Leibish continued to press his claim that diamonds should be certificated to protect against the falling dollar. But when the meal arrived, Solomon raised his hand to end the conversation. "A good lechau shouldn't be spoiled by business talk. Besides," he went on as the waiter filled their glasses with water, "today is the holy Baruch Mordechai's *yahrzeit*."

"Ahh," responded Leibish nodding his head, "Baruch Mordechai the water carrier."

"Better known as 'the Nistar,'" Solomon corrected as he prepared to recount the story. He knew Leibish was familiar with the tale, but it was a story that could be repeated over and over again and still one never tired of hearing it. Or at least Solomon never tired of telling it.

Baruch Mordechai, Solomon hastened to point out, was his ancestor. And although the diamantaire was a descendant of a distinguished Hungarian family, he considered "the Nistar" his most famed precursor.

W HEN BARUCH MORDECHAI was a youngster, he received a blessing from the Chassam Sofer. The precise content of the sage's benediction was a guarded secret, but it was known that his words were intended to protect the child from the temptations of pride. No one, however, could have imagined this to be the child's problem. Pride was the least of young Baruch Mordechai's worries.

The boy appeared to be a pious fool. All day long he would sit with a *sefer* in front of him — whatever was open or was placed before him — and mouth the words with a blank look of incomprehension on his face.

To the children of Baruch Mordechai's shtetl, the boy was the subject of mockery and the target of pranks, destined to be the village idiot. To the elders, Baruch Mordechai was a pitiful lad who they feared would never wed. But these conclusions were premature.

While Baruch Mordechai was still a child, Solomon recalled, a ferocious fire burned his family's house to the ground along with everything they owned. As simple as Baruch Mordechai may have been, he was wise enough to realize he had no future in that village. He approached the Ksav Sofer for advice and was advised to travel to the Land of Israel.

"**S**OLOMON, my friend," Leibish interrupted, "I know this story, and you know I do. I know every comma and exclamation point and every place you pause for effect. Let's just eat our goulash and mamaliga quietly and pretend you related the tale in its entirety. How's that?"

"Leibish, I'm surprised at you," his companion said in mock rebuke. "Surely you know me well enough to assume there is a point I wish to make. Retelling my favorite story is only the means to an end."

"Couldn't we skip ahead to the end now?"

"What's your rush, my impatient friend? There's plenty of time until the palatchinkas are served." And with that, Solomon went on with his tale.

A WEALTHY RELATIVE offered to help Baruch Mordechai's family in its plight. He lent them a large sum of money and underwrote the boy's journey to *Eretz Yisrael*. The journey was eventful and difficult, culminating with Baruch Mordechai's late-night arrival in Jerusalem. All that night and most of the next day he wandered through the streets of the Holy City, his wide eyes staring vacantly at the strange sights arranged before him. A merchant finally noticed this gentle youngster and, out of curiosity as much as kindness, welcomed him into his home. The host was impressed by Baruch Mordechai's outstanding piety but equally baffled by the boy's simplemindedness and ignorance.

To earn his keep, Baruch Mordechai accepted a job as a *shamash* in a shul. The simple work seemed custom-made for the boy, whose quiet kindliness slowly captured the hearts and the sympathy of the Jerusalemites. But after years of placing *sefarim* and *siddurim* on the shelves and straightening out the chairs, Baruch Mordechai elected to switch professions and become a water carrier. This way, he figured, he would be able to devote more time to Torah study, which for him consisted of mouthing words over an open *sefer*.

To the consternation of all, Baruch Mordechai had engaged in this meaningless exercise for as long as they had known him. The words of Torah would forever elude this pitiful ignoramus, they said, and many wondered what motivated him to while away hours feigning Torah study.

O NE PIOUS JERUSALEMITE, however, had somehow gotten a different impression. One Purim after Baruch Mordechai had consumed enough wine to drop his defenses, this old man called him to deliver a *shiur* before everyone present.

The hundreds assembled were convinced that this was intended as a Purim stunt, although some felt it was in poor taste and out of character for the elder who had initiated the request. To hear Baruch Mordechai mumble disjointed Talmudic verses in utter imbecility would surely be amusing, but it would just as surely embarrass the water carrier needlessly.

Yet to everyone's amazement, the young man rose to the occasion, delivering a dazzling *shiur* that impressed all the accomplished scholars of the city and left the rank and file with their jaws gaping and their eyes bulging in disbelief.

Baruch Mordechai was no simpleton after all, but an

erudite scholar with a genius for concealing his knowledge. His whole life had been a fulfillment of the Ksav Sofer's blessing, but it was to end in remorse the moment he became sober and realized what he had revealed.

Not long after that fateful Purim, Baruch Mordechai's holy soul was summoned to the Heavenly Academy. The *mekubalim* of Jerusalem convened and determined that he was one of the thirty-six righteous individuals whose piety supports the world.

"**T**HIS is what we are missing today," Solomon concluded, returning to his lechau with gusto. "*Nistarim*. We don't have the secret righteous anymore. These days everything is Madison Avenue, showy and chintzy. Even our *tzaddikim* are not as anonymous as they used to be."

He looked up at Leibish for a sign of agreement, but his colleague shook his head slowly. "Solomon," Leibish said with the utmost gravity, "I know a *nistar* today, a genuine *nistar*."

"Ah c'mon," Solomon chided him, "then you weren't listening to my story."

"But I was," Leibish waved his fork in protest. "In fact, it was only upon hearing you describe Baruch Mordechai working as a *shamash* that I realized. A genuine *nistar*, I tell you."

"Nu, so which yeshiva is he in?" Solomon questioned with perked interest.

"He's, well, er, a janitor."

"A what?"

"A janitor. In a shul in Crown Heights. He doesn't even know me, but I have kept my eye on him for the last few years, and there is no mistake about it. The man is a bona fide *nistar*.

"He looks and acts like some executive, not like the *nebbach* type at all. Even the most degrading tasks he performs with care and dignity. Watching him take out the garbage, mop the floor, clean off the tables, and so on, it's... it's like watching the *kohen gadol* perform the *avodah* in the *Beis Hamikdash*.

"You would imagine that a person in charge of replacing all the *sefarim* would stack them up in a rush and then thrust them onto their shelves. Not Mendel the janitor. He lovingly lifts up every *siddur* and *sefer* and gently plants a kiss on each one before returning it to its spot.

"I have never seen or heard of a janitor with such respect for what men are doing in the *beis midrash*. If someone is learning, Mendel cleans around him so as not to disturb him. And if you have ever been in a shul or *beis midrash* when people are cleaning up, you know that their outstanding trait is usually not *kavod haTorah*."

"**F**UNNY you should say that," Solomon responded, "because come to think of it, I know a *nistar*, too. There is a guy who has a cleaning service in my neighborhood and is even more pious. He cleans about ten homes on my block and every week another story circulates about the man's righteousness.

"Just this week my neighbor Feinberg reported that when Mendel — funny, he has the same name — was vacuuming under their couch he found a notebook with the name 'Bruchie Feinberg' written on the cover. He examined the pad and noticed that it also said '*Halacha,* Rabbi Bernstein, Tues. 7:30-8:45'. It was already a quarter to eight. Obviously, Mendel concluded, Bruchie had lost her notebook behind the couch and gone to class without it. How would she take notes that night? he wondered. No one was home but Mendel was so worried that he ran the seven blocks to the school in the freezing cold. Then, since it was an evening seminary for women, he didn't want to walk in and waited outside until he found a student who promised to deliver the notebook to its owner right away.

"And this," Solomon continued, "is a mere drop in the bucket. Nothing Mendel finds — no matter how small — goes unreturned or unrepaired. He never even mentions it to his employers.

"The most amazing thing," Solomon emphasized, "is that this is a real intelligent guy. He's not an immigrant like you or me. From the looks of him, he could have a seat on the stock market, yet he is going around cleaning houses."

BUT LEIBISH was unimpressed. "If I were to tell you some of the things my Mendel does in the shul," Leibish countered, "you would see that I am talking about a man far more pious than yours."

"Then I haven't done him justice," Solomon responded. "I observe Mendel first-hand on a weekly basis when he cleans our home. I'm telling you, the man has walked straight out of *Pirke Avos.* Why, my Mendel..." Solomon stopped short and gave a robust laugh. "I started this discussion by bewailing the dearth of *nistarim* today. Now it seems we've got too many. But if your Mendel is what you say he is, I would be very anxious to meet him. Just tell me when is the next time I can get a glimpse of him working at the shul and I'll take a ride over."

"The same goes for me," Leibish echoed. "Let me know when there is something worth seeing by you and I'll be right over."

On that note, the two diamond dealers shook hands, recited the proverbial "*mazel und bracha,*" and parted company.

"**H**ELLO LEIBISH? This is Solomon. Listen, Mendel is just finishing cleaning up over here, and he told me he has to leave soon *for Crown Heights.* I think we've solved the Mendel mystery."

"It's the same Mendel?!" Leibish asked incredulously.

"Listen, I want you to come over here right now and offer him a ride so we can find out a little about him." The enthusiasm in Solomon's voice betrayed his appetite for detective work.

The eagerness was shared by his friend, who didn't need any more encouragement to jump into his car and head off to Boro Park. In less than half an hour, Leibish pulled up in front of Solomon's house, where his fellow sleuth was busy stalling an unsuspecting Mendel.

"Leibish!" Solomon called out in pseudo-astonishment.

"What a surprise! Where are you headed?"

"Crown Heights."

"Perfect," Solomon responded, "got room for two?"

"Of course, come on in."

"Are you sure it's O.K.?" Mendel whispered to Solomon as they climbed into the car.

"No problem," Solomon assured him. "Leibish, I would like you to meet Mendel, eh... pardon me," he said, turning to his cleanup man, "what's your last name?"

"Shreiber."

"Nice to meet you. Where can I drop you in Crown Heights?" Leibish asked Mendel innocently.

"Please don't go out of your way," Mendel demurred. "Anywhere near Kensington and Empire is just fine."

"The shul there?"

"That's right."

Leibish caught Solomon's eye in the rearview mirror and he turned back to Mendel.

"I thought I'd seen you around there."

"I'm the janitor," Mendel offered, saving his driver the embarrassment of asking the next question. "The shul is very good to me: I hold down several jobs, so they let me make my own hours."

"This isn't exactly the safest time of day to be travelling to Crown Heights," Solomon interrupted. "Couldn't you go earlier?"

"I wish," Mendel replied, "but I don't have any other time. In fact," he added, his voice now almost a whisper,

"I have yet another job to get to when this is over."

Leibish and Solomon exchanged looks of bewilderment. "Where do you go from here?" Leibish asked.

"I work a night shift at a printing press in Lower Manhattan."

"Manhattan?!" they both chimed in. "Without a car?"

"I only have to change trains once," Mendel shrugged.

BY THIS POINT both Solomon and Leibish were bursting with curiosity, but they did not want to offend Mendel by asking the wrong thing. In the back of their minds they were also beginning to wonder if their "*nistar*" wasn't more than a little bit eccentric. Or at least unhealthily hooked on working his way to earning a fortune.

Solomon figured that sticking to small talk would be the best tactic for discovering more about the mysterious man. "If you work the night shift," he began, "I imagine you don't get up until early in the afternoon."

"I have to be at work at nine," Mendel corrected. "I also like to get up before *davening* to learn a little with my boys before they leave for *yeshiva*."

"Where do you work?" Solomon prodded.

"An accounting firm in downtown Brooklyn."

"Also janitorial work?" Solomon blurted out, unable to conceal his fascination.

"I'm a CPA," Mendel answered barely audibly.

BY NOW Leibish had grown impatient with Solomon's indirect line of questioning. He feared the car ride would be over before they learned the secret of Mendel Shreiber. Something was really askew. Here was an obviously intelligent man — a CPA no less — doing the most menial and debasing jobs in addition to his normal profession. Leibish was itching to ask him straight out what obsessed him to work so hard, but before he could articulate the question Solomon inquired which yeshiva Mendel's boys attended.

"B'nei Dovid," responded the CPA, also printer, also janitor.

"Your son isn't Shaya Shreiber, is he?" Leibish asked in amazement.

Mendel nodded.

Leibish was suddenly very choked up. "Mendel here is the father of one of the next *gedolim*," he told Solomon solemnly. "My boys learn in B'nei Dovid and they say that in *middos* Shaya is probably already one of the *gedolei hador*, and in learning he is possibly two *decades* beyond his age.

"As a matter of fact," Leibish added, remembering an obscure detail, "they say his younger brother, who learns somewhere out of town, is even more advanced than Shaya."

Mendel's only comment was a semi-silent *"Baruch Hashem."*

SOLOMON SAT BACK and began to take stock. "Mendel, I never knew you had such illustrious children. Maybe you're related then to this famous Chanie

Shreiber, the one who directs the Jewish Education Network in Boro Park."

Mendel's silence spoke for itself.

"I can't believe it," Solomon exclaimed. "Chanie Shreiber is a household word. My daughters talk about her and quote her all day and night." Another barely audible "*Baruch Hashem*" could be heard.

Leibish could no longer contain himself. "Stop the car," he ordered impulsively. Solomon complied. "Mendel, eh, Reb Mendel, you owe us an explanation. You have the most beautiful and illustrious children, absolute prodigies, *bli eyen hara*, and you are a CPA, yet you spend the majority of your day cleaning out washrooms. What is it that's driving you? Are you worried you won't be able to provide a big enough dowry for your children?"

Mendel desperately turned to Solomon for support but his would-be protector didn't come to his defense. He was looking just as mystified as Leibish.

"*Rabosai,*" Mendel glanced awkwardly at the floor, "I don't like speaking about myself. However, since you insist, I will explain. I only beg you to keep driving, lest I be late for work."

Mendel's request was honored and the car resumed its journey. Mendel took a deep breath and plunged into the past:

"**F**OUR YEARS AGO we were living a relatively comfortable life in Flatbush, where we owned a large home. I was a partner in the same accounting firm I work for today. I always felt that if I could find a way to work shorter hours without earning less, I would be able to spend more time learning. The idea was very appealing to me and I pursued it.

"My plan was to purchase some kind of business that would require minimal involvement on my behalf but turn a handsome profit. I discovered much too late that such enterprises only exist in fantasies.

"Anyway, before I knew it, I had borrowed over a quarter of a million dollars to cover the purchase of candle-making machinery and installation in the basement of my home. My calculation was very simple: candles are something we always use for Shabbos, *Yom Tov*, and *yahrzeits*, and only three candle manufacturers cater to the religious market.

"One of these three was retiring and offered to sell his equipment to me for a 'steal.' I figured that without overhead, since I could house the entire operation in my basement, I could really run an efficient operation.

"Wisely, I didn't abandon my position in my partnership to begin this endeavor, but that is where my wisdom ended. My naiveté was incredible. I had believed the fellow who sold me his equipment when he told me that he was retiring from this line because he was 'past it.' It never occurred to me that the only thing that was obsolete was his machinery.

"I ended up buying a quarter of a million dollars worth of antiquated, uncompetitive junk. The other two candle manufacturers had modern equipment that could produce a dozen candles cheaper than I could produce one. I was stuck.

"Several friends and store owners learned of my plight and offered to place sizeable orders, but I wouldn't allow it.

Why should they spend more than the going rate merely because I was foolhardy?

"**T**HANK GOD I was able to unload the machinery. I only received a mere fraction of what I paid for it, but at least it was out of my house and no longer haunting us, unlike my gargantuan debt.

"I had borrowed a fortune — and that was after I had exhausted all my own personal resources in the enterprise. With about two months to pay off the debt and no savings left, I sadly sold our lovely home to the highest bidder and rented a cramped apartment for my family. But I was still shy the lion's share of the money and I was running out of time. I finally had no choice but to take out a loan to pay off my earlier debts. And since it's only permissible to borrow money when you know you'll be able to pay it back on time, I was in a predicament. I therefore took on as many extra jobs as I could to enable myself to take out additional loans. I had no other choice. I still have a long way to go, but every year I see the debt diminishing."

"One second," Solomon interrupted in disbelief, "I don't understand. You certainly had other options. You could have asked your creditors for an extension..."

"You could have declared bankruptcy," Leibish offered.

"Pushed them off or delayed them," Solomon continued. "You might have even considered leaving town for a little while until things quieted down."

Mendel waved his hands in revulsion. "All these ideas and many more were suggested to me, but I never considered a single one of them. I borrowed the money and I am obliged to pay it back. If it means mopping floors, and emptying garbage, so be it."

Leibish pulled up in front of the shul, and Mendel reached down to open the car door. "You know, I thought it would be hard for me, that I would feel ashamed to do this type of work. But strangely enough, when I remember why I'm doing it, I feel blessed. I never felt prouder in my life. Thanks for the ride."

As Leibish swung the car around in front of the shul to drive Solomon back home, he let out a prolonged sigh. "Maybe he *is* a *nistar*, but it sure seems hard on him."

"I don't know about that," Solomon mused aloud. "With such exceptionally fine children you can't help but feel that God is rewarding him for his integrity with a very special blessing. And I can't think of many other full-time CPAs that match him for genuine dignity and pride."

They both instinctively turned to throw a glance at the shul before driving back to Boro Park. The two merchants fell silent with awe and admiration as they watched Mendel Shreiber through the window of the shul begin sweeping the floor with his back upright and his head held high.

Heard from: Rabbi Yaakov Hopfer

Balance Sheet

Months	Chessed	Teshuvah	Torah	Tefillah	Tzeddakah	Aveiros
Tishrei Cheshvan						
Kislev Teves			**Sound Investment**			
Shevat Adar						
Nissan Iyyar						
Sivan Tammuz						
Av Ellul						
					Prepared by	Index No.
					Date	

❀

וכמה שנואה ומגונה מדה זו לפני הקב״ה
שמסלקנו עבור זה מעל פניו כמו שנאמר לא
ישב בקרב ביתי עושה רמיה.

שפת תמים פרק א'

Fraud is so odious and despicable to
the Holy One, blessed be He, that God
casts out the offender from before
Him, as it says, ''He may not dwell in
my home, one who defrauds.''

Sfas Tamim: 1

Payday

HOME OF THE SHLAH and the Pnei Yehoshua, Frankfurt am Main was, until the beginning of the nineteenth century, a city abounding in Torah learning and fear of Heaven. But just one decade later, the fumes of the so-called "Enlightenment" began to drift west from Berlin. Taking their cue from the French Revolution, Enlightenment agitators worked with the government to tear down the Jewish ghetto's figurative walls.

By 1818, the Jews were granted so much equality that German law forbade the public dissemination of Torah knowledge. All religious teachers were banished from the city along with the local phrenologists and all the other Neanderthals, and a fifty-gulden fine was levied against anyone superstitious enough to support Torah study. The *chevra kadisha*, which insisted on perpetuating archaic Jewish burial ritual, was dissolved, synagogue upkeep was curtailed, and the local *mikvaos* were either destroyed or drained. All the funds donated by the Rothschild family for religious institutions were transferred to the silk-gloved hands of the Reform.

As in the days of Rabi Akiva, the Torah faithful had to go underground. Indeed, the lot of religious Jewry in Frankfurt am Main had become so bleak that desperate measures were called for. The community acted wisely in beseeching the Chief Rabbi of Moravia to leave his prestigious position in Nikolsberg. They could never match the honor, acclaim, or salary that Rabbi Samson Raphael Hirsch enjoyed there, but they presented the Rabbi with a mission that he — and the entire generation — could not afford to refuse.

FROM THE DAY he arrived, Rav Samson Raphael Hirsch became a champion of the Orthodox cause. On every issue, he provided an undaunted, eloquent challenge to the Reform authorities and their government supporters who threatened religious life in the area. Rav Samson Raphael was able to nab the wily foxes and torch them by their tails.

Playing on the country's preference for separating church and state — which Bismark had just accomplished regarding the Catholic Church — Rabbi Hirsch fought tirelessly to emancipate the Orthodox from the shackles of the tyrannically secular Jewish governing body.

Autonomy was finally achieved, and Rav Samson Raphael Hirsch wasted no time establishing a new school system under his personal direction, based on the dictum of *"Torah im derech eretz."* Perceiving the needs of the hour, Rav Hirsch boldly constructed a curriculum steeped in Torah but nonetheless acceptable to those seeking a secular education for their children. This left him with the enormous task of convincing the embattled community to send their children to his brave new school, and to support it financially.

Since his arrival in Frankfurt am Main Rabbi Samson Raphael had been under tight public scrutiny, but that paled next to the inquisitions he was now subjected to. Rabbi Hirsch weathered the suspicious probes, however, and not a stitch of *shatnes* was found when he was slid under the microscope.

FRANKFURT JEWRY found him knowledgeable in every area of Torah. And just as he was able to analyze esoteric matters with scientists and secular scholars, he was equally comfortable assuaging the concerns of the laymen.

People were taken by the giant's gentle manner. He never scolded any of his *baalei battim* or reproached a pupil in public. He was a fighter and a revolutionary, yet he had the demeanor of a gentleman. Every day he could be seen spreading crumbs outside his window for the hungry sparrows of the Rhineland.

Above all, the community was impressed by the scholar's integrity. Some initially wondered why this foreign upstart had insisted on personally collecting the funds for his projects. Their theories were not especially complimentary to the Rabbi. But once the townsfolk had occasion to meet Rabbina Hirsch and to attend his classes, they realized how baseless their accusations were.

Nonetheless, Rabbi Hirsch was forever concerned about his appearance in the public eye. His personal conduct and manner were a *kiddush Hashem* of grand proportions. In his interpersonal relations and his performance of *mitzvos* between man and his Creator, every action was considered and calculated. Rav Samson Raphael's salary was paid by the Orthodox community and he considered himself accountable to them for his wages. Accountants were stunned by his meticulous recording of every expense and outlay of what he deemed communal funds.

AS THE VENERABLE RABBI GREW OLDER, one financial concern was particularly on his mind. His annual salary was paid in full on the first of the secular year. In his typical piety, Rabbi Hirsch feared that he might die during the course of the year, leaving "unearned" communal money in his family's hands. He therefore took several measures to ensure that his passing would not result in what he considered unfair gains for his heirs.

From Rav Samson Raphael Hirsch's perspective, this anxiety was understandable. Despite his incredible humility, he realized what he had accomplished during his lifetime. He had single-handedly effected a revolution and a renaissance of religious Jewry in Frankfurt and throughout Germany. As the father of neo-Orthodoxy his commentaries and responsa would be studied reverently for generations to come. After bringing so much *nachas* to his Maker and so much good to his People, he did not want his good name sullied by the slightest tarnish.

His sincerity did not go unrewarded. On the 27th of Teves, the final day of the secular calendar, his holy soul was summoned to the Heavenly assembly, *December 31, 1888.*

Heard from: Rabbi Shimon Schwab

A Joint Effort

AMONG THE SPIRITUAL giants of Chassidus, Rabbi Menachem Mendel of Kotzk was a colossus. A saint with no tolerance for pretense, he could bore through the depths of another's soul with only a look, or a few words.

The Kotzker Rebbe was totally removed from and unaffected by the world of the mundane, yet he was intricately involved in daily life and the goings on around him. He constantly sought to make peace between man and his fellow man, and between the Children of Israel and their Father in Heaven.

If, for any reason, a chassid was unable to reach that understanding by his own efforts, the Kotzker would nudge him toward reconciliation with one of his pithy sayings, which combined profound insight with a sober dose of reality. "Where does the Creator live?" he once asked. "Wherever he is admitted. This is even true of an earthly king," he continued. "When garbage blocks the gates of his palace, he is unwilling to enter."

The Kotzker also said, "Some people wear their faith like an overcoat, warming only themselves. But some light a fire with their *emunah* and also warm others." "Man is born with jealousy," began another adage, "but desire is a matter of habit. My hope is that you don't sin, not because it is forbidden, but because there isn't enough time."

R ABBI MENACHEM MENDEL MORGENSTERN OF KOTZK resisted the mantle of leadership. But with the passing of the legendary Reb Simcha Bunim of P'shyscha, it fell upon him, along with the responsibility for the spiritual lives of thousands of chassidim.

One of his most renowned protégés was Reb Yitzchak Meir of Ger, author of the "Chiddushei Harim" and founder of the Gerrer dynasty. With the Chiddushei Harim, his grandson, Reb Yehuda Aryeh, author of the "Sfas Emmes," and his son, Reb Avraham Mordechai, the "Imrei Emmes," Ger established a burgeoning bastion of Torah that flourishes to this day.

Among Reb Avraham Mordechai's contemporaries in Poland was another spiritual heir. Revered and respected by chassid and *misnagid* alike, the Amshenover Rebbe, Reb Yaakov Dovid Kalish, led his devotees to dizzying heights of piety and purity in the years prior to World War II.

Like the Amshenover Rebbes before and after him, Reb Yaakov Dovid was a disciple of the Kotzker Rebbe in his steadfast commitment to *emmes*. Truth sprouted forth from Kotzk, the chassidim say, and it took firm root in Amshenov.

LIKE THE GERRER REBBE and other *gedolei Torah*, the Amshenover Rebbe heard and felt the rumblings of a "new world order." But rather than escaping from Poland and leaving his flock behind, the Amshenover decided to stay. Some of his more prominent and affluent chassidim urged him to flee while he still could, but the Rebbe declined. "If I go," he thought selflessly, "who will take care of those that stay?"

No, the Amshenover Rebbe would not abandon his community. Late one night, as the Amshenover *beis midrash* was still brimming with chassidim learning, *davening,* and exchanging words of wisdom, Reb Yaakov Dovid took his uncle and brother aside and charged them with a mission: "As you know, the Amshenover dynasty was born in the *beis midrash* of Reb Simcha Bunim and the Kotzker. Since then it has moved from place to place, nurturing new generations of chassidim. Whatever the future has in store, you must not let the vile marauders stamp out this precious legacy. Wherever the Lord leads you, reestablish the Amshenover court."

Stirred by Reb Yaakov Dovid's plea, uncle and nephew expeditiously prepared for their task by joining up with the Mirrer Yeshiva situated in Vilna. From this city they would begin their incredible trek across Siberia to Japan and later Shanghai, straying far from the madness of Europe.

At each leg of the journey, young Reb Yitzkl contemplated the challenge looming before him. As he crossed the Sea of Japan, everything seemed to come into focus: true, the motley masses pressed together on the old tramp steamer were just a speck of humanity adrift in a sea of darkness, yet these survivors would dazzle the world with their Torah and their deeds. What lay ahead they did not know, but they would never forget where they had come from, and what they had left behind.

As he watched the black waters of the ocean recede behind the boat, Reb Yitzkl's thoughts harked back to the men of his *shtiebel*. There was "Yossel *der Shneider*," a tailor by profession. Before performing any mitzva, Yossel would rub his hands together with the joy and anticipation of a starving man about to partake of a feast. There was "Nosson *der Bakker*," who owned the local bakery; he would celebrate his birthday by distributing bread to all those in need. And "Michoel *der Malach*," an angelic fellow, who seemed to prefer fasting over eating. Each member of the *minyan* had a disparate personality, and his fate — like that of Reb Yitzkl's uncle, who also remained behind — was probably being sealed as he sailed. Suddenly, he recalled the thick envelope, probably this vanishing community's only hope for a memorial.

E VERY DAY Reb Yitzkl would look at the envelope entrusted to him and pray for the chance to discharge his duties. Somehow, he felt the Almighty would guide him to the right place at the right time. But until then, the envelope weighed heavy on his heart.

After the debacle known as World War II burned itself out, Reb Yitzkl and his uncle Reb Shimil'a made their way to the United States of America. By the time they reached the West Coast, the chassidim who preceded them had already purchased a shul and a home for Reb Shimil'a in New York.

With his nephew in tow, the "new" Amshenover Rebbe headed east to establish his court. But Reb Yitzkl was left in the lurch. How would he fulfill *his* mission and sanctify the money placed in his care by the martyrs of Amshenov? He, too, wished to found a court, and the

14,000 zlotys tucked in the tattered envelope would pay for the cornerstone of the shul he would build.

Uncle and nephew had barely arrived in New York when Reb Yitzkl set about fulfilling his commitment. As it turned out, he was shy the lion's share of the cost of building a shul, but it was a start. Nonetheless, the young Rebbe was tormented: he didn't want to just start, he wanted to finish!

Where could he get additional funds? "Try the Joint Distribution Committee," Reb Shimil'a advised. "They help refugees get started in this country."

"But they only give money to people who have nothing. Once they hear about my 14,000 zlotys, they'll assume I'm a *gvir*."

"14,000 zlotys?! That's all?" Reb Shimil'a made a quick calculation. "You're talking about just over a thousand dollars. Besides," he reminded him, "according to *Halacha*, that money isn't really yours. It belongs to the community."

"But it's my responsibility."

Reb Shimil'a thought for a minute. "If it will make you feel better," he said, "you could transfer the money, making it technically not yours before you apply for financial aid."

"Uncle," Reb Yitzkl protested, "I don't like that idea. It may not entail an outright deception, but I don't believe it's really honest. I guess the only thing to do is to present my case to the Joint and hope for the best."

Reb Shimil'a objected. "The Joint is run by Jews that are not always sympathetic to East Europeans — they won't understand! I know how important it is to you to build a shul. Don't risk what may be your only chance!"

In deference to his uncle, Reb Yitzkl nodded sheepishly. A few days later, he made an appointment at the Joint's office in Manhattan.

NEW YORK CITY in the mid-1940s was a town on the verge of an explosion. Everywhere you looked, the city showed signs of doubling in size in a very short time.

As the organization in charge of settling and subsidizing as many Jewish immigrants as possible, the Joint Distribution Committee was doing its part to help. The Joint distributed funds, arranged housing, found jobs, and provided many more services to its downtrodden wards. It was difficult work accommodating such a clientele and persuading this clientele to be accommodating. The *Europishe* Jews were not anxious to leave their mentality or appearance behind. The assimilated Jews of the Joint couldn't understand why.

Irwin Buchwald was one member of the perplexed personnel. Although he spoke Yiddish fluently, he was troubled by what the language represented. It wasn't that he disliked Jewish Jews, it was just that Americans — of any race or creed — were supposed to be clean-shaven and worldly. Obviously, religious refugees from Europe were never going to fit in.

Indeed, as far as he was concerned, it was a waste of time for them to even try. Buchwald felt it would be a lot wiser to send them off to Palestine, where they would be much happier.

ONE DAY in the autumn of 1946, Irwin Buchwald took the trolley from his home in the Eastbrook section of Queens to the subway station on Atlantic Avenue. From there he would travel to Manhattan to the Joint's headquarters at 57th and Madison. The trip was just long enough to make him anxious about his job and the people he had to deal with. "Why, I'll bet half of them are rich. They just want even more money," he muttered under his breath. "They probably came here with jewels sewn into their pockets... and expect us, the 'goyim,' to give them more."

By the time Irwin reached his office he was in a lousy mood. All morning, he would be giving away money to people he felt didn't deserve it.

One of these "unworthies" was Rabbi Yitzchak Kalish. His appointment was scheduled for 1:15, but by 2:45 he still hadn't shown up.

A funny thing happened to him on the way to the city: he was engulfed in an epidemic known as "World Series Fever."

That afternoon at Ebbets Field, the Brooklyn "Bums" and the St. Louis Browns were going to play baseball, and the outcome would determine who would win the pennant. Thus, Rabbi Kalish found his trolley station mobbed with people scurrying about, talking in small groups, and gushing with excitement.

REB YITZKL miraculously found a seat on the trolley, opened up his *sefer*, and resumed his learning. He hadn't gotten very far before the man to his left peered at him over the waxed tips of his handlebar mustache and asked urgently, "Do you know the score?"

"The score?"

"Yes. I'm anxious to know the latest score!"

"Let me think."

Reb Yitzkl wasn't sure what the gentleman meant, but he wanted to be of some help. Mentally, he began to review *Shas* and chassidishe *sefarim*. After deep concentration and prolonged cogitation he turned to his neighbor and apologized: "I'm sorry, I'm not familiar with it."

Unbeknownst to Reb Yitzkl, the young man had gotten off three stops earlier. To make matters worse, Reb Yitzkl should have, too.

Lost and confused (he still wasn't sure what the score was), Reb Yitzkl straggled to a nearby subway station. So did hundreds of jubilant Brooklyn Dodger fans.

The din was so loud that Reb Yitzkl feared he was under attack. Then he saw the smiling faces, joyous comraderie, and excited gesticulations of the throngs of men pouring onto the platform. "This must have something to do with the score," he thought to himself.

When the train came clanging down the track, he patiently waited while waves of baseball fans jammed the subway doors, filling it to capacity. But when the second stream of cars came along, the same thing happened.

IT WASN'T until all the short-sleeved spectators were well on their way home that Reb Yitzkl finally got on a subway that took him to the Joint's headquarters. He was three and a half hours late.

Back at the Joint, Irwin Buchwald had a splitting headache. He put on his sweater and mumbled something to his co-workers about going home early. As he walked out into the huge waiting room, he saw a young, frazzled Rabbi sitting quietly in the corner.

"Can I help you?" he asked.

"My name is Yitzchak Kalish. I have an appointment with Mr. Buchwald."

"My name is Buchwald. And you *had* an appointment. You're late!"

"I'm sorry... I got lost."

"I should make you come back again tomorrow."

Reb Yitzkl sighed. "If that's what you want..."

Buchwald stared at the Rabbi, then softened. "No. Follow me."

REB YITZKL obediently walked behind the brusque bureaucrat past rows of non-descript desks manned by non-descript people.

Reaching his office, the clerk collapsed into the chair behind his desk and pulled out a new file which he marked "Kalish, Isaac."

"I assume you're applying for a grant," Buchwald began matter-of-factly, preparing to rattle off his standard litany of questions and record the standard answers. "Are you currently employed?"

"No."

"Are you planning to get a job?"

"Yes."

"What kind of work do you do?"

"I am a Rabbi."

Irwin Buchwald frowned distastefully. "Another one. It seems as if everyone from Europe is a Rabbi!" he thought to himself. "Where do you live?"

"Brooklyn."

"Do you have any money?"

"Yes."

"Where were you bor..." Buchwald stopped short. He could have sworn he'd heard an affirmative reply to the money question. "Nah..." he dismissed the fleeting thought, "must be my headache."

"Number of relatives living with you?"

"Fourteen thousand, one hundred ten."

"What did you say?"

"Fourteen thousand, one hundred ten."

"You've got that many relatives?"

"No, I have that much money. Fourteen thousand, one hundred ten zlotys. I believe it comes out to $1,008.45."

"Let me get this straight. You have a thousand dollars, yet you come here asking for money?"

"No and yes."

"Don't get talmudic with me!"

"I'm not. I am simply answering your questions in the order you posed them. The money is not really mine — it's my community's. They want it used for a synagogue. I am asking for a grant on my own."

IRWIN BUCHWALD stopped his questioning. It was the first time any interviewee had ever admitted to having any money. Why was this fellow telling him this? Everyone always had money — at least something. But this Kalish Rabbi was owning up to owning a small fortune. Maybe he had done something really illegal. Or maybe he had already received a grant in the past and was looking for an alibi to explain his ill-gotten gains.

Buchwald stared at the frail man and suddenly constructed a third and infinitely more plausible scenario: maybe he was honest. Admirably honest. He could see it in his clear, earnest eyes. Momentarily moved, the bureaucrat regained his composure and reverted to type.

"If you qualify for this grant, how will you use this money?"

"As I mentioned, for a synagogue."

"And how do you plan on making a living?"

"I will be the Rabbi."

"Rabbi, there are hundreds of Rabbis and dozens of shuls!"

"But I must reestablish the Amshenov court, I..." he stammered, tears in his eyes, "I promised!"

Buchwald tried to fathom the sincere young Rabbi in front of him. "What makes you think you can succeed? Even if you do qualify for a grant — and I'm not saying you do — how are you going to make a living?"

Reb Yitzkl's clouded countenance dissolved into a

smile. "Let me tell you a story. The Kotzker Rebbe once gave the great Reb Yechiel Meir of Gostynin the honor of blowing the *shofar* on Rosh Hashanah. But try as he might, Reb Yechiel could produce only the faintest sound.

"After the prayers, the Kotzker congratulated Reb Yechiel on his accomplishment. Some thought the Rebbe was making fun of him, but the Kotzker was quick to explain by elucidating the verse 'The great *shofar* is blown, and a still, small voice is heard' — even though a small sound is heard, if a great person is behind it, the *shofar* will do its job. My uncle, Reb Yaakov Dovid of blessed memory, may the Lord avenge his death, was a great person. I am merely the still, small voice."

A shudder involuntarily swept through Irwin Buchwald's body. "Stay here," he ordered.

For the first time all day, Reb Yitzkl became worried. As Buchwald left his seat and began conferring with his colleagues, Reb Yitzkl heard Reb Shimil'a's warning ringing in his ears: "They won't understand."

He struggled to remain calm. "Amshenov had its roots in Kotzk," he reminded himself. "Kotzk had its roots in *emmes*. I cannot carry on the tradition based on a false foundation!"

He was also concerned about having so much money. "Maybe they'll want proof that the money's mine," he fretted. "Or they'll confiscate it. Or I'll have to pay some sort of tax. Maybe they'll tell me to leave, and I'll never get the funds we need."

AFTER FIFTEEN MINUTES that seemed much longer, Irwin Buchwald and about twenty co-workers marched into the office, looking very official. Reb

Yitzkl didn't know whether to run or remain. Buchwald solved the dilemma for him.

"Rabbi, you qualify for the grant."

Reb Yitzkl resumed breathing and praised the Lord out loud.

"Not only that, my friends and I would like to become the first dues-paying members of your shul. And if you don't mind, would you give us a blessing?"

Heard from: Rabbi Simcha Schustal

The Customer is Always Right

ABE WOLFSON looked up from his counter and the jeweler's loupe nearly popped out of his eye. He straightened out his jacket, fumbled for his tongue and offered, "Er... Rabbi Kamenetsky, eh, how can I help you, I mean, how can I help 'the Rabbi'?"

"Of all times for my shop to be empty," Abe muttered to himself. "Here Reb Yaakov Kamenetsky, the *Gaon* of Lithuanian Jewry, walks in, and there is no one to witness the event. They'll probably never even believe me. *Vey iz mere*, what a boon this could have been for business.

"I know," he thought in an instant, "whatever he purchases, I'll get him to sign a receipt. I'll tell him it's some kind of warranty."

While Abe was ruminating, Reb Yaakov removed a dazzlingly ornate new silver *kiddush* cup from a gift-wrapped box and placed it on the counter. Just then three customers entered Wolfson's Jewelry Shop and the proprietor's hopes of making capital out of his illustrious patron soared. But the Rabbi's cup had not yet runneth over.

The three customers went straight over to the watch display near the window and promptly engrossed themselves in microquartz technology. Wolfson tried desperately to direct their attention to the counter. When his less-than-subtle gesticulations failed, he called out loud, "I have something over here that I think you may be interested in seeing." He stood on his toes and jerked his head toward Reb Yaakov, winking so hard his eye ached. Finally, the threesome picked up the hint and crowded around the celebrity in their midst and the ebullient jeweler.

"**C**OULD YOU PLEASE estimate for me the value of this *becher?*" Reb Yaakov requested.

"What?!" the man behind the counter exclaimed. Surely the Rabbi wasn't thinking of selling such a thoughtful — and expensive — gift. Wolfson's other customers looked at each other in disbelief.

Quite unaware of the controversy he was generating, Reb Yaakov repeated his request in the same gentle tone. Abe shrugged his shoulders, placed the cup on his scale, examined it, and quoted the Rabbi a price.

Reb Yaakov reached into his pocket to remove his wallet, but Abe stopped him midway, gesturing with his hand that there was no need. "I do appraisals for free," he said rather hastily, but he barely sounded convincing.

The Rabbi pressed to pay for the services rendered but the jeweler became more emphatic. Defeated, Reb Yaakov thanked Abe effusively for the favor and departed.

Meanwhile four individuals remained frozen in their positions, dumbstruck by what they had just seen. Everyone present was well-acquainted with Reb Yaakov Kamenetsky. Aside from his erudition and brilliance, he was reputed to be a man of unmatched piety and saintliness. But what they had witnessed negated everything they had ever heard.

EVEN ORDINARY PEOPLE far less righteous than a leader of the Jewish People would not go into a store to determine the value of a gift they had received. It was as puzzling as it was crass.

The foursome could not keep their curiosity to themselves, and soon hundreds of people around town were gossiping about Reb Yaakov's bizarre behavior and apparent breach of etiquette. It didn't take long for their rumbling to reach the *Gaon's* own ears, and it obviously troubled him.

Reb Yaakov felt he had only one recourse: to address the incident in his upcoming Rosh Hashanah *drasha*. By the time he stepped up to the podium before *tekias shofar* two weeks later, the rumors had reached fever pitch and the capacity crowd was hungry for a confession. What they got was something else.

Reb Yaakov related to the assembled that he was given the *becher* by the shul and, as such, he viewed it as part of his salary.

He ruled that everything he earned was taxable — even the fifty cents, twenty-five cents, and *chai* cents congregants had pledged to their Rabbi during a *Mi shebeirach* decades earlier in Toronto — and he had to know how much to report to the Internal Revenue Service. Without a professional appraisal how would he know the exact value to declare to the authorities?

His congregants were contrite beyond measure. Reb Yaakov's explanation seemed so obvious. How could they have suspected otherwise? No one was more guilt-ridden than Abe Wolfson. That day, he resolved to give people the benefit of the doubt, especially *gedolim* like Rabbi Kamenetsky, who had taught him a thing or two about appraising.

Heard from: Rabbi Simcha Schustal

Balance Sheet

Months	Chessed	Teshuvah	Torah	Tefillah	Tzeddakah	Aveiros
Tishrei						
Cheshvan						
Kislev						
Teves						
Shevat						
Adar						
Nissan						
Iyyar						
Sivan						
Tammuz						
Av						
Ellul						

Final Accounting

Prepared by

Date

Index No

יְמֵי הָאָדָם שֶׁהוּא חַי עַל הָאֲדָמָה כֻּלָּם חַיִּים
וְקַיָּמִים לָנֶצַח דְּהַיְינוּ שֶׁמִּכָּל יוֹם וָיוֹם נַעֲשָׂה
בְּרִיאָה רוּחָנִית קְדוֹשָׁה לְע״ל בְּבוֹא זְמַנּוֹ
לְהִפָּקֵד מִן הָעוֹלָם בָּאִים כָּל יָמָיו לְמַעְלָה עִמּוֹ
לְהָעִיד עָלָיו לִפְנֵי אֲדוֹן הַכֹּל. וְע״כ צָרִיךְ כָּל
אָדָם לְהִזָּהֵר שֶׁיִּהְיוּ כָּל יָמָיו שְׁלֵמִים בִּקְדֻשָּׁה.

אהבת חסד פרק י״ב

Every one of man's days is imbued
with eternal existence, for with every
day a holy spiritual creation is formed
for the World to Come. When he
dies, all his days will escort him
above and attest to his conduct before
the Supreme Master. Therefore, man
must be careful that all his days are
replete with holiness.

Ahavas Chessed: 12

Honor Above All

IF YOU ASK most Americans when the Civil War took place, chances are they'll scratch their heads, jog their memories from elementary school, and reply, "around 1860." But another civil war occurred one hundred years later. This one was fought at home *and* thousands of miles away. It divided generations, families, and friends. It cost 50,000 American lives and millions upon millions of dollars. It was Viet Nam.

To anyone who lived through it, the Viet Nam era was an unforgettable clash of cultures: the traditional Buddhist mentality of Viet Nam versus the capitalist interests of France and America. Hawks versus doves. Old versus young.

By 1967, more than 325,000 American soldiers were stationed in Viet Nam, participating in the world's first TV war. It was a bloody show. Every night, Americans sat in the comfort of their living rooms and watched their sons give their lives to save another nation's honor. Almost thirty boys a day were killed in the line of duty, with hundreds more wounded. In fact, the U.S. Army suffered more casualties each week than the South Vietnamese Army it was supposed to be helping! Nearly 400 U.S. planes had been downed by 1967. And America had six years of combat still ahead of her, in a conflict that was to last 18 months longer than World War II.

For boys over the age of 18, 1967 was a time of choices: they could dodge the draft by seeking refuge in Canada or Sweden; they could enlist in the Army, Navy, or Air Force and hope for a safe assignment; they could sign up for the National Guard and stay stateside; they could declare themselves conscientious objectors and sit out the war behind bars; they could apply for a Divinity deferment; or they could risk being drafted. Each choice carried implications that could change, and in some cases end, the chooser's life.

JEFFREY GROSS was born in 1949. January 28th, to be exact. And when the great draft lottery was held eighteen years later, Jeff's number came up. Literally. It was 73. According to the Selective Service System, if your number was under 140, you could expect to be drafted. And so for Jeffrey Gross, the choice had to be made, and soon.

Complicating his decision was the fact that Jeff wanted to attend medical school. If he was really serious about becoming a doctor, he couldn't fool around with his future by opting for either a CO deferment or a one-way trip to Canada.

So Jeff decided that the best way to beat the draft was to enlist under the Berry plan, which would keep him out of the Army's clutches until he finished med school. "At least this way I know who's going to be paying for my education," he told his parents, "my dear old Uncle Sam."

Jeff spent the next few years at Ohio State medical school. While he was only moderately religious, every day Jeffrey Gross faithfully whispered devout prayers for the war to end before he went on active duty.

But it didn't. The U.S. was getting more and more embroiled, the action was hotter than ever, and the Viet Cong were spilling American blood like water. Medical personnel were especially vital to the war effort. After all, they were the ones who sewed, patched up, operated, and cured the wounded so they could go out and get shot up again. If you were unlucky enough to be sent into the field as a paramedic, statistic-based rumor had it that you would last three days.

D R. JEFFREY GROSS had not only heard the rumors, he had seen the facts. From his base at Fort Huachuca, Arizona, he examined hundreds of men who had made it back alive (although not necessarily in one piece) before their discharge. For some it was the loss of an eye or an arm that destroyed their morale. For others, it was the loss of a friend.

Jeff knew what the future held in store. And he pulled every string, performed every favor, and paid off every officer he could to avoid it.

For the moment, luck was with him. When his overseas assignment came, he didn't go to Hue (it didn't exist anymore; as the officer in charge stated at the time, "We had to destroy Hue to save it."), Da Nang or My Lai.

He didn't even go to Tan Son Nhut, the huge air base that served as the first stop for thousands of American troops. He was sent to Heidelberg, Germany.

In Heidelberg, Dr. Gross' practice revolved around NATO more than 'Nam. Contrary to popular belief, the United States maintained a hefty military presence in Europe. Even though America was bogged down in war, her commitment to her NATO allies had to be kept. And Jeffrey Gross was only too happy to help.

Most of his days were spent taking care of the accidental cases of broken arms and incidental cases of viruses. "It's not bad," he wrote his parents, "as long as I forget it's Germany."

Throughout his fledgling medical career, Jeff tried to circumcise newborns whenever possible — even though they weren't Jewish — figuring that it was good practice for when the mitzva of *milah* would present itself. As an obstetrics resident at Ohio State, he had had the opportunity to perform hundreds of circumcisions. "Do the circ, jerk," the third-year residents would command the lowly interns, but years after his internship, Jeff was still glad to be the "jerk."

ONCE when Jeff was stationed briefly at Fort Benning, outside Savannah, in "Joja," young Captain Mark Meyers had a special request. "Dr. Gross, would you be willing to circumcise my son according to Jewish law?"

This was the first time Jeff had ever been asked to do a traditional *bris*. "I don't know much about it," he replied honestly.

"Well, you've got eight days to learn," Captain Meyers grinned.

Jeff waded through the literature, but all he found was one article in a 1951 *New England Journal of Medicine* and another in a 1962 copy of *Clinical Pediatrics*. Both left a lot to be desired. So in the finest military tradition, he decided to be all that he could be and found a *mohel*. Fortunately, he didn't have far to look.

FOR OVER TWENTY YEARS, Reb Yosef Samuels had performed *brisim* for the Jewish community of Atlanta. Reb Yosef introduced the young doctor to the intricacies of *priah* and *metzitzah*, *hatafas dam*, and much more.

Patiently and painstakingly, he went over the *halachos* of *bris milah*, explaining when the *bris* may be performed on Shabbos and when it must be postponed. But in his tutorials, Reb Yosef did more than just teach the laws; he also conveyed the significance of *milah* as an affirmation of Abraham's ancient covenant and a guarantee of the redemption of the Jewish People.

Exposure to the sagacious *mohel* and the time-honored, biblical rite catalyzed Jeff's dormant religious upbringing, strengthening his commitment to Judaism and to the performance of *bris milah*. With Reb Yosef's coaching and his own estimable medical skills, he became a first-rate *mohel*, except for one flaw: he wasn't totally observant. Thus, Rabbi Samuels made him promise to use his instruments and acumen only on Jewish children, and only where no kosher *mohel* was available.

Jeffrey Gross pledged his agreement. He even arranged

for Reb Yosef to join him at Fort Benning for the *bris* of Captain Meyers' son. In the next three years, he performed several *brisim*, mainly for the sons of officers stationed overseas.

BUT LITTLE DID JEFF KNOW that his pact with Reb Yosef would soon be tested. It all started with a phone call from Rabbi Steven Arnold, the Jewish chaplain assigned to Jeff's division.

"Dr. Gross, you are known as the best *mohel* in USAEUR, certainly at the 130th Station hospital. I know that since your arrival in Heidelberg you have been anxious to perform *brisim* on Jewish babies, so let me hand you the biggest 'assignment' of your career: Iron Mike's wife had a boy last Wednesday in Weisbaden."

"Iron Mike Smithson?"

"The one and only."

"I didn't know he was Jewish."

Some men are born to be soldiers. Iron Mike Smithson must have had a pre-natal head-start even on them. Everything about the man said "military" in capital letters.

Iron Mike had been first in his class at West Point. He served two tours of duty in Viet Nam, receiving so many medals and ribbons that he didn't have room for them all on his dress uniform, despite the dimensions of his colossal chest.

Jeff thought about it. "I suppose I can perform the *bris*, but I'll have to see if I can get leave from the hospital to travel to Weisbaden."

"Oh, that won't be a problem."

"Why are you so sure?"

"Because Colonel Smithson's father-in-law happens to be the CINC-AT."

"The Commander-in-Chief, Atlantic Forces?"

"That's right."

Between Iron Mike and the CINC-AT, Jeff Gross was momentarily stunned. So much so that he forgot to ask the most critical question regarding *milah*.

"I suggest you brush up your technique," the chaplain continued. "You're going to have some very important guests looking over your shoulder."

Jeffrey Gross wasn't the kind of person to get nervous. But he was very much aware of his "audience." One false move or inopportune remark could result in his being transferred from the cool corridors of the military hospital in Heidelberg to the hot, deadly jungles of Viet Nam.

T HE FIVE DAYS between Chaplain Arnold's call and Jeff's appointment passed all too quickly. That Monday, he was taken by MPs to the maternity ward in Weisbaden to examine the baby. Still recovering from her caesarean section, Mrs. Smithson wasn't available for the usual pre-*bris* consult.

On Wednesday, Jeff arose earlier than usual. He mentally went through the procedure, checked his medical bag, reviewed his uniform — which was noticeably lacking in decorations of any kind — and uttered a silent prayer to Heaven (and his mentor, Reb Yosef) that all should go well.

As Dr. Gross' jeep pulled up outside the medical center in Weisbaden, he saw row after row of staff cars from various divisions of the U.S. Army and its NATO allies. He also noticed private cars, no doubt carrying American politicians and maybe even a reporter or two.

"This must be some party!" Jeff remarked to the MP who drove him. "I just hope the guest of honor doesn't make a scene."

INSIDE, the waiting room on the second floor had been cleared to make way for fifty guests. An array of delicacies stretched from one end of the room to the other. Jeff could see cakes, fish, *hors d'oeuvres* and liquor. At the far end, he could also see Iron Mike Smithson and his patriarchal-looking father-in-law pumping hands and bearhugging the brass.

Like radar, Chaplain Arnold zeroed in on the young doctor and quickly escorted him to where the colonel and CINC-AT were standing.

"Gentlemen," Rabbi Arnold addressed his two superior officers, "let me introduce you to the man of the hour, Dr. Jeffrey Gross."

Jeff automatically began to salute, but shifted swiftly to accept Iron Mike's outstretched hand. In a second, the bone-crusher's set of pincers had bonded Jeff's five fingers into a single flipper. He hoped the damage would wear off before he had to operate.

"Doctor, I hope your hand is steadier than mine at

this point. I think I would rather face a full division of Viet Cong than that knife of yours."

Jeff managed a weak smile, which was rather difficult since he was still reeling from the handshake. He desperately tried to think of something clever and witty to say, but he was too much in awe of the myth surrounding the man and too much in agony over the pain surrounding his knuckles. Finally he said, "I'm sure you won't feel a thing."

Both Colonel Smithson and his father-in-law laughed heartily. "How long have you been performing these circumcisions, son?" asked CINC-AT, an immaculately attired man in his early sixties with a shock of gray hair and a fatherly manner that put Jeff at ease.

"About four years, sir," Jeff replied, his eyes drifting down to the commander's nametag, which read: "DeMartino."

DeMartino! Suddenly, bells and whistles, alarms and sirens, horns and Klaxons, and tocsins and flashing lights went off in his head. "Oh, my gosh!" he thought. "I forgot to find out whether or not the kid's Jewish!"

J EFF BEGAN to panic. His mind raced with the speed of an SST: "If the baby's not Jewish, I can't do the circumcision. If I don't do the circumcision, I'll embarrass both Iron Mike and his five-star father-in-law. If I embarrass them, I'll be handed a one-way ticket to Viet Nam — if I don't get court-martialled and sent to the brig for insubordination first."

Finally, he got hold of his rampaging thoughts. "Before you freak out, find out," his inner self admonished.

Casually, almost too casually, Jeff asked CINC-AT, "Sir, may I have your daughter's name for the circumcision prayer?"

"Her name? Why, it's Maria."

"I see. And she hasn't converted to Judaism by any chance, has she?"

"No-o, not that I'm aware of."

Fortunately, Iron Mike had been drawn into a half-dozen other conversations by a corps of well-wishers. Out of the corner of his eye, Jeff could see him excitedly talking to his army buddies.

J EFFREY GROSS wanted to run and hide. In his mind's eye, the reporters were having a field day, writing headlines like BABY BAWLS, SOLDIERS BRAWL, DOC GOES AWOL and JEWISH SURGEON WOULD RATHER FIGHT THAN STITCH.

All too soon, Jeff could see Iron Mike tearing himself away from a corps of well-wishers and coming toward him to get the show on the road. "There must be a way out of this mess," Jeff muttered to himself. "Maybe I can diagnose the baby as ill. But too many doctors around here would disagree... Maybe I can tell them *I'm* ill. But that will only postpone the circumcision..."

From out of nowhere, an idea flashed in his mind. It was a risk, but he had no choice. Jeff took a deep breath and turned to his commander-in-chief.

"Excuse me, General."

"Yes, son?"

"May I ask the General for his advice on a personal matter?"

"Certainly, my boy."

"General, if you made a vow to someone and then you were put in a position where you had to break that vow or jeopardize your career, what would you do?"

The General smiled. "You sure know how to ask tough questions. To be honest with you, I don't know how I would respond in your particular case. But I will tell you that 'Honor Above All' is a motto I believe in and try to live by."

Dr. Gross took another deep breath and came out with it: "Then General, I cannot ritually circumcise your grandchild."

"What?!"

"Several years ago," Jeff went on calmly but quickly, "I made a vow to an old man, and maybe even to God, that I would not perform the Jewish circumcision ceremony on a non-Jewish child. And Jewish law states unequivocally that the religion of the child is determined by the mother. For this reason, if I am to be faithful to any code of honor, I may not perform this ceremony..."

At that moment, Iron Mike came bustling back in. "Let's get moving. I told the nurses to bring in the baby..."

General DeMartino turned to his son-in-law. "Dr. Gross cannot circumcise the child."

"What do you mean, he can't circumcise my son?"

"Mike, the doctor says he can't do it," his father-in-law repeated.

"He must," Colonel Smithson shot back. "Everything has already been arranged."

"The child is not Jewish," the General explained.

"Not Jewish?" Colonel Smithson exploded. "He's as Jewish as I am!"

"I'm afraid you know more about military history than about your own heritage," CINC-AT chided his son-in-law. "According to Jewish law, the religion of the child follows the mother, *not* the father."

I RON MIKE was livid. "Dr. Gross, I *order* you to perform the circumcision of my son," he said stiffly. "If you refuse, you will be transferred to a tactical unit, where you can practice your surgical skills on those who really need them."

Jeff could already feel Iron Mike's iron grip doing a repeat performance on his neck. He turned chalky and involuntarily gasped for air.

"Dr. Gross," the General interrupted. "You will not perform this circumcision. And that's *my* order!"

The crowd in the room fell silent as father and grandfather began raising their voices. It was obviously a stand-off, but as they say in the Military, R-H-I-P, "Rank Has Its Privileges" — and it was obvious to everyone who outranked whom.

"May I have your attention," General DeMartino called out. "Dr. Gross has informed us that for ideological reasons, he cannot circumcise the child at this time." Jeffrey Gross felt about two inches tall and shrinking as some one hundred and fifty eyes stared down at him.

"However," CINC-AT continued, "I know you all join with me in congratulating Colonel Smithson and my daughter Maria on the birth of their son, Lincoln."

From the crowd, Jeff could hear a lot of murmuring, followed by a few hearty "Congratulations!" and "Mazel Tovs!"

"I would now like to call upon the father,"General DeMartino went on, "to say a few words..."

Jeffrey Gross never heard Mike Smithson's speech. He felt ill and fearful that he would be the subject of the address, he silently slithered his way out of the medical center, where an MP was waiting to return him to Heidelberg.

BACK AT the 130th Station hospital, Dr. Gross was bombarded with questions. "How did things go? Did you meet CINC-AT? Are they going to put you up for a ribbon?"

Jeff couldn't even begin to tell his colleagues what had happened. Or why. He could only wait for the inevitable transfer orders. As far as he was concerned, it was just a matter of time before he would be sent to Viet Nam. Actually, "sentenced to Viet Nam" would be more accurate.

He was right about being transferred. But he was wrong about the destination. Within three days, he was sent home to the U.S. A personal note from CINC-AT explained the change.

"You did what you had to do. Now it is my turn. On my orders, you are to report to the base nearest to your hometown, where you are to finish your tour of duty. Coercion has no place in my army. Honor above all. Anthony P. DeMartino."

Heard from: Dr. David Epstein

Day of Judgment

SITTING ALONE at his desk at the *Jüdenrat*, formerly the Jewish Community Council of Levov, Dr. Jozef Parnas tried to assess the damage of the "Blitz" pogrom. The loss of human lives and property was as unfathomable as it was inestimable.

The first detachments of the German Army arrived in Levov the same day the Russians retreated from the city. The Nazis didn't waste any time in "getting down to business." They called the Ukrainians to war against the Bolsheviks — by striking out at the Jews.

The Ukrainian masses were happy to oblige. Under the aegis of German officers, the militia and populace seized Jews on the street, and men, women, and children hiding in their homes were rounded up and carted off to prison courtyards from which they never emerged. Eyewitnesses confirmed that the Brygidki prison alone was awash in the blood and brains of two thousand Jews tortured to death there.

Pleased with the success of the initial pogrom the Germans gave the Ukrainian nationalists three days to avenge the death of an obscure Pole killed by a Jew in Paris in 1926. The result was the brutal murder of thousands more innocent Jews.

DR. PARNAS had little time to ponder the heinous aftermath; as head of the *Jüdenrat*, his primary function was to meet the economic demands of the Nazis. Since much of Levov had been destroyed by the German advance on the city, they deemed it only appropriate that the Jews should pay for its reconstruction and compensate the marauders for the havoc wreaked. This "compensation" was set at 22 million rubles.

The Jews actually viewed the fine with a sense of relief. They hoped that they would now be able to barter for their lives and be spared more frenzied pogroms. Thus, long lines of donors laden with cash, thousands of kilos worth of gold and silver watches, jewelry, *menorahs*, and wedding rings formed in front of the *Jüdenrat*.

The community's zeal to cooperate didn't satisfy the Nazis, however, and thousands of Jewish intellectuals, professionals, and prominent merchants were taken hostage to expedite payment. Dr. Parnas tried to intercede on their behalf, as he had for countless Jews before, but the Gestapo reminded him that his sole responsibility was to do his commanders' bidding unstintingly and unquestioningly. Needless to say, these hostages were never heard from again.

PARNAS THOUGHT he had reached the limits of human endurance... until he received a *nissayon* that anyone would dread: he was ordered to provide five hundred healthy workers.

Until now, if the Germans had wanted workers they had simply snatched them. Levov itself housed numerous labor camps, or *Erzeihungslager* (educational institutions) as they were deceptively dubbed, and the infamous Janowska *Zwangarbeitslager* (forced-labor camp). Clearly the new Nazi directive, charging the *Jüdenrat* with filling slave-labor quotas, was aimed at psychologically crushing the Jews.

The consequences of disobeying such an order were patently clear. Nonetheless, Dr. Parnas' response to the Nazis was terse: "I will not provide you with men."

The Germans did not anticipate such daring recalcitrance. Their strategy was to obliterate not only the Jewish People, but the Jewish soul. They never dreamed both would be so courageous or so resilient. With the methods they employed they had assumed that their terrified prey wouldn't have the gall to maintain their dignity or communal responsibility.

The poor wretch who can no longer hope for anything beyond another morsel of food, or less tortuous labor, is easily conquerable. Honor, however, is the most puissant form of resistance, and the most contagious. It must be eliminated immediately before it can spread, and the Nazis had a remarkably pragmatic way of curtailing that which they did not desire.

MOBILE SS UNITS surrounded the *Jüdenrat*. Erwin Schultz, chief of *Einsatzkommando* (Liquidation Group) 5; SS-Brigadeführer Otto Rasch; General Fritz Katzmann, SS and Police Leader in the Galicia district; SS Untersturmführer Gustav Willhaus;

Gestapo heads Engels and Weber; and *aktions* supervisor Wepke broke into Dr. Parnas' office and threatened him with every torture the Nazi mind could conceive. But he was intractable.

Undaunted, the cunning Engels adopted a different policy: "Nothing can stop us from achieving our goal," he growled at Dr. Parnas. "Before you force us to rip you and your family limb from limb, consider the lot of Levov Jewry. Certainly they would rather you deliver five hundred workers than make us kill every one of them in retaliation against your insubordination. It is time for you to act wisely, not rashly."

Dr. Parnas curtly reiterated his refusal to hand over Jews to German dominion.

The Nazis felt it inadvisable to simply kill off the head of the *Jüdenrat*, lest his martyrdom trigger mass heroism. Once the *Jüdenrat* implemented the selections, he could be butchered without risk.

And so, in their own chillingly efficient way, SS officers promptly arrested Dr. Parnas, the *Dayannim*, the *gabbaim* of the local synagogue, and nine other members of the *Jüdenrat*. At ten o'clock Sunday morning they would all report to the *Arbeitsamt* (the Jewish labor office) to see if Parnas had changed his mind. It was Wednesday morning.

THE DAYS passed exceedingly slowly for Dr. Parnas, but not slowly enough. He had only four days to make his fateful decision. It wasn't as if the Germans were asking him to send Jews to their death, he thought; they were looking for laborers. Perhaps confinement in a labor camp would actually be in the workers' best interests. At least there they would be granted steady food rations.

There was no legal way of acquiring food in Levov. Hunger, disease, cold, and inadequate housing were rampant. Jews were forbidden to use public transportation, and they were subject to a curfew most of the day. Without the "help" of the Gestapo and its Ukrainian cohorts, famished Jews dropped in the streets of their despicable rat- and typhus-infested ghetto.

Moreover, Dr. Parnas' mind raced, if the Germans had threatened to kill every Jew in Levov, there was no reason to doubt them. Everything the Jews owned had been confiscated by the Nazis, and gentiles were never arrested for tormenting a Jew, or even murdering him. Every day hundreds of Jews were herded onto trucks and driven to the forest to be executed. And rumors of major upcoming *aktions* coursed through the city.

SUNDAY MORNING the shackled Jews were brought to the *Arbeitsamt,* where hundreds of spectators had congregated. At ten o'clock, Dr. Parnas was shoved out of an armored truck and into a crowd of shell-shocked comrades. If imprisonment hadn't weakened his resolve, the Nazis reasoned, surely exposure to the more vulnerable members of the *Jüdenrat* — who had spent the last four days in incredible, unspeakable anguish and affliction — would.

Dr. Parnas' message to his colleagues was laconic and to the point: "I do not know what will befall me. I fear you will not see me again, but I beseech you to conduct the affairs of the *Jüdenrat* judiciously and *honorably.*" The last word he repeated for emphasis.

A second later the doors opened, and Engels, Wepke, Weber, and other Gestapo agents burst into the room and began to rant. Engels ordered that the building employees be held hostage until the *Jüdenrat* provided five hundred healthy workers early the next morning. If the quota was met on time, all the captives would be freed. "The decision," Engels said, turning to Dr. Parnas, "is yours."

Parnas hesitated. All eyes focused squarely upon him. Some of the storm troopers aimed their rifles while others brandished their bludgeons.

Taking a last look at all the noble souls he had worked with under these inhuman conditions, Dr. Parnas turned to his demonic taskmasters and declared, "My decision is final."

The head of the *Jüdenrat* was marched outside, thrown to the pavement, and tied to the truck that had transported him. As a bloodthirsty mob gathered, sadistic SS officers clad in heavy spiked boots stomped on the seventy-year-old doctor until the truck roared off, taking Dr. Parnas to his Maker.

Compared to other residents of Levov, Dr. Parnas' physical suffering was brief, but his mental agony was immeasurable. So was the courage of this brave Jew who humbled his captors. Even under the whip of Satan incarnate, he acted with dignity and honor.

Heard from: Gideon Greif

Life of Deaths

IN A SMALL OFFICE adjacent to the prep room, Dr. Mattias briefed the team that would assist him in the open-heart surgery. Benny Lerner, an intern at North Bronx Hospital, had sat through many similar briefings since the start of his rotation in the surgery department. But this case was different — so different that Dr. Moore, the head of North Bronx's Infectious Disease Department, addressed the assembled.

After three months of studying under Dr. Moore, Benny had developed a strong attachment to him. As a doctor, Moore was unsurpassed in his field; as a human being he was a paragon. Lerner's specialization and fascination was internal medicine and he was the lead car in the long train of Moore groupies. From the day he met the ID specialist, Benny had yearned to be Moore's chief resident.

Now it looked as though that particular dream just might be fulfilled, since not too many doctors were anxious to treat his clientele. The tide began to wash in in late 1982, at first in dribs and drabs and later in great waves. The patients varied in age, background, and severity of symptoms, but all were suffering from "the Syndrome." Every major hospital in America had its complement of Syndrome patients, but North Bronx, catering largely to intravenous drug users and other high-risk subcultures, had more than its share.

Initially both professionals and laymen assumed the Syndrome was some form of retribution for the decadence and depravity of its victims. But Moore and his staff quickly and grimly concluded that the deadly virus struck not only countercultural elements but innocent bystanders as well.

Little Esti Roth, the subject of the briefing, was one such casualty. Plagued by congenital heart disease, she had already undergone open-heart surgery twice, during which her heart was stopped while a heart-lung machine pumped numerous units of blood into her system. One of those units had been contaminated with the virus.

THE VERY MENTION of the Syndrome made the surgical team shiver. It was the early days of the epidemic and everyone was afraid. Nightmares were commonplace, anxieties endemic. A splash of blood or an inadvertent jab with a needle — the everyday occurrences of hospital life — became traumatic. A headache set off alarms; a rash appeared and people thought, *It's beginning.* Some workers at North Bronx refused to go near Syndrome patients, and the administration's harsh disciplinary measures did little to allay their fears.

For his part, Moore presented the surgical team with documented evidence that it was safer to remain in a room with a Syndrome victim than to cross the Grand Concourse. Furthermore, he emphasized, Syndrome patients too often lived in terror of abandonment, a dread not just of death but of dying alone. They were exiles, as Camus wrote of victims of an earlier plague, and it would not help if their caretakers treated them like lepers, — wrapping themselves in layers of protective clothing or leaving food outside their doors.

Moore had taken the opportunity to address matters not directly related to the operation, but part and parcel of hospital care in North Bronx. But his impassioned appeal made no impact. Shielded in an armor of gauze and batting, gloves and face masks, the team looked like a corps of snowmen as they trooped through the waiting room into the operating theater.

As he padded by, Benny Lerner was shocked to see a *frum* couple. It was obvious that it was their daughter who was scheduled for surgery, and he shuddered at their inevitable grief and embarrassment: the Syndrome simply did not touch the religious community.

S INCE MATTIAS had little respect for interns in training, he magnanimously assigned Lerner to be the "step-'n-fetch-it" for this operation. Under different cardiac surgeons, Benny had been permitted to hold the retractors, position the instruments, and once or twice sew up the chest. Mattias, however, liked to work with the same people each time and felt that with a scrub and circulating nurse on hand, an intern needn't be anything but a "gofer." Thus, Benny's role in the lengthy operation was confined to removing a unit of blood from the refrigerator, handing medications to a nurse to decant, adjusting a surgical assistant's face mask, and frequently securing Mattias' eyeglasses.

Towards the end of the surgery, however, the anesthesiologist noticed that the I.V. wasn't flowing well, and he instructed Benny to change the tape on the back of the patient's hand. As the intern did so, he found himself stealing a glance at the little girl's bloodless face. All at once, he saw her for what she was: not the potential carrier of a terrifying disease, but a small, suffering child.

She couldn't have been more than four years old. His mind flashed back to the couple outside: they were probably only a year or two older than he was. For all he knew the father might have been a grade ahead of him in yeshiva.

LERNER was twenty-six and still new to dying. His career in infectious diseases would make him a plague doctor battling the most fearsome epidemic of our time. But years of fighting a losing struggle against death would neither desensitize nor destroy a man whose first encounter with the plague began with Esti Roth in OR #4.

Benny was the intern assigned to monitor Esti's recovery. Every day he checked her blood pressure, pulse, respiration, temperature, fluid balance, *and* emotional state. The little girl's delicate beauty and iron will created a magnetic field which captured those brave enough to risk her company, and Benny Lerner was Esti's biggest catch. He loved to talk to her and tease her, and his visits were far more frequent than duty demanded.

Benny understood that besides her devoted parents, he was all Esti had. Long before she contracted the Syndrome, her heart condition rendered her housebound and virtually friendless. She had never even played outdoors. Yet her personality was delightfully effervescent.

Esti's infatuation with Dr. Lerner was evident from the drawings she made for him every day. Morning, noon, and night she assiduously wielded her crayons, depicting scenes she imagined occurred in the outside world.

Benny would analyze the artwork with the Roths and then squabble with them over who had been given the better picture. These mock arguments drove Esti *meshugah* and she loved every second of them. Gazing out from under a fluff of black bangs, her often melancholy brown eyes became electrified with joy at the competition over her creations.

With Benny bringing home five pictures a day on average, his apartment soon took on the appearance of an Esti Roth retrospective, and he invited her to tour the exhibition after her release from the hospital.

Far dearer than the drawings, though, were the precocious little four-year-old's stories from the weekly Torah portion, which she gleefully related to Dr. Lerner on Friday afternoons. Mrs. Roth primed her daughter well, and Benny simply could not go home for Shabbos without Esti's *dvar Torah*.

E STI RECUPERATED RAPIDLY from her operation and was released from the hospital on schedule. Although she had cleared this hurdle, Benny knew only too well that she would be back at North Bronx. She might enjoy a stretch of good health, but in the end everyone with the Syndrome crashes. Once the body's immune system breaks down, infections run riot and even a minor ailment can become fatal.

Esti's descent into what hospitals tactfully call the "final event" came all too soon. She was admitted to North Bronx with *Pneumocystis carinii*, a pneumonia rare among the population at large but common — and deadly — among Syndrome victims. By this time Benny had joined Moore's team of epidemiologists and was adept at treating symptoms, meliorating pain and comforting loved ones. In Esti's case he was one of them.

He understood what her parents were going through. They were confronting a *nissayon* that no one they knew had ever undergone. Seeing Esti slide in and out of lucidity, victim of a disease that struck the dregs of society, was unbearable. Exposure to the squalid lives of other North Bronx patients plagued with the Syndrome did nothing to lessen their burden.

Yet the Roths' courage amazed the young doctor. They didn't question their lot, nor did Esti. During his years in yeshiva, Benny had been taught about *emunah*, but this was his most powerful lesson.

Benny wished he could tell them that medical advances might yet save Esti, but there were none. Science was engaged in an uphill footrace against time without making any progress at finding a cure. And even if major breakthroughs had been made, the Roths would still have considered themselves in the hands of God.

Only that granite-like faith carried them through the subsequent months of horror. Sometimes Esti seemed to have been swallowed up by her swelled limbs, and other times she seemed to rally, lulling her family into false hopes of remission. Benny's treatment came to resemble a rearguard action in war, fighting one battle at a time. But he drew sustenance from caring for Esti and easing her parents' pain.

A T THE AGE OF FOUR-AND-A-HALF Esti already had a partial understanding of what death meant. Whenever Benny would try to detach himself from her and withdraw to a safer emotional distance, she would ask if he would be able to visit her after she died. "Who will tell you stories from the *parshah*," she asked one day, "when I go to live with *Hashem*?"

Silence blanketed the room. Mr. and Mrs. Roth looked at each other and began to weep. So did Benny. His professional objectivity was long since shattered, and she slew him with arrows of angst.

L ERNER ALWAYS KNEW how the story of Esti would end. The only thing that surprised him was the velocity: there was not enough time to prepare himself. He always felt incredulous at the death of someone as young as Esti, and he half-expected an authoritative voice to grant her a reprieve. But as a doctor, he knew that not every story has a happy ending.

As Esti descended into a fugue state, laboring for breath, Benny felt it important to prepare the Roths for the conclusion of her life of deaths. Esti's skin turned pale as tallow as she began her final crash. The demise of a Syndrome victim is among the ugliest known to medicine and he detailed the possible scenarios. To his relief and astonishment, Esti's parents didn't flinch.

Labor Day weekend Benny left the hospital to visit his family. He knew Esti's death was imminent, and begged his stand-ins to take special care of her in his absence and to contact him if the need arose.

THE SUN SHONE brilliantly on the balmy morning of his return. But the beautiful weather was all but lost on the staff and infirm of North Bronx. Benny had been gone from the hospital for only four days, but it seemed like much longer and he couldn't wait to visit Esti.

Benny had felt a twinge of guilt about leaving her in her condition, and he'd prayed more fervently than ever for a breakthrough that would arrest the Syndrome in its deadly tracks. He contemplated Dr. Rieux's conclusion in *The Plague* that his job was no longer to cure but "to detect, to see, to describe, to register, and then to condemn." No matter how his medical career would develop, Benny felt that he could never adopt such a policy with the Estis he would encounter.

It wasn't until the early afternoon that Benny had a chance to visit her. Bounding breathlessly up the stairs to her floor, he burst into her room. But Esti's bed was empty and there was no sign of her parents.

Lerner swallowed hard and retreated to the doctors' lounge. Staggering over to a desk, he gripped a pen and a sheet of paper and wrote:

Dear Esti,

THINGS YOU DIDN'T DO

Remember the day I removed your sutures too early? I thought you would tell the other doctors of my mistake -- but you didn't.

And remember the time I was nervous about draining blood, so I put on gloves and a face mask? I thought you'd say you were scared -- but you didn't.

And the time I kept missing your vein with the I.V. needle and you developed bleeding under the skin? I thought you'd ask for someone else to do it -- but you didn't.

And the time I hurt your feelings by criticizing your drawing? I thought you'd get sore with me -- but you didn't.

And the time I guessed the ending of your parshah story. I was sure you'd yell at me -- but you didn't.

Yes, there are lots of things you
didn't do,

but you put up with me and
you always greeted me with a
smile. You never cried, or
complained when I didn't have
time to visit you. There
were so many things I
wanted to make up to you
when you recovered from
the disease --

but you didn't.

Heard from: Dr. Arthur Smerling

Piskei Halacha
of Harav Hagaon Rabbi
Shlomo Zalman Auerbach

❀ ... on **"Robbed Blind"**

A merchant overpaid by a customer need not
seek him out to return the extra money if this
involves leaving his business unattended (and he
can find no one to tend the shop in his absence)
in a crime-ridden area.

❀ ... on **"Home, Sweet Home"**

If a landlord charges his tenant only a
nominal rent on the assumption that he could
pay no more, but after the tenant's demise he
is discovered to have been wealthy, מעיקר הדין the
landlord may not demand compensation from the
tenant's heirs. It is within his rights, however, to
request compensation.

❧ ... on **"Special Delivery"**

With the crew's help, a woman can give birth on a plane. Consequently, if an unscheduled landing is made to accommodate a woman in labor, she should not be billed for the expenses. This is the case even if the airline was unaware of her pregnancy, provided that she didn't know she had to inform them. If, however, she opts for the suggestion that the plane land before she gives birth, and she agrees to defray the cost of this emergency landing, she must indeed pay for the expenses.

❧ ... on **"The Best Policy"**

Once a gentile insurance firm issues coverage for a stolen item, the policy holder is not *obliged* to return the money if the item is later retrieved, since he did not defraud the company by reporting that it was stolen when it was not. However, it is most appropriate and praiseworthy if he does return the coverage, which could conceivably sanctify God's name.

❧ ... on **"Wheels Within Wheels"**

If someone is paid with an item that's traceable to a person who lived generations earlier, he need not seek out the original owner's heirs and return the object. Over time, items change hands, ownership is transferred, and one can never ascertain if any object genuinely belongs to the person from whom he receives it.

✤ ... on **"Windfall"**

One who redeems stolen items from a thief need not surrender them to their rightful owner until this owner reimburses him for the expenses incurred during the redemption.

✤ ... on **"To Teach a Lesson"**

In the event that a principal hires a teacher, whether or not he stipulates that it is for a trial period, and the teacher does not work out, the principal is not obliged to recompense the teacher from the school budget — even if such recompense constitutes the teacher's sole income. However, the principal is *permitted* to imburse the teacher from the school budget, and it is proper and meritorious if he does so.

✤ ... on **"Holy Smoke!"**

One may not collect insurance on any item not specifically covered by his policy. Furthermore, one may not alter damaged goods such that they *will* be covered by his policy.

❦ ... on **"All Wrapped Up"**

If, on the advice of a halachic authority, someone submitted stolen articles to the police in order to apprehend a thief, he is no longer *responsible* for returning the items to their owners.

❦ ... on **"Matzos Mitzva"**

If someone promises to ensure that remuneration is provided for services rendered for a second party, he may not absolve himself of this responsibility by assuming that the second party will arrange payment.

❦ ... on **"A Gem of a Mitzva"**

If a landlord was מתייאש, relinquishing his claim to the debris on his roof, any item found there מעיקר הדין belongs to one who has rented that space.

❦ ... on **"Diamond in the Rough"**

Someone who has no means to pay his debts, must nonetheless repay them all, even if he is legally bankrupt and even if this entails selling his personal possessions.

❦ ... on **"Payday"**

If an employee is paid in advance for a specific period of employment but he dies before completing it, his estate need not refund the money intended to cover the remainder of this period. Doing so bespeaks exceptional piety.

It is important to note that the halachic decisions above were rendered for the specific stories appearing herein. A competent halachic authority must be consulted for applicability in any related situation. Even in the particular aforementioned cases, however, certain factors could alter the ruling: e.g., the *psak* on "Special Delivery" is exclusively referring to an *ex post facto* situation. As in all cases where life is in danger, all precautions — at any cost — should be taken; re "To Teach a Lesson " such a decision is largely based on prevailing wage agreements (מנהג המקום); re "Diamond in the Rough" *Beis Din* has the authority to determine what possessions the debtor must relinquish to pay his debts (מסדרין לבעל חוב); re "Payday" the situation depends on the intention (אדעתיה דהכי) of the employer.

Glossary

Glossary

The following glossary provides a partial explanation of some of the foreign words and phrases used in this book. The spelling, tense, and definitions reflect the way the word or phrase is used in *Above the Bottom Line*. Often, there are alternate spellings and meanings for the words. Foreign words and phrases translated in the text are not included in this section.

AINEKEL — grandchild

ATTAROS — (pl.) ornaments adorning a SEFER TORAH

AVEIRAH — sin

AVODAH — ritual worship performed in the Holy Temple

BAAL TESHUVA — penitent

BAALEI BATTIM — lay individuals

BALABATISH — respectable

BAR MITZVA — 1. thirteen-year-old Jewish boy who assumes the religious responsibilities of an adult; 2. the ceremony confirming a bar mitzva

BARUCH HASHEM — lit. the Lord is blessed; thank God

BARUCH SHE'AMAR — lit. blessed is He Who spoke; prayer recited during SHACHARIS

BATTIM — black leather boxes that encase the TEFILLIN parchment

BECHER — (Yid.) goblet

BEIS HAMIKDASH — the Holy Temple

BEIS MIDRASH — house of study used for both Torah study and prayer

BEN ZEKUNIM — son born to a couple in their old age

BENTCHER — booklet containing the grace after meals

BITUL TORAH — wasting time that could be spent learning Torah

BLI EYEN HARA — lit. without the evil eye; expression invoking Divine protection for children, good health, good fortune, etc.

BRIS MILAH — Jewish rite of circumcision

CHAI — eighteen

CHALILA — God forbid

CHALLAH — special loaves eaten on SHABBOS

CHANUKAH — the Festival of Lights

CHASSAN — bridegroom

CHASSIDIM — (pl.) devoutly religious followers of a REBBE

CHASSIDUS — type of Jewish mysticism

CHASSUNAH — wedding

CHAZAL — contraction of *chachameinu zichronam livracha*, our sages of blessed memory

CHEDER — lit. room; yeshiva elementary school

CHEVRA KADISHA — lit. Holy Society; group that provides for the religious needs of the community, particularly in the area of the care and rites of the dead

CHILLUL HASHEM — desecration of God's name

CHINUCH — education

CHOL HAMOED — The intermediate days of SUKKOS and PESACH

CHUMASH — any of the five books of the Torah

CHUPAH — 1. wedding canopy; 2. the wedding service

CHUTZPAH — nerve, audacity

DAVEN — (Yid.) pray

DAYANNIM — judges

DERECH ERETZ — proper conduct

DIVREI TORAH — Torah thoughts

DRASHA — learned discourse

DREY — (Yid., colloq.) misguide, equivocate

EMMES — absolute truth

EMUNAH — faith

ERETZ YISRAEL — the land of Israel

EREV PESACH — Passover eve

EREV SHABBOS — Sabbath eve

FARHEIR — (Yid.) oral examination in GEMARA

GABBAI — warden of the synagogue who collects and dispenses charity

GADOL (GEDOLIM) — lit. great one; a giant in Torah scholarship

GAON(IM) — lit. brilliant one; honorific for a distinguished sage

GEDOLEI HADOR — the generation's greatest Torah scholars

GELT — (Yid.) money

GEMARA — 1. commentary on the MISHNA (together they constitute the Talmud); 2. a volume of the Talmud

GEMILUS CHASSADIM — deeds of lovingkindness

GENUG — (Yid.) enough

GOYIM — (pl.) gentiles

GUTTE YID — (Yid.) goodhearted Jew

GVIR — man of substantial means

HACHNASSAS KALLAH — dowering a bride

HACHNASSAS ORCHIM — hospitality

HAKADOSH BARUCH HU — the Holy One, blessed be He

HALACHA — Jewish law

HARBATZAS TORAH — dissemination of Torah

HASHAVAS AVEIDA — returning a lost object

HASHEM — lit. the Name; respectful reference to God

HATAFAS DAM — drawing of the blood during circumcision

KABBALA — the body of Jewish mystical teachings

KADDISH — mourners' prayer in praise of God

KALLAH — bride

KAVOD HATORAH — honor for Torah

KIDDUSH — sanctification; prayer recited over wine to usher in the Sabbath and festivals

KIDDUSH HASHEM — sanctification of God's name

KLAL YISRAEL — community of Israel; all Jewry

KOLLEL — post-graduate yeshiva composed of young married students who receive stipends

KRECHTZ — (Yid.) mournful sigh

LAMDAN — scholar

LEBIDIKE VELT — (Yid.) lively and wonderful world

LIMUDEI KODESH — Jewish studies

MAARIV — the evening prayer service

MACHZOR — holiday prayerbook

MALACH — angel

MATZAH(OS) — unleavened bread

MATZOS MITZVA — MATZAH baked specifically to fulfill the MITZVA of eating on PESACH

MAZEL — luck

MAZEL TOV — congratulations

MECHANECH — educator

MECHUTANIM — your child's in-laws

MEKUBALIM — kabbalistic scholars

MELAMED — teacher

MERE — (Yid.) me

MERKAZ SHOMREI STA"M — organization centered in Jerusalem that promotes a high standard of SIFREI TORAH, TEFILLIN, and MEZUZOS

MESHUGAH — crazy

MESHULACH — 1. emissary; 2. itinerant collector of TZEDDAKAH

METZIAHS — (pl.) bargains

METZITZAH — suctioning of the blood during BRIS MILAH

MEZUZAH — small piece of parchment inscribed with a Biblical passage and affixed to the door frame

MI SHEBEIRACH — lit. He Who blessed; prayer for the sick

MIDDOS — character traits

MIGRASH HARUSIM — Russian Compound in Jerusalem

MIKVE(OS) — ritual bath used for purification

MINCHA — the afternoon prayer service

MINYAN — quorum of ten adult Jewish males; the basic unit of community for certain religious purposes, including prayer

MISHNA — the earliest codification of Jewish oral law by Rabbi Yehudah HaNasi

MISHNAYOS — sections of the MISHNA

MISNAGID — opponent of CHASSIDUS

MITZVA(OS) — commandment

MIYACHED YICHUDIM — mystical term implying spiritual achievements of the highest order

MOHEL — one who performs the religious ceremony of circumcision

MONTAG UND DONNERSHTIK — (Yid.) Monday and Thursday

MOTZEI SHABBOS — Saturday night

NACHAS — satisfaction

NEBBACH — (Yid.) unfortunate

NESHAMA — soul

NIGGUN — melody, tune

NISSAYON — trial of faith

OY VEY — (Yid.) expression of woe

PARNASSAH — livelihood

PARSHAH — weekly Torah portion

PAYOS — sidelocks

PESACH — Passover

PETIRA — demise

PIRKE AVOS — section of MISHNA that deals with ethics

POSEIK(IM) — halachic authority

PRIAH — peeling back of the membrane during BRIS MILAH

PSAK — halachic ruling

PURIM — joyous festival commemorating salvation from genocide

RABOSAI — gentlemen

RAV — Rabbi

REBBE(IM) — 1. rabbi; usually a Talmud teacher; 2. instructor; 3. chassidic leader

RECHOV — street

REFUAH SHELEIMAH — complete recovery

ROSH CHODESH — the new moon

ROSH HASHANAH — beginning of Jewish year

ROSH YESHIVA — yeshiva dean

SEDER — Passover ceremony commemorating the Exodus from Egypt

SEFER (SEFARIM) — book of religious content

SEFER (SIFREI) TORAH — Torah scroll

SEUDAH SHLISHIS — the third Sabbath meal, usually begun just before sunset and lasting past nightfall

SHABBOS — the Sabbath

SHACHARIS — the morning prayer service

SHAILAH — halachic query

SHAMASH — synagogue caretaker; rabbi's assistant

SHAS — lit. the six orders of the MISHNA; the Talmud

SHATNES — mixture of wool and linen prohibited by the Torah

SHAVUOUS — holiday commemorating the giving of the Torah

SHEL ROSH — TEFILLIN placed on the head

SHIN — Hebrew letter

SHLEP(PING) — (Yid.) dragging

SHMATTE — (Yid.) rag

SHMOOZE — (Yid.) chat

SHMURA MATZAH — MATZAH that's been guarded since the harvest, lest it become leaven

SHMUESS — ethical discourse

SHNORRER — (Yid.) alms collector

SHTETL — (Yid.) village

SHTICK — tricks

SHTIEBEL — (Yid.) small, informal, intimate room for prayer and study

SHUL — (Yid.) synagogue

SHULCHAN ARUKH — lit. set table; the Code of Jewish Law

SIDDUR — prayerbook

SIMCHA — lit. joy; celebration

SOFER — scribe

SUKKAH — temporary dwelling inhabited on SUKKOS

SUKKOS — week-long autumn festival during which one dwells in a SUKKAH

TACHANUN — supplications recited during SHACHARIS and MINCHA

TALLIS — four-cornered prayer shawl with fringes at each corner, worn by men during morning prayers

TALMID(EI) CHACHAM(IM) — Torah scholars

TALMIDIM — students

TASHMISHEI KEDUSHAH — religious articles

TEFILLIN — black leather boxes containing verses from the Bible bound to the arm and head of a man during morning prayers

TEHILLIM — Psalms; Book of Psalms

TEKIAS SHOFAR — blowing of the ram's horn on ROSH HASHANAH

TORAS COHANIM — sacred book of priestly law

TREIF — (Yid.) lit. torn; non-kosher; unacceptable

TZADDIK — righteous man

TZEDDAKAH — charity

TZITZIS — fringes worn by males on a four-cornered garment

TZURIS — (Yid.) troubles

VEY IZ MERE (Yid.) "woe unto me"

YAD — ornament which helps in the reading of the Torah

"YAGATA UMATZASA, TA'AMIN" — through labor results will be achieved

YAHRZEIT — anniversary of the day of death

YARMULKE — (Yid.) skullcap

YERUSHALAYIM — Jerusalem

YESHIVA — academy of Torah study

YETZER HARA — evil inclination

YICHUS — lineage

YID — (Yid.) Jew

YISHUV — lit. settlement; early settlement of Jews in ERETZ YISRAEL

YOM KIPPUR — the Day of Atonement

YOM TOV — holiday

YONTIFF — (Yid.) holiday

YUNGERMANN — (Yid.) young married man

ZECHUS — merit

Q. What brand new publication has more subscriptions than Jewish periodicals that have been around for a quarter of a century or more?

A. Hanoch Teller's **StoryLines**, a tri-annual "story-letter" for the whole family.

Here's Why:

Each inspiring tale in **StoryLines** is an original gem written by the king of storytellers, **Hanoch Teller**, whose stories have delighted and uplifted Jewish audiences for over a decade.

Attractively designed and produced on high-quality paper, each issue has a timely story about the holiday it heralds. Acclaimed by parents and educators alike, each issue of **StoryLines** includes: a feature-length story annotated with a vocabulary-expanding glossary, a biography of a *tzaddik* or *tzaddekes* for teenagers, an easy-to-read tale for beginners, a cartoon episode of "Velvel the Wagon Driver," a teachers' guide for effective use of all the material, and much more.

StoryLines subscribers can take advantage of spectacular savings on books and cassettes not available elsewhere.*

Join the **StoryLines** sensation and receive a delightful "story-letter" three times a year: Rosh Hashana, Chanuka, and Purim. It's entertaining, intriguing, informative, and educational. You'll cherish every word. Subscribe today — don't be left out!

* *StoryLines* is only available through subscription

HANOCH TELLER's
StoryLines
Stories for the whole family
37 West 37th St. 4th floor. New York,N.Y. 10018

127 Woodstock Ave. London NW11 9RL   Arzei Habirah 46/7 Jerusalem 97761